D1453552

Interpreting Interpretation

INTERPRETING INTERPRETATION
The Limits of Hermeneutic Psychoanalysis

ELYN R. SAKS

Yale University Press   New Haven and London

Printed in the United States of America.

Library of Congress Cataloging-in-Publication Data
Saks, Elyn R., 1955–
Interpreting interpretation : the limits of hermeneutic
psychoanalysis / Elyn R. Saks.
p. cm.
Includes bibliographical references and index.
ISBN 0-300-07603-7 (alk. paper)
1. Psychoanalysis. I. Title.
BF173.S265 1999
150.19'5 — dc21   98-35063
CIP

A catalogue record for this book is
available from the British Library.

The paper in this book meets the guidelines
for permanence and durability of the Committee
on Production Guidelines for Book Longevity of
the Council on Library Resources.

10 9 8 7 6 5 4 3 2 1

Contents

Preface / vii

CHAPTER 1
Introduction / 1

CHAPTER 2
The Hermeneutic Analytic Thinkers / 18

CHAPTER 3
The Models / 80

CHAPTER 4
The Plausibility of the Story Model of Hermeneutic
Psychoanalysis / 120

CHAPTER 5
The Plausibility of the Other Models of Hermeneutic
Psychoanalysis / 163

CHAPTER 6
The Weak Form of the Argument from Patient
Rejection Revisited / 207

CHAPTER 7
Implications for Theoretical Psychoanalysis and
Other Concluding Thoughts / 220

APPENDIX
The Reality of the Story Model and the Applicability
of the Argument to Its Variants / 231

References / 247
Index / 255

For Melvin Lansky, Stanley Jackson,
and the late Martha Harris

PREFACE

Why would a law professor write a book on hermeneutic psychoanalysis? The short answer, in my case, is that I have been
interested in psychoanalysis for years. Indeed, I began training
as a lay analyst at the Los Angeles Psychoanalytic Society and
Institute several years ago. I became interested in *hermeneutic*
psychoanalysis when, in writing an article on the problem of
competency and unconscious delusions, I discovered that hermeneutic psychoanalysis purported to solve the problem. My
first treatment of the theory was a twenty-page section of a
long article on this legal problem. Realizing that I needed to
say much more, however, I wrote an article devoted entirely
to hermeneutic psychoanalysis as it bore on the problem. My
colleagues convinced me that I should write a piece on hermeneutic psychoanalysis itself—its meanings and problems—and
not cramp the analysis by the need to relate it to a particular
legal dilemma. The relation of hermeneutic psychoanalysis to
this dilemma now takes up but a few pages in the last chapter.

As is appropriate in a psychoanalytic work, I have confessed
the genetic roots of my project, at least the manifest ones. But
how did I come to focus on the specific aspects of hermeneutic
psychoanalysis analyzed in the following pages? In the course
of thinking about the legal problem, I realized that the hermeneutic solution was hard to pin down because, despite their
similar vocabularies, the hermeneuts seemed to mean very different things. Thus I constructed the five models of hermeneutic psychoanalysis that compose chapter 3.

The heart of the work, however, is what I call the argument from patient rejection—the argument that patients would reject hermeneutic psychoanalysis if informed of its true nature. In thinking about the models, I became aware that the argument from patient rejection did not apply in the same way to all of them. Thus I identify and analyze different versions of this argument as it applies to the five models.

One of the models—the story model—is particularly vulnerable to the argument. I suggest that patients both will and should reject the story model because it asks them to believe interpretations that do not purport to be possibly true—a normatively undesirable expectation. Consider in this light whether any right-minded patient would, or should, want to believe recovered memories of sexual abuse that are only "narratively," but not "historically," true. Some story theorists, indeed, apply the concept of narrative truth to apparent memories of sexual abuse. I do not wish the reader to get lost in this example—the problems are more systemic and fundamental—but the potential implications are disquieting to say the least.

Why do I focus so on the patient? First, until now, I have always seen psychoanalysis from the patient's point of view (being a patient myself). Second, in an earlier phase in my career, I represented psychiatric patients and children. As an attorney, I was trained to be entirely client-centered. I was obliged to counsel clients when I thought they were making a poor choice, but ultimately they decided. The lawyer's job is to do what the client wants, not what she thinks he needs. Thus, in basing the central argument of the book on what patients will want, I am being true to my training as a lawyer.

But, apart from my personal history, one may wonder why we should particularly care what patients think in this instance. The answer is simple: Psychoanalysts have a duty to be candid with their patients. Once patients are informed of the nature of at least some versions of hermeneutic psychoanalysis, they will reject them, and these versions of hermeneutic psychoanalysis will self-destruct. Patients, then, have the power to doom such versions of hermeneutic psychoanalysis. My arguments do not establish that hermeneutic psychoanalysis is wrong in its characterization of psychoanalysis, just that if it is right, it may be a desperately unhappy vision of psychoanalysis.

It is my hope that, as a law professor with a long-standing interest in psychoanalysis, I have been able to say something about one currently fashionable version of the discipline that will be useful to psychoanalysts interested in theory, as well as to those interested in the practical ramifications of hermeneutics generally. Although I do not pursue the implications of my argument for other areas of hermeneutic theory, scholars in those areas may well be interested in my findings.

Many people have contributed enormously to this project; I certainly have not worked in isolation. I thank first the dean of the University of Southern California Law School, Scott Bice, as well as the administrators of the Law School and the faculty generally, for providing a working environment conducive to scholarship. In addition, I am very grateful to Albert Brecht and the staff of the USC Law Library for their excellent research assistance. I am also most appreciative of Rosemary Hendrix for her wonderful secretarial assistance.

For reading drafts and making many helpful comments, several colleagues have my deep gratitude: Scott Altman, Gerald Aronson, Richard Bonnie, Richard Craswell, David James Fisher, Ronald Garet, Benjamin Kilborne, Jill Kowalik, Jeffrey Levine, Martin Levine, Alexander Meiklejohn, Daniel Ortiz, Uriel Procaccia, Michael Shapiro, Larry Simon, Christopher Slobogin, Nomi Stolzenberg, Catharine Wells, and participants at a USC workshop.

Several of these people deserve special mention. Scott Altman and Dick Craswell always read my work most attentively and gave me extremely helpful comments. Jerry Aronson made some very perceptive suggestions. Ron Garet gave a wonderful commentary at my workshop. Catharine Wells's critique pressed me to distinguish more carefully among kinds of hermeneutic psychoanalysis. And Alexander Meiklejohn, as always, gave me excellent editorial assistance, marking up my pages so much that I could hardly see the type. I am deeply grateful to all of these people.

Several students furnished wonderful research assistance: Todd Bates, Paul Davis, Michael Hercz, Steven Kim, Maria Ronchetto, Heather Spragg and Julie Stillman. I am most appreciative of their help.

I would also like to thank my editor, Gladys Topkis, for her help and support in writing this book. As all who have worked with Gladys Topkis know, she is an extraordinary person of many talents and gifts.

I also thank the people closest to me for giving me the love, security, and well-being that enable me to write: my parents, Barbara and Bert, and my brothers, Warren and Kevin. Kenny Collins, my freshman English teacher and close friend all these years, taught me to love to write. My dear friend Steve Behnke has been there since I first met him in law school: bright, irreverent, loving, supportive. And my special friend, Will Vinet, through his nurture and support, has provided a great sense of well-being. I feel the deepest love and appreciation for all of these people.

Finally, I wish to thank the people to whom this book is lovingly dedicated: the late Mrs. Martha Harris, Dr. Stanley Jackson, and Dr. Melvin Lansky—my three analysts, who, through their generous and skillful attention, have helped me to love and to work.

Interpreting Interpretation

I

Introduction

Like other disciplines in our universities, psychoanalysis has lately been reinterpreted as a hermeneutic discipline. Indeed, many traditional hermeneuts have singled out psychoanalysis, among the human sciences, as the exemplar of a hermeneutic discipline, and many psychoanalysts proclaim themselves converts to the hermeneutic reading of their discipline. An equally large number of psychoanalysts, however, repudiate that reading and reaffirm traditional understandings. The arguments for their repudiation are many, but in this book I am concerned with one in particular: the idea that, if patients were informed of the true nature of psychoanalysis on the hermeneutic reading, they would reject psychoanalysis as a form of therapy. I call this objection the argument from patient rejection (of whatever version of hermeneutic psychoanalysis is being rejected).[1]

The structure of this book is straightforward. I make, essentially, four claims, and I attempt to provide their warrants. The first claim is that there are verbal expressions that can be labeled hermeneutic. My description of what counts as hermeneutic provides the warrant for this claim. Although I discuss hermeneutics in general and hermeneutic psychoanalysis in particular in more detail below, for now I can say that the hermeneutic position in psychoanalysis is characterized by being antiscientistic, antiscientific, acausal, and meaning-centered.

The second claim is that there is an overrepresentation of

1. One might also speak of features of hermeneutic psychoanalysis that would lead patients to accept it; but that would be a different book.

such statements in selected writers. I quote from a number of writers in chapter 2 to suggest that this claim is true. But I cannot really provide a warrant for the claim as I have not, of course, sampled the whole universe.

The third claim is that these hermeneutic writers can be grouped in five categories. My warrant for this claim is simple — the pleasures of taxonomy.

The fourth and most important claim is that these hermeneutic psychoanalytic theories will estrange — and possibly damage — patients insofar as they offer them stories that, while they organize patients' lives, are not held by their tellers to be true. Alternatively, if these theories do not so damage the patient, they should be regarded as damaging because of our ethical and legal zeitgeist. I do not provide a warrant for the first part of this claim, inasmuch as I do not do empirical research in this work — although I offer reasons for suspecting it is true. I do provide a warrant for the second part of this claim; that is what the bulk of this book is about.

What is hermeneutics? And what is hermeneutic psychoanalysis?[2] The name of Hermes, the messenger of the Greek gods, gave rise to the Greek verb *hermeneuein*, from which the term "hermeneutics" derives. *Hermeneuein* means "to make something clear, to announce or to unveil a message" (Thompson 1996, 360–61) — in short, to *interpret*. John Thompson neatly summarizes the early history of hermeneutics: "The discipline

2. The history of hermeneutics in general and of hermeneutic psychoanalysis in particular is vast and sprawling. There are numerous accounts of this history. For succinct renditions of the history I have found Thompson and Inwood helpful, and I rely extensively on them. For thoughtful accounts of hermeneutic psychoanalysis I have found Fisher (1990), Strenger (1991), and Steele (1979) especially helpful, and I have relied extensively on them too. To do full justice to the questions, What is hermeneutics? and What is hermeneutic psychoanalysis? would require another work.

of hermeneutics first arose, one could say, with the interpretation of Homer and other poets during the age of the Greek Enlightenment. From then on, hermeneutics was closely linked to philology and textual criticism. It became a very important discipline during the Reformation, when Protestants challenged the right of tradition to determine the interpretation of the holy scriptures. Both classical scholars and theologians attempted to elaborate the rules and conditions which governed the valid interpretation of texts" (Thompson 1996, 360).

From its origins as a discipline concerned with the interpretation of texts, particularly religious texts, hermeneutics has grown to encompass considerably more. According to Michael Inwood, hermeneutics developed in three central phases. First, Friedrich Schleiermacher focused on a systematic theory of the interpretation of texts and speech. Second, Schleiermacher's biographer, Wilhelm Dilthey, extended hermeneutics to the understanding of all human behavior and products by reorienting it toward the foundations of the *Geisteswissenschaften,* or the "human sciences." Third, Martin Heidegger expanded hermeneutics even further: whereas Dilthey is concerned with understanding in the cultural, in contrast to the natural, sciences—particularly the interpretation of the products of past societies—Heidegger is concerned with the interpretation of the being who interprets texts and other artifacts, namely, the human being or *Dasein:* "Understanding *Dasein* is more like interpreting a text overlaid by past misinterpretations (or penetrating the self-rationalizations of a neurotic) than studying mathematics or planetary motions. Hermeneutics no longer presents rules for, or a theory of, interpretation; it is the interpretation of *Dasein.* But hermeneutic phenomenology gives an account of understanding, since a central feature of *Dasein* is to understand itself and its environment" (Inwood 1995, 353). For Heidegger, understanding is a matter of "projecting what we are capable of." The anticipatory character of understanding "is a reformulation, in ontological terms, of what is commonly called the 'hermeneutical circle'" (Thompson 1996, 360). This concept recognizes the inherent circularity of all understanding: the fact that one can understand the parts only in terms of the whole, and the whole in terms of the parts.

Hermeneutics has continued to develop since Heidegger. Hans Georg Gadamer, who was strongly influenced by Heidegger, establishes a connection between the anticipatory character of understanding and the related notions of prejudice, authority, and tradition. Gadamer claims that our negative conception of prejudice is itself a prejudice stemming from the Enlightenment and keeping us from seeing that understanding always requires prejudgment or prejudice: "We are always immersed in traditions which provide us with the prejudices that make understanding possible. Hence there can be no standpoint outside of history from which the totality of historical effects could be grasped; instead, understanding must be seen as an open and continuously renewed 'fusion' of historical 'horizons'" (Thompson 1996, 361).

Jürgen Habermas challenges Gadamer's complacent view of the link between understanding and tradition, since tradition may be a source of power that distorts the process of communication. Instead, Habermas calls for critical reflection. Paul Ricoeur, in turn, tries to mediate this dispute by reemphasizing the concept of the text.

Hermeneutics, then, has grown vastly in its dimensions: "The appreciation of texts and works of art, the study of action and institutions, the philosophy of science and social science: in all of these spheres, problems of understanding and interpretation are recognized as central" (Thompson 1996, 361). The hermeneutic movement has extended to disciplines as diverse as philosophy, literature, history, and the social sciences. Although hermeneutics began by making a distinction between the natural sciences and the human sciences, many today would reject such a distinction and claim that all understanding is interpretive. For example, Richard Rorty, a member of the hermeneutic-influenced pragmatist school, sees hermeneutics as what discourse must become when we leave the realm of "normal science" in all areas of human inquiry. Nevertheless, many hermeneuts would "want to defend the peculiar character of social and historical enquiry. For the *objects* of such enquiry are the product of *subjects* capable of action and understanding, so that our knowledge of the social and historical world cannot be sharply separated from the subjects who make up that world" (Thompson 1996, 361).

As one scholar argues, "What makes an approach 'hermeneutic' is that it gives some priority to the knowing subject's contribution in constituting and structuring the facts of the matter to be understood. That is to say, what makes an approach hermeneutic is that it holds that the nature of understanding is central to understanding that something is true" (Balkin, personal communication). In the psychological realm, the hermeneutic approach may be understood to be a "rejection of two different approaches to the human sciences — positivism and behaviorism — on the theory that understanding social facts and social behavior requires a sympathetic understanding of the meanings created by other minds" (Balkin, personal communication).

Psychoanalysis involves interpretation, a search for the meanings of the "texts" — dreams, associations, parapraxes — that psychoanalytic patients produce. Consequently, it is not surprising that important hermeneutic thinkers should have come to see psychoanalysis as a paradigmatic hermeneutic enterprise.[3]

3. Indeed, although Freud was committed to the belief that psycho-

Habermas and Ricoeur are the seminal psychoanalytic hermeneuts, although they in fact see psychoanalysis as a mixed hermeneutic and nonhermeneutic discipline. Many psychoanalysts and psychoanalytically informed thinkers have since climbed on the bandwagon, most now seeing psychoanalysis as purely hermeneutic. I shall look at a number of these thinkers in some detail later.

What, more precisely, makes hermeneutic psychoanalysis hermeneutic? David James Fisher (1990) describes the hermeneutic psychoanalysis of Habermas and Ricoeur in ten propositions:

> 1. Psychoanalysis concerns itself with texts, "a set of signs that can be deciphered or understood through the rules and guidelines of exegesis" (5); these texts include dreams, neurotic symptoms, jokes, myths, and works of art, among others;
>
> 2. Freud's scientistic self-misunderstanding of metapsychology notwithstanding, psychoanalysis is not a branch of the natural sciences, but a distinctively human science (5);
>
> 3. Hermeneutic psychoanalysis is suspicious of consciousness—it is aware of the risks of false consciousness and is attuned to the illusions, deceptions, and self-deceptions of consciousness, striving to be a demystifying activity (6);

---

analysis was a natural science, at the same time he subscribed to some propositions that were decidedly hermeneutic. It is perhaps no accident that he called his most famous book *The Interpretation of Dreams*. (In saying this, I do not mean to suggest that every use of the word "interpretation" makes one a hermeneut. Still, a careful reading of Freud suggests some hermeneutic features in his work.)

4. Hermeneutic psychoanalysis is cognizant of transference and resistance (6);

5. "Psychoanalysis is a dialogue taking place within the field of speech" (7);

6. Psychoanalysis is an intersubjective discipline; "the psychoanalyzed analyst does not bracket out his subjectivity, but uses his subjectivity in a controlled, conscious way in order to facilitate the dialogue committed to mutual understanding" (9);

7. Psychoanalysis serves a narrative function (9);

8. Psychoanalysis has norms of validity and proof appropriate to a hermeneutic discipline, the notion of the hermeneutic circle playing a key role in this conception of validity (10);

9. Hermeneutic psychoanalysis has a distinctive goal—to overcome "irrational internal distortions in the service of enlightenment" (11);

10. "Psychoanalysis is linked to the disciplines and techniques of freedom" (11).

Not all contemporary hermeneuts would either base their explication on Habermas and Ricoeur or endorse all of these propositions, at least in this form. For instance, many do not speak in terms of a "suspicion of consciousness" or of "enlightenment." Still, whether they use this language or not, most would probably endorse the general substance of these ten propositions.[4]

4. Some of Fisher's ten propositions would be subscribed to by psychoanalysts of all stripes and therefore are not distinctive of hermeneutic psychoanalysis. For example, both hermeneutic and natural science approaches to psychoanalysis are attempts to make the bizarre plain, so to speak. To the extent that Fisher denies this, he is misappropriating as sole property of the hermeneuts features common to all of psychoanalysis.

Other commentators have discussed what makes hermeneutic psychoanalysis hermeneutic. Carlo Strenger, for example, characterizes hermeneutic psychoanalysis in terms of five theses: first, that the metapsychology should be discarded; second, that psychoanalysis should avoid subpersonal terminology and use only personal terms; third, that psychoanalysis does not explain behavior in terms of causes; fourth, that psychoanalysis is concerned with meanings; and fifth, that there are always many possible interpretations of human behavior, and psychoanalysis is one of them (1991, 38–40).

Robert Steele, another commentator who discusses what makes hermeneutic psychoanalysis hermeneutic, characterizes hermeneutics in general in terms of its position on understanding and language: understanding is situational and historical, and language is the medium through which we understand; on meaning and method: the methods of the natural sciences and the interpretive sciences are radically different—the hermeneutic method being dialogue—and all method is already interpretation; on history: the "hermeneutic spiral" captures both the synchronic and the diachronic dimensions of interpretation; and on self-reflection: humans are a distorted text needing interpretation, and interpretation must be a process of getting beneath the surface of what is meant. He then turns to hermeneutic psychoanalysis, which he characterizes in terms of the same basic tetrad (1979, 389–411).

Such summaries of the basic features of hermeneutic psychoanalysis, of course, obscure important differences among hermeneuts. For example, some hermeneutic analysts stress the contrast between psychoanalysis as a human science and as a natural science, as the early philosophical hermeneuts did. Others focus on the multiplicity of incommensurable interpretations inevitable in the human sciences, as some later philosophical hermeneuts do.⁵ Similarly, Irene Fast distinguishes, among those concerned with narrative, between those who explore narrative structure in psychological terms and those who address questions of referentiality or congruence ("If associations, interpretations, life histories are narrative constructions, what is the relationship between them and actual historical events?" [1993, 3]).⁶ The first perspective sees narrative as the

5. For this distinction among hermeneutic psychoanalysts, see Phillips 1991.

6. A prominent example of the first type, for instance, is Jerome Bruner, who has written widely about narrative as fundamental to being human: he explores how we narrate, the conditions of narrative, and what it says about our minds and the human condition. See, e.g., *Acts of Meaning* (1990), in which Bruner argues that psychology made a wrong turn in moving toward computer metaphors; it should be concerned with meaning-making, embodied in folk psychology. The impulse to tell stories is perhaps innate and may even explain the structure of human grammar. Bruner speaks here of certain characteristic features of the impulse to narrative: narrative requires, "first, a means for emphasizing human action or 'agentivity'. . . . [S]econdly, that a sequential order be established and maintained. . . [Thirdly], . . . a sensitivity to what is canonical and what violates canonicality in human interaction [and] [f]inally, . . . something approximating a narrator's perspective" (1990, 77). Bruner suggests that selves are somehow constituted by the stories we tell about ourselves. And he is at pains to stress how integrally related folk psychology/narrativity and culture are. Bruner does also take some positions that should be roughly thought of as alternative metaphysics positions in my schema (see below). Thus he claims that "knowledge is 'right' or 'wrong' in light of the perspective we have chosen to assume. Rights and wrongs of this kind—however well we can test them—do not sum to absolute truths and falsities." He implies that this does not lead to an "anything goes" relativism, although he is concerned about the charge of relativism to which his constructivism might expose him. Bruner also seems to endorse Rorty's concept of truth, following James, as "what is good in the way of belief." Although Bruner then takes some positions that make him suitable for classification in terms of my schema, his basic project is outside my purview and falls into Fast's first category.

way we organize our experience and explores the vicissitudes of that organization. The second is more concerned with philosophical problems that are, in part, the focus of this book.

This brief review of hermeneutics and hermeneutic psychoanalysis lays the groundwork for what follows. The focus of this book will be to understand one central claim that hermeneutic psychoanalysts often make: that psychoanalytic interpretations are concerned with *meaning* rather than with facts or causes. The book critiques several models for understanding this hermeneutic claim. As suggested above, the argument of the critical portion of this book runs as follows:

1. There has been an attempt to understand psychoanalysis as a hermeneutic discipline;
2. There is more than one way to do this—indeed, there are at least five;
3. Psychoanalytic interpretations must make claims to truth;
4. Psychoanalytic interpretations may also need to make claims to causal explanations of behavior;
5. Hence, only those versions of hermeneutic psychoanalysis that are consistent with these propositions are appropriate applications of psychoanalytic treatment; we should reject the rest.

The organization of the book is as follows. In chapter 2, I present eight hermeneutic thinkers, largely in their own language, so that the reader will get a feel for what they say. These thinkers often seem to speak the same language—use the same words and concepts, images and analogies—and some commentators see them as holding essentially the same position.

Yet the commentators are mistaken; in the third chapter I sketch five different models of the meaning of the hermeneutic claim that interpretations seek after meaning, not facts or causes. I give these models names descriptive of their positions. First, the clinical psychoanalysis theorists mean simply that psychoanalysts are interested in the aims, purposes, and wishes underlying behavior, not its neurophysiological antecedents. At the opposite end of the spectrum, the story theorists mean that psychoanalysts simply tell stories that give meaning to patients' lives. The alternative metaphysics theorists agree that psychoanalysts are interested in actual aims, purposes, and wishes but propose a radically new metaphysical understanding of knowledge, truth, and reality. The metaphor theorists suggest that analysts uncover metaphoric truths about patients when they interpret behavior. Finally, the interpretations-as-literary-criticism theorists mean that interpretation yields noncausal truths about patients' underlying psychological states. I make some effort to classify the eight hermeneuts I describe in chapter 2, although the point of chapter 3 is not to offer a definitive reading of any of the hermeneuts, but to establish the viability of the five models.

In chapter 4 I critique the story model of hermeneutic psychoanalysis, which is most vulnerable to the argument from patient rejection.[7] The basic structure of the argument from patient rejection of the story model is as follows:

7. The argument from patient rejection, although not by that name, has been suggested by a number of commentators. See, e.g., Grunbaum (1984); Sass and Woolfolk (1988); Sass (1993); Freeman (1985); Eagle (1980). (Eagle also makes the same kind of argument as to therapists as well. See Eagle, 1984, 166–67.) See also, e.g., Shapiro (1993, 395–421) (criticism of nonreferentiality of interpretations in hermeneutic view). The virtue of my account, I think, is that it spells out and defends more clearly than before the different steps of the argument as well as the fact that it has empirical, normative, and conceptual components. (Earlier commentators have seemed to make the empirical point alone.) Similarly, my account has the virtue of showing how the argument is affected in light of the earlier distinction among the kinds of hermeneutic psycho-

1. Patients will not accept a version of psychoanalysis that provides them with stories that do not purport to be at least possibly true; as an empirical matter, that is, patients will reject a psychoanalysis so understood;

analysis. Earlier commentators have simply applied the argument to all hermeneuts, not realizing that there is a strong and a weak version of the argument, and of the strong, a more and a less sophisticated version. These versions have varying degrees of cogency.

Other criticisms of hermeneutic psychoanalysis are equally important and deserve fuller study. The most sustained critique is Adolf Grünbaum's. See Grünbaum (1984). See also Blight (1981) (given the Great Epistemological Divide between the natural and the human sciences, psychoanalysis is forced to align itself with hermeneutics; but, based on a Popperian vision of the unity of the sciences, the Great Epistemological Divide is a myth and ought to be rejected); Eagle (1984) (the hermeneutic view inadequately deals with the problem of reliability and the associated one of criteria for knowledge; even as pure therapy, we need to go beyond hermeneutics to determine therapeutic effectiveness; the value of psychoanalysis that truth is "not only enlightening but freeing" [171] is ultimately rejected and negated by hermeneutics); Edelson (1985) (references to subjectivity, meaning, complexity, and uniqueness do not provide epistemological justification of psychoanalysis as a hermeneutic science, with the case study at its center, exempt from the ordinary canons of scientific method and reasoning; Edelson also gives detailed reasons for rejecting the view that psychoanalysis studies meanings, not causes, and therefore is not a natural science); Holzman and Aronson (1992) (first, the hermeneutic view accepts a logical distinction between scientific and other realms of explanation, but in fact there are no qualitatively different kinds of explanation—"all theories are provisional statements subject to change on the basis of test" [80]; second, unlike interpretation of other texts, the analyst's interpretive efforts confront the resistance of the text to be deciphered; third, the hermeneutic view offers no "rules of procedure" [80]; fourth, the hermeneutic view implicitly embraces Cartesian dualism); Holzman (1985) (restates the first two arguments in Holzman and Aronson [1992]; argues against the effort to counterpose causes and reasons; and argues against the view that psychoanalysis requires a different set of investigative methods from natural sciences because it is not

2. Patients *ought* not to accept a psychoanalysis so understood; it is normatively undesirable to believe interpretations that do not purport to be at least possibly true;

3. Psychoanalysts ought not to secure their patients' acceptance of psychoanalysis by lying to them about the truth-status of their interpretations; even if placebos are acceptable in some contexts, they are not acceptable here;

4. Alternative understandings of the story model of psychoanalysis under which the interpretations' truth-status seems not to be an issue at best radically alter the nature of psychoanalysis and at worst are subject to the same objection as the story model itself.

In short, there are both empirical and normative components of the argument from patient rejection of the story model. As we shall see, there is a conceptual, definitional component of

---

ahistorical and context-free, citing Grünbaum's point that neither are some of the natural sciences); Hanly (1996, 445–57) (criticism of narrative approach of Spence, Schafer, and others from perspective of critical realist).

Other commentators criticize the critics of hermeneutic psychoanalysis. See, e.g, Phillips (1987) (criticizes Grünbaum's critique of Habermas, Ricoeur, and the view that motives are not causes of but reasons for human behavior); Terwee (1987) ("aims to show that Grünbaum's critique of the hermeneutical conception rests on basic misunderstandings and very significant errors in interpretation" [347]; Grünbaum simply adopts the empirical-analytical conception of science and assumes that alternative viewpoints are implausible without arguing that they are; Terwee defends Habermas in particular against Grünbaum's arguments against him).

Other commentators try to find an acceptable path somewhere between a hermeneutic and a natural science conception of psychoanalysis. See, e.g., Strenger (1991).

this argument that applies to some versions of the story model as well.

Chapter 5 looks at the remaining models of hermeneutic psychoanalysis in light of the argument from patient rejection. The clinical psychoanalysis and alternative metaphysics models seem to escape the criticism that applies to the story model. Neither asks patients to believe interpretations that do not purport to be possibly true, although the alternative metaphysics model offers a novel conception of truth.

The alternative metaphysics model's dependence on a novel conception of truth, however, invites a more sophisticated version of the argument from patient rejection. The idea here is that this model depends on a conception of truth that is so problematic that it is *as if* patients were being asked to believe nontruths. Alternatively, the alternative metaphysics model might be too subjectivistic or relativistic to offer a satisfying account of truth. The chapter will point out various problems with making the argument from patient rejection in this way—although the argument may have some merit.

The metaphor model also escapes the argument from patient rejection, at least in its strong form. Because the analyst believes her interpretations are metaphorically true under this model and wants her patient to believe they are true only in this sense, this model withstands the strong form of the argument from patient rejection. It may, however, be subject to a weak form of the argument, according to which patients empirically will reject a psychoanalysis so understood because they find it unacceptable and normatively ought to do so for the very same reason—and not because it asks them to violate their moral norms about belief.[8] Conceivably, patients might find the meta-

8. If the principle that one ought not to believe nontruths has moral force, then arguments incorporating this principle might rightly be deemed strong because they provide a sturdier foundation for predict-

phor model objectionable because, as I read it, psychoanalysis then offers patients so little in the way of knowledge—so little, in particular, in the way of knowledge about their own minds. Additionally, analysts do not practice psychoanalysis as if they were offering only metaphoric truths.

The interpretations-as-literary-criticism model is also not subject to the strong version of the argument from patient rejection. Still, it is problematic in offering an interpretation of interpretation that is not causal—it is simply in the nature of psychoanalytic interpretation to reveal causes. Moreover, it may be subject to the weak version of the argument from patient rejection: patients may be dissatisfied with a conception of psychoanalysis under which it reveals noncausal truths by non-interpretive means. And once again, analysts appear as they practice to be offering causal truths.

Chapter 6 reevaluates the weak form of the argument, suggesting that there is not a serious problem if psychoanalysis does not appear to be as certain different models characterize it: analysts can simply practice, and conceptualize the way they practice, differently. Moreover, although one could then argue that the therapy would not be analysis, why should we care? I offer reasons for thinking we should care. Yet I also propose that the important issue for patients deciding whether they can accept a particular therapy is empirical, namely, whether the therapy works. The weak form of the argument from patient

---

ing "patient rejection." Arguments lacking this principle, and hence less predictive, I term weak. It is also true that the weak argument has a normative and conceptual component (as we shall see), which might lead those anxious for a therapy to be analysis—patients and analysts alike— to reject it. Still, I think the normative force of the strong argument is stronger and thus lends greater weight to the prediction of rejection in that case.

rejection, then, is not as persuasive as the strong, although it does have some merit.

A conclusion discusses the implications of the various models for an issue other than patient acceptance, namely, what they mean for theoretical psychoanalysis; examines other important questions raised by this study, questions that could be the subject of further research; and ties together the findings of this book.

The Appendix asks in more detail whether any theorist genuinely holds the story model or whether it is a straw man. It first argues that, to the extent that some of these thinkers take a more moderate position, it is still subject to the argument. But it concludes that a number of thinkers do seem to take the more radical position and have influenced a cadre of clinicians who clearly do take it. Perhaps none of these people recognizes what their language commits them to, but commit them it does.

Finally, one must ask whether referring to all the thinkers in the different models as hermeneutic is a misnomer. Some might claim that hermeneutics is about understanding truth, so that the story model, for example—or any model of hermeneutic psychoanalysis that is not concerned with truth—is not really hermeneutic at all. The hermeneutic approach is concerned with *how* things are true and with the possibility that there are different modalities of truth. Recall, for instance, that Gadamer's great opus is called *Truth and Method*. Similarly, the old *verstehen* hypothesis says that knowledge is one thing in the human sciences and another in the natural sciences. Hermeneutics, then, is not ambivalent about the importance of truth, but it emphasizes that the nature of the thing to be understood may put the truth conditions of statements about that thing and methods of ascertaining their truth on a special footing. If this is right, the story model, for one, is not a model of hermeneutic psychoanalysis.

I do not intend in this book to enter a debate about the correct purview of the term "hermeneutic." It may well be that all philosophical hermeneuts embrace some colorable conception of truth. On the other hand, a number of commentators have criticized them, as we shall see, for problematic conceptions of objectivity and truth. The central point is that, even if some of the psychoanalysts I discuss distort the philosophical hermeneutic tradition, they conceive of themselves — and are conceived of by other analysts — as hermeneutic psychoanalysts. Indeed, one may wonder whether these several positions are not actually closer than they appear, especially considering how alike they all sound. At the least, the apparently unproblematic views threaten to become problematic in the wrong hands.

2

The Hermeneutic Analytic Thinkers

I have selected eight representative thinkers who have written about hermeneutic psychoanalysis for consideration in this chapter. They are a disparate group in many ways: some are practicing psychoanalysts, some are not; some have written extensively about hermeneutic psychoanalysis, some have not; some have written at one time, some at another; some have one clinical view, some another. Indeed, several of these thinkers might reject the idea of being grouped with the others. But that is part of the point: these people sound quite a lot like each other but are actually very different. I select these eight thinkers, then, because they seem fairly representative in many ways, not the least of which is that they often sound alike but really take quite different positions. I do not discuss one important class of hermeneutic psychoanalysts, perhaps the most important historically—namely, Ricoeur and Habermas.[1] They are prominent examples of the class of mixed hermeneuts, and I ignore them because their mixed version of hermeneutics is not subject to the argument from patient rejection and may raise unnecessary complications.[2]

In presenting the views of these eight hermeneutic thinkers, I quote fairly extensively from their work. I wish to give the reader a feel for how they speak about their subject. Interpreting these interpretivists, as it turns out, is a fairly difficult

1. See, e.g., Habermas (1971); Ricoeur (1970 and 1981).

2. In essence, the mixed version of hermeneutics may be saved from the argument by virtue of the *non*hermeneutic portion of the mix; other effects of the mix in terms of the argument I leave for others to explore.

business, and I want readers to be able to decide for themselves what each is saying.

Indeed, I do not take myself to be writing intellectual history in this work at all. Although I present five stylized models of positions these hermeneutic thinkers may be taking and offer some thoughts on how to classify each of the thinkers whose language I present, my primary goal is not to give a definitive reading of any of them. Indeed, most of the thinkers I treat here have written widely, so that arriving at a final reading of their work would require systematic presentation of their views at differing times of their careers. I attempt no such presentation.

My goal, rather, is to use their language as a springboard from which to formulate various plausible hermeneutic views— and then to assess the views themselves. At the same time, I wish to give enough of their language to enable the reader to see that each model is a plausible interpretation of hermeneutic psychoanalysis. I leave for others the task of arriving at comprehensive views of the theories of these practitioners. So long as each of my stylized models seems a plausible version of hermeneutic psychoanalysis, my goal in presenting these thinkers will have been accomplished.

I wish in presenting these writers to focus on one central feature of the hermeneutic sciences: their taking the supreme category to be that of *meaning* (Atwood and Stolorow 1984). The hermeneuts, as noted, often say things like psychoanalysis seeks after meaning, not causes, or meaning, not facts. What do they mean by this? It is the possible answers to that question that will generate the five stylized models of hermeneutic psychoanalysis.

Although George Klein never identified himself as a hermeneutic psychoanalyst, several features of his thought lend themselves to that characterization, and commentators have counted him as either a hermeneut or at least a precursor of hermeneutics.[3] Klein saw the central task of psychoanalysis as deciphering meaning rather than identifying the neurophysiological substratum of behavior. Indeed, psychoanalysis was actually, according to Klein, two theories: the clinical theory, which was concerned with the analysand as a meaning-creating subject, and the metapsychological theory, which was concerned with the analysand as a natural object that is subject ultimately to the laws of physics. The clinical theory was primary, and Klein recommended that psychoanalysts devote themselves to further adumbrating and validating that theory.

Klein's affinities with the hermeneutic tradition may be seen initially in his linking of clinical psychoanalysis more closely to the humanistic disciplines than to natural science: "The analyst's job of explaining has much in common with the historian's obligation of narrative construction and with the playwright's responsibility for depicting a logic of motivation. I am skeptical whether conceptions of mechanisms or physiological models, on the other hand, can lead deductively to concepts of intentionality of the sort that serve the aims of clinical explanation" (1976a, 30, 31).

In a move that will later appeal to many hermeneuts, Klein

3. Depending on one's definition of "hermeneutic," of course, Klein will either count or not count as a hermeneut. For example, he is unambiguously concerned with meaning as a central category, and he objects to the scientism of the metapsychology. But he is arguably not antiscientific (see below)—he thinks that clinical psychoanalysis can be studied scientifically—and to the extent that that is an important part of hermeneutic psychoanalysis, Klein is not a hermeneutic analyst.

analogizes interpretation to literature. He points out that the discovery of the analyst has traditionally been the province of the novelist, to whom we are most beholden for "our hypotheses concerning the meaning of man's behavior" (52). As Klein later puts it, "Psychoanalysis looks upon human development in terms of milestones and of solutions occurring in a context of given limits. Again, psychoanalysis is, in this respect, most related not to biology but to the aims of the dramatist and the novelist, for it parallels the intentions of dramatic structure and reflects the basic appeal of drama" (55).

Klein's emphasis on the role of meaning in the psychoanalytic process places him most squarely in the hermeneutic tradition. According to Klein, "The fundamental intent of the psychoanalytic enterprise [is] *unlocking meanings*" (48). A central ingredient of the clinical mode of explanation is that "its accounts are in terms of reasons and origins, significance and meaning" (50). He continues,

> Psychoanalysis, first of all, attempts to specify coherences in behavior in terms of purpose, not only conscious intention but also that arising out of the dynamics of aborted wish, conflict, defense, anxiety, guilt, and unconscious fantasy. When an analyst sees a pattern of behavior functioning as a "defense," for example, he is stating the *significance* of a pattern of behavior; he is making a statement about its purpose or intention. The coherences to which an analyst becomes sensitized are unique in their distinctive concern with purpose — aims frustrated, conflicted, aborted, regressed, defended against. This discovery of intention is the primary objective of the analyst in the psychoanalytic situation, and the primary function of

his extraphenomenological concepts of meaning-fulness. (52)

"The analyst's distal foci, then, . . . are behavioral coherences that exemplify purpose and significance. The main point of psychoanalytic work is to unlock such meanings" (53).[4]

According to Klein, it was Freud's genius to bring problems of meaning and significance back into psychology: "He developed a taxonomy and a code for deciphering the meanings of personal relationships in their conscious and unconscious aspects. Psychoanalysis imputes meaning to behavior by showing the significance of myth in our lives, those inner phantoms of fantasy which render objects significant, and which lead us to establish and react to relationships" (53).

When Klein says that the function of psychoanalysis is to decipher meanings, he is thinking of the clinical theory, as opposed to the metapsychological theory. He has clearly distinguished two psychoanalyses or shown that psychoanalysis presents itself in two guises: "the psychology in terms of which Freud interpreted dreams and symptoms and slips of the tongue —the distinctive meanings that behaviors acquire when interpreted in terms of sexual and aggressive wishes, conscious and unconscious events, displacement of aims, transference, unconscious fantasy, and related principles; and on the other hand a theory—the theory of metapsychology—which explains that clinical theory" (43). What is distinctive about psychoanalysis as clinical theory, then, is its orientation to intentionality:

4. See also Klein (1976a, 54) ("psychoanalysis is a psychology of the *meanings and syntheses arising out of crises in an individual's lifetime*"); Klein (1976a, 55) ("The core, then, of the clinical psychoanalytic enterprise is in the meanings that emerge from the dialectics of the directed forces to which a person is subject; that is, the forces resulting in dilemma and conflict and the opposing conditions from which evolve patterns of behavior which are viewed as ego syntheses").

"The central objective of psychoanalytic clinical explanation is the *reading of intentionality;* behavior, experience, testimony are studied for meaning in this sense, as jointly exemplifying directive "tensions," avowed, disavowed, repressed, defended. This orientation to explanation generates concepts that reflect a picture of individual development as a problem-solving, meaning-seeking, meaning-organizing venture, involving and resulting from the constant resolution of incompatible aims and tendencies. Applied to the understanding of symptoms, for example, such explanation consists in going back from a symptom not to the workings of a mechanism which is itself actually or potentially observable, but to a life-history context in which the symptom becomes intelligible as exemplifying an aimful solution. (27)

Whereas the clinical theory is concerned with "why" questions, the metapsychology is concerned with "how" questions, that is, with specifying causal texture in the sense of mechanics: "In this other side of psychoanalytic explanation, the terms of explanation have nothing to do with the subject's own vantage point; it is the person *observed as a physical process* that is the main objective. . . . [T]he experience of the subject and his aims become 'objects' for study. They are no longer aims and intentions within reach of the subject's experience, but structural facts of the psyche, 'properties' of an object" (29).

But what is the relationship between the clinical theory and the metapsychology? Psychoanalysts tend to take the clinical concepts for granted and to think of the metapsychology as the basic theory that explains those concepts, but according to Klein, they have things all wrong. The clinical theory is the most distinctively psychoanalytic. The clinical concepts are not less theoretical or abstract than the metapsychological concepts—indeed, they constitute a general psychological theory.

The essential problem with the metapsychology and with modern proposals for replacing it is not that they are inherently implausible, but that they are "simply irrelevant to the clinical psychoanalytic enterprise" (47): "The essential *clinical* propositions concerning motivation have nothing to do with reducing a hypothetical tension; they are inferences of *directional* gradients in behavior, and of the *object relations* involved in these directions. . . . The key factors, then, in the psychoanalytic clinical view of motivation are relational requirements, encounters, crises, dilemmas, resolutions, and achievements—not a hypothetical 'tension' reduction" (47–48).

Physiological terms cannot substitute for psychoanalytic terms descriptive of meanings of object relations:

> Meaning and purpose—conscious and unconscious —define *principles* of regularity that are *translatable* to, but not *reducible* to, physiological and neurophysiological specifications. . . . It is not simply that the psychoanalytic situation cannot provide the data for a physiological conception of psychoanalytic facts. It seems to me that no such data could ever substitute for the constructs of personal meaning which constitute psychoanalytic psychology, which is of an entirely different level of perceived order, involving different units of analysis. These cannot be known from, or deduced from, principles of physics and chemistry, or from mechanical, physiological, or cathectic models. Therefore it is of secondary, not primary, importance for

psychoanalysts to concern themselves with translations to physiological models of explanation. (56)[5]

Although Klein sees psychoanalysis primarily as the clinical theory and not the metapsychology, and although he likens psychoanalysis so conceived to a humanistic discipline, he does not regard psychoanalysis as nonscientific—as beyond the possibility of verification or falsification. Indeed, he sees questions of validation as crucial, although beyond the scope of his current work.

Thus, Klein points out that the clinical concepts are closer to the activities of clinical observation and the focus of the analyst's intentions than the metapsychological concepts, and he goes on to stress that they are therefore also more responsive to the data and capable of systematic modification. Klein argues that we must attempt to assess psychoanalytic concepts further, based on systematic efforts to link these concepts to the observed data of the psychoanalytic situation and on the responsiveness of the concepts to modification by observation. The strategy of inferring from data to lawfulness is a matter vital to the development of psychoanalysis.

In short, for Klein, psychoanalysis is "in the class of theories

5. Klein concretely applies his ideas about the two psychoanalyses to a number of Freudian concepts in an effort to disentangle the clinical from the metapsychological in these concepts. A well-known example is his piece called "Freud's Two Theories of Sexuality," (1976b, 72–120). Here he argues that the clinical theory, for Freud, emphasizes the meaning of sexuality, while the drive-discharge theory is one of ameaning. These two theories fail to make contact with each other. Drive theory needs the specification of an energic unit; these units could not be those of psychoanalysis, whose units are cognitive ones of meaning. Klein concludes that we need testing of the clinical theory in its own terms. On the significance of testing the clinical concepts, for Klein, see below.

that concern themselves with the 'why' of behavior, that try to state reasons rather than causes, that try to say that a behavior has a certain meaning, derived from the *history* of this meaning in the person's life, that try to speak of the *psychical* functions through which the meaning is expressed" (56). If Klein's theory ought to be regarded as hermeneutic, it ought to be so regarded because of its fundamental focus on meaning.

ROY SCHAFER

The Early Schafer

Roy Schafer has been a prominent spokesperson for a hermeneutic vision of psychoanalysis. A prolific writer, Schafer has undergone certain transformations in his views over the course of time; yet he has remained basically hermeneutic since at least *A New Language for Psychoanalysis* (1976). I divide my discussion of Schafer's work between his early hermeneutic period—the period of *A New Language*—and his later hermeneutic period—the period of *The Analytic Attitude* (1983) and *Retelling A Life* (1992). To simplify, in his early period Schafer asks us to focus on the clinical psychology (understood in terms of his action language) as opposed to the metapsychology; in his later period, he asks us to focus on psychoanalytic interpretations as narratives.

One of the main thrusts of *A New Language for Psychoanalysis* is Schafer's idea that analysts should focus on wishes and intentions, not on causes in the sense of happenings in the body. In other words, analysts should focus on Freud's clinical theory and abandon the metapsychology: "It is high time we stopped using this mixed physicochemical and evolutionary biological language altogether" (1976, 3).

Schafer identifies at least two problems with the metapsy-

chology. The first is the anthropomorphism that pervades it —
an "inescapable consequence or correlate of Freud's mecha-
nistic and organismic mode of theorizing" (102).[6] The second
problem is that the natural science approach "excludes meaning from the center of psychoanalytic theory. . . . But meaning
(and intention) is the same as 'psychic reality'—that which is
at the center of clinical psychoanalytic work" (199). As Schafer
puts it elsewhere, "The biological language of functions cannot
be concerned with meaning. . . . the primary psychoanalytic
language is a language of and for meanings and the changes
they undergo during development and during the psychoanalytic process" (89).[7]

Thus Schafer is convinced that we should reject the metapsychology in favor of the clinical theory.[8] And he wants to see
psychoanalysis as a form of humanities, not of natural science.
His investigation here "involves turning attention to the roots
of psychoanalysis in the humanities. These roots have been all
but lost sight of in this, the heyday of the medical-scientific
program for psychoanalysis. . . . Psychoanalysis is necessarily
closely related to the humanities in that its raw data are meanings and subjective experience, and its methods are those that
promote the clarification and organization of meaning and experience along certain lines. Psychoanalysis is a special form of
knowing about human existence and history" (25).

Now as we have seen, meaning is at the center of clinical psychoanalytic work. And what meaning amounts to, in
essence, is psychic reality: " 'Psychic reality' refers to subjec-

6. See also Schafer (1976, 110-11).

7. Indeed, Schafer suggests that the two problems that the metapsychology poses are related. See Schafer (1976, 103).

8. In language that is more prominent in his later work, Schafer also
points out that the natural science approach is but an "option" (1976,
68-69).

tive meaning, especially unconscious meaning" (89). Schafer gives a concrete example: "In explaining why a person gives up the efficient use of his or her eyes, we would base our clinical explanation on that which has found disguised expression in 'looking,' which is to say, the latent *meaning* of looking. We would say that having taken on the significance of certain drive activities and gratifications, looking was being dealt with as if it were these very activities and gratifications — *which, in psychic reality, it is*" (87). He adds, "We speak of these analyzed meanings as the analysand's psychic reality" (90).

Indeed, psychoanalysis itself is a process of creating "a more comprehensive, unified, and intelligible past and present for the patient, . . . and, on this account, it even provides some vague outlines of a future" (49). It does this, among other things, by "filling in crucial gaps of a particular kind in the analysand's memory, in the awareness of certain crucial meanings and connections, and in intrapsychic and interpersonal experience" (49). In short, "analysis creates a new or another version of the life and mind of the patient" (49).[9]

What are Schafer's views about the nature of truth and reality in these early days? His first cut on the nature of reality and our access to it is in the context of his exploration of several visions of reality inherent in psychoanalytic thought and practice — the comic, romantic, tragic, and ironic. He terms these views "visions of reality," he says, "to emphasize that they are partly subjective, or not completely disprovable, ways of looking at experience and imposing meaning on it" (55):

9. Note that Schafer shares another feature with the hermeneutic analyst who wishes to focus on meaning, namely, wishing to focus on the reasons for an action, rather than on its causes. See, e.g., Schafer (1976, 205).

The term *vision* implies judgments partly rooted in subjectivity, that is, in acts of imagination and articles of faith, which, however illuminating and complex they may be, necessarily involve looking at reality from certain angles and not others. As visions influence the determination of facts and their interrelations and implications, clashes between visions cannot be settled by simple appeals to "the evidence." It would not be correct to regard these clashes merely as matters of opinion. (23)[10]

Even more important than Schafer's views on the status of these visions of reality are his views on the truth of the personal reality that analyst and patient come to agree on as the patient's life history in the course of an analysis. Is the psychoanalytic life history of the individual patient objective and true? Schafer says his concern is with

> an understanding of what analysis necessarily is. I propose, therefore, that the analytically created life history, while not fictive, is also not what one might call the absolute truth. How could it be when it has been wrought by two specific collaborators working at a specific point in time, under specific conditions; and also when, as I mentioned earlier, the collaborating side of the analysand's ego itself has

10. Even in these early years, Schafer sometimes puts the point in language closer to that which he will frequently use later: although we "seem to be seeing the phenomena as though they were accessible without mediation, that is, as prior to and independent of some rendition of them, and which therefore seem to stand there innocently open to multiple approaches, . . . this is an illusion. There are no virginal phenomena" (1976, 201–02).

been shaped by the influences it is the business of the analytic collaboration to modify? . . . If it is permissible to say so, the version becomes less fictive as the analysis is extended in range and made more precise. . . . Nevertheless, however close the approximation to truth—and it can be considerable and of considerable value to the analysand—in the end, one is still left with a version of one's life and mind. It cannot be otherwise. (49–50)

Thus, "the emerging analytic life history is to be viewed as a joint creation of patient and analyst—not a fiction but not simply factual either, being subject to a degree to the limitations, individualities, and visions of the two participants in the analytic process" (1983, 56).

Schafer cites a personal communication from Loewald bearing on this issue:"In a sense, every patient, and each of us, creates a personal myth about our life and past, a myth which sustains us and may destroy us. The myth may change, and in analysis, where it becomes conscious, it often does change. The created life history is neither an illusion nor an invention, but gives form and meaning to our lives, and has to do with the identity Erikson speaks of" (50).

The Later Schafer

In considering the later Schafer—the Schafer of *The Analytic Attitude* and *Retelling A Life*, for example—I shall organize the discussion into three parts: first, his conceptualization of the psychoanalytic process; second, his contrast between his worldview and that of the positivist; and third, his conception in particular of the truth and verifiability of psychoanalytic interpretations.

According to Schafer, "Psychoanalysts may be described as people who listen to the narrations of analysands and help them to transform these narrations into others that are more complete, coherent, convincing, and adaptively useful than those they have been accustomed to constructing" (1983, 240). Or, as Schafer puts it elsewhere, "People going through psychoanalysis—analysands—tell the analyst about themselves and others in the past and present. In making interpretations, the analyst retells these stories. In the retelling, certain features are accentuated while others are placed in parentheses; certain features are related to others in new ways or for the first time; some features are developed further, perhaps at great length. This retelling is done along psychoanalytic lines" (1983, 219). In a word, psychoanalysis is a "telling and retelling along psychoanalytic lines" (1983, 218).

This conception of analysts as retelling the patient's life implies "a perspective on the analyst at work, specifically that he or she takes everything in the analytic situation as a text that requires interpretation or that might, by suitable interventions, be developed to the point where it is enough of a text to yield to psychoanalytic interpretation" (1992, 176). Yet "like any other text presented to the world, the analysand's text does not remain in his or her control" (1992, 176).[11]

In what do the analyst's retellings or narrative revisions consist? The concept of retelling, for Schafer, "subsumes four overlapping terms: redescribing, reinterpreting, recontextual-

11. Thus the analyst focuses on not only the content of the telling, but also the action of telling itself—and its disruptions. See Schafer (1983, 186, 223, 228).

izing, and reducing" (1983, 187).[12] As a schematic example, Schafer cites the case of an interpretation that deals with reaction formation against sadism. Here, "the analyst is *redescribing* ostensible kindness as a defensive move, or *reinterpreting* as defensiveness what the analysand has already interpreted and presented as evidence of sheer kindness, or *recontextualizing* ostensible kindness by placing it in a setting of infantile as well as current danger situations, or *reducing* the manifest forms and occasions of forced kindness to prototypic childhood situations of danger and defense (for example being good out of fear of abandonment)" (1983, 187).

An interesting feature of Schafer's position follows from his view of analysis as tellings and retellings. Unlike Donald Spence, who sees all reconstructions in essence as constructions, Schafer sees all constructions as reconstructions. The reason is obvious: because the patient is always constructing, the analyst is always necessarily reconstructing what has already been constructed: "Each analytically revised account of the past is necessarily a reconstruction of that which has already been constructed differently" (194).

Indeed, even accounts of the present, for Schafer, are always reconstructions: "Accounts of the present (the here and now) are reconstructions in the same way as accounts of the past, as described above, except that they feature acts of perceiving rather than remembering." Because "every perception is itself a construction (an interpretive selection, organization, and formulation), the perceived present may not be regarded as a reality that is simply given, self-evident, or prenarrational. Like the facts of the past, the facts of the here and now exist only in narrated versions of them" (195).

12. For a rather different description of retellings than Schafer's customary one, see Schafer (1983, 194).

Schafer also wishes to insist that analyst and analysand are coauthors of the text being interpreted (1992, 177). And just as analyst and analysand mutually influence each other, so interpretations of the present and interpretations of the past mutually influence each other: "The past is used to make the present more intelligible, and the present is used to make the past more intelligible, which is to say more coherent, continuous, and convincing" (188).[13]

Thus, there is a "complex circularity and narrativity of working simultaneously with the here and now reconstructions of transference and resisting and the then and there reconstructions of the vicissitudes of early development. Those then and there reconstructions remain, however, part of the here and now of the analytic narrative enterprise. How else could it be?" (201).[14]

Schafer also stresses the importance of the "second reality"— the largely unconscious reality that emerges as the chief locale or scene of effective psychoanalysis (161).[15] The second reality "is the reality of unconscious mental processes, and it is characterized by modes and contents of a special sort" (244). "This second reality is as real as any other. In many ways it is more coherent and inclusive and more open to your activity than the reality you now vouch for and try to make do with" (235). "The second reality of psychoanalysis is more akin to the reality constructed in poetry, story, visual arts, and myth. It both supplements and competes with pragmatic conventionalized reality. Both kinds of reality are constructions. Each construction has its uses" (255).

A related point that Schafer is at some pains to emphasize

13. See also Schafer (1983, 196, 201, 208).
14. One reason it could not be otherwise is given by the very nature of transference. See Schafer (1983, 203).
15. See also Schafer (1983, 244).

is the primacy of the history of the analysis itself. He asks, "Is there a narrative form that is methodologically more adequate to the psychoanalytic occasion [than the traditional case history]?" and he answers, "I believe there is. It is a story that begins in the middle which is the present: the beginning is the beginning of the analysis" (238).[16] Indeed, ideally all material in the analysis "should be at least implicitly interpreted with reference to its function in the analytic dialogue and thereby maximized in its significance and utility. There are no 'other issues' pure and simple; there are only alternate, even if often tangential and delayed, approaches to the issues of the analysis itself" (207).[17] And so "the history that the analyst comes to believe in with most justification is the history of the analysis itself" (206).

Schafer also believes that the history of the analysis (as of the life of the patient) is more like a set of histories that is retold from multiple perspectives than a final, definitive account. Thus there is no single, definitive account of an action, an analysis, a life (204, 206).

Implicit in Schafer's theory of the nature of the psychoanalytic process is his postmodern worldview, which he contrasts with Freud's positivistic worldview. Schafer's worldview shapes and gives form to his narrative conception of psychoanalysis: "Freud established a tradition within which psychoanalysis is understood as an essentialist and positivist natural science. One need not be bound by this scientific commitment, however; the individual and general accounts and interpretations Freud gave

16. See also Schafer (1983, 209, 239).
17. Indeed, Schafer goes so far as to say that "reconstruction of the infantile past is a temporally displaced and artificially linearized account of the analysis in the here and now." (1983, 203). See below on the interrelation between past and present.

of his case material can be read in another way. In this reading, psychoanalysis is an interpretive discipline whose practitioners aim to develop a particular kind of systematic account of human action" (212).

The positivist model is flawed for a number of reasons. "According to [that] model," Schafer says, "the investigator discovers, studies, and theorizes about facts that exist as such apart from the investigator's interrelated theoretical and methodological precommitments" (188). "At least for the analytic observer, the subject and object are clearly distinct. Reality is encountered and recognized innocently. In part it simply forces itself on one, in part it is discovered or uncovered by search and reason free of theory" (234).[18]

The problem with thinking of analytic projects—say, normative life-historical projects—as simply fact-finding expeditions, is that "each such expedition is prepared for what is to be found: it has its maps and compasses, its conceptual supplies, and its probable destination. This preparedness (which contradicts the empiricists' pretensions of innocence) amounts to a narrative plan, form, or set of rules" (238).[19] As a result, "in psychoanalysis, as in all other fields of inquiry, there can be no theory-free and method-free facts" (188). A simple positivistic conception of analytic work is inadequate. The facts are what the analyst makes them out to be (257).

Schafer concludes from these difficulties that we must adopt a different worldview:

> Today, . . . this positivist stance in relation to data
> seems obsolete. I think it is now necessary to ac-

18. And see Schafer's description of the positivist's position on such questions as "When and where is a phallus?" and the nature of selfhood. See Schafer (1983, 284, 184).
19. See also Schafer (1992, 189).

cept some form of the following interrelated propositions: one cannot distinguish sharply what the analyst finds and what the analyst introduces as a narrative organization; no absolute distinction between analytic subject and object is tenable; all perception is interpretation in context; and all proposed analytic interpretation is therefore reinterpretation that requires both recontextualization of what has been told and reduction of that telling to one or another psychoanalytic storyline. (184)

"Thus, in considering analytic knowledge," Schafer says, "we confront this triple circularity: conventional distinctions between subject and object, between observation and theory, and between past and present no longer hold" (203).

The positivistic telling, in brief, "is only one way of giving or arriving at an account of the subject in the world, and it is incoherent with respect to the epistemological assumptions inherent in psychoanalytic inquiry, that is, those assumptions that limit us always to dealing only with *versions* of reality" (234).

Schafer is clear that rejection of the positivist vision of the world lands him squarely in the camp of the hermeneuts, and Schafer declares himself to be a hermeneut:

What has been presented here amounts to a hermeneutic version of psychoanalysis. In this version, psychoanalysis is an interpretive discipline rather than a natural science. It deals in language and equivalents of language. Interpretations are redescriptions or retellings of action along the lines peculiar to psychoanalytic interest. Action can only be named or described from one or another point of view, that is, on the basis of certain presuppositions and in keeping with certain aims. (255)[20]

A central feature of Schafer's hermeneutic vision of psychoanalysis, as we have seen, is that we can have no unmediated access to reality—all facts are constructed. Reality is always mediated by narration. Far from being innocently encountered or discovered, it is created in a regulated fashion (257). As Schafer puts it elsewhere,

> one can never have unmediated access to . . .
> events, for the events can exist only in narrative
> accounts that have been or may be developed by
> the analysand or analyst for different purposes and
> in different contexts. On my understanding, this
> pluralistic and relativistic conception of "events" is
> put forward in many modern theories of knowl-
> edge. In psychoanalysis, the versions of significant
> events change as the work progresses, and with
> these changes go changes in what is called the ex-
> perience of these events, for the narrative accounts
> and the experiences are inseparable. . . . the analyst
> views [the analysand's] experience as always being
> constructed or reconstructed; it can be encoun-
> tered only in explicit or implicit narrative accounts.
> (186)[21]

As an example of realities that are constructed—and of how Schafer construes their constructedness—consider his descriptions of self and other as narrated:

20. See also Schafer (1983, 191).
21. See also Schafer (1992, 50, 55, 56).

We are forever telling stories about ourselves. In telling these self-stories *to others* we may, for most purposes, be said to be performing straightforward narrative actions. In saying that we also tell them *to ourselves,* however, we are enclosing one story within another. This is the story that there is a self to tell something to, a someone else serving as audience who is oneself or one's self. When the stories we tell others about ourselves concern these other selves of ours, when we say, for example, "I am not master of myself," we are again enclosing one story within another. On this view, the self is a telling. From time to time and from person to person, this telling varies in the degree to which it is unified, stable, and acceptable to informed observers as reliable and valid. (218)

About narrations of the other, he says, "Additionally, we are forever telling stories about others. These others, too, may be viewed as figures or other selves constituted by narrative actions. Other people are constructed in the telling about them; more exactly, we narrate others just as we narrate selves. The other person, like the self, is not something one has or encounters as such but an existence one tells. Consequently, telling 'others' about 'ourselves' is doubly narrative" (219). In short, self and other are an existence one tells—not something one "has" or "encounters."

Schafer seems to be saying here that the realities of self and other are simply narrations. In fact, however, Schafer takes the facts to be more complicated than that: "Evidence does not consist of simple, narratively unmediated, objective facts. What is called the evidence is, like all other evidence, theory laden; it is constructed in that uncertain area between what is found and what is created, and it is that 'evidence' that is used to support reasoning which, unreflectively, is taken to be simply logical, factual, and conclusive" (1992, 54).[22] Schafer's commitment to the constructedness of reality is evident in many areas. Thus, for Schafer, acts are narrated.[23] Experiences are narrated or constructed too: "One learns how to construct experience" (1983, 248). And naturally, if reality is constructed, it follows that the events and items of reality involved in psychoanalysis are constructed too: "One must, first of all, accept the proposition that there are no objective, autonomous, or pure psychoanalytic data which, as Freud was fond of saying, compel one to draw conclusions. . . . What have been presented as the plain empirical data and techniques of psychoanalysis are inseparable from the investigator's precritical and interrelated assumptions concerning the origins, coherence, totality, and intelligibly of personal action."[24] Schafer notes as variables crucial to the stories an analyst tells the analytic attitude and the analyst's theoretical stance.[25]

For Schafer, then, facts are constructed—from transference, to life-historical events, to self. They are constituted by narratives. Language "occupies center stage in theoretical thinking

22. See also Schafer (1992, 182).

23. See, e.g., Schafer (1992, 44). Indeed, not only is the telling or presenting of a version of an action a narration; so is the version itself. See Schafer (1992, xiv). Moreover, even the barest, most minimal account of an action is itself a narrative. See Schafer (1992, 45).

24. See, e.g., Schafer (1983, 212). For the general claim, see also Schafer (1983, 213). Schafer also makes the claim as to specific items involved in psychoanalysis. See, e.g., Schafer (1983, 239) (traditional developmental accounts); (1983, 204) (life-historical facts); (1983, 209) (biographical material); (1983, 189, 243) (psychoanalytic experience); (1983, 195, 220) (transference); (1983, 183) (the "second reality"); (1983, 209) (inner emptiness); (1983, 231) (inability); (1983, 255) (introspection); (1992, 54) (self-deception).

25. See Schafer (1992, 20) and (1983, 212), respectively.

and research. Language is seen as that which makes the world that it tells about" (1992, 148).

I now wish to consider two themes that are related to Schafer's view that facts are constructed. First, multiple constructions are possible in the case of any fact. And second, one has some choice about which construction to adopt.

Schafer says he "invoke[s] the idea of narration precisely in connection with the inevitability of alternative descriptions" (1992, xiv). Acts and events come into being in narrative or at least narratable form, "and that form is almost infinitely changeable" (1983, 251). And so, for example, "when the analysand is viewed as being engaged in narrative performance, he or she will be understood to be giving only one of a great number of possible accounts that could be given of these life events" (1983, 186). His account "must be regarded as merely one version of the story-content to which reference is being made" (1983, 252).

The account Schafer is recommending, he says, "necessarily limits one to constructing some version or some vision of the subject in the world. One defines situations and invests events with multiple meanings. These meanings are more or less adequately responsive to different questions that the narrator . . . wants to answer; they are also responsive to the rules of context that the narrator intends to follow and to the level of abstraction that he or she wishes to maintain" (1983, 234). And so, an individual analysis, for example, "produces not one history but a set of more or less coordinated accounts of life history. And thus it is that different analytic approaches based on different assumptions produce different sets of life histories that support these assumptions" (1983, 205).

That so many versions of things are possible permits Schafer to make his familiar claim that there is "no one, final, true, all-purpose account of that event" (1983, 253).[26] It also leads to the second point that I wish to stress about Schafer: his belief that one has some choice about which of the many possible constructions to adopt. The "proposition that drive is a narrative structure," for example, means that it is "an optional way of telling the story of human lives" (1983, 225).[27] One often fails to recognize that one has such choices: "Because [a particular] story is so familiar . . . [one is] not ordinarily prepared to recognize it as a story" (1992, 50).

Yet, while one has choices about which narratives to use, the narratives themselves to some extent constrain choice: when one chooses a storyline, one must "observ[e] such constraints as it exercises on narrators working within the conventions of how these deceptions are to be presented" (1992, 56). And so Schafer prefers "storyline" to "metaphor"

> because, in my estimate, it has more obvious generative and regulatory connotations. Storyline suggests that there are a number of versions of the story that may be actualized, provided only that the storyteller observes enough of the conventional constraints (follows the "line"). These conventional constraints are not ordinarily extremely limiting, but there is usually a point beyond which attentive readers or listeners will begin to question whether a different story is now being told; for example, a consistent emphasis on experiences of relaxed plea-

26. See also Schafer (1992, 44).
27. Schafer gives several other examples of his claim. See, e.g., Schafer (1992, 55) (deception); (1983, 249) (disclaiming forms of action); (1983, 220) (transference). Indeed, even "viewing psychoanalysis as a therapy itself manifests a narrative choice" (1983, 220).

sure in the context of giving an account of defense will be thought to be changing the story unless it is made clear that and how that relaxed pleasure is necessary to the story of defense. (1992, 47)[28]

Although one's choice about how to describe, and so constitute, the world may have some constraints, it remains just that—a choice. Consider Schafer's discussion of one's choice about the "rules regulating the creation of reality":

The rules regulating the creation of reality may be conventional, in which case no questions are likely to be raised about the world and how we know it; if needed, consensual validation will be readily obtained. But things can be otherwise. Once certain rules are defined, they may prove to violate convention in a way that is incoherent or at least not understandable at a given moment. In this case, the place of these rules requires further investigation and interpretation. Those rules that inform truly original ideas may necessitate revision of accepted ideas about the rules that "must" be followed and the kind of reality that it is desirable or interesting to construct. (1983, 235)

Schafer's worldview, different from the positivist worldview, has constructivism and perspectivism at its center:

To agree that analysts interpret interpenetrated or cohabited texts is to accord to constructivism and its corollary, perspectivism, an essential place in psychoanalysis and to put into permanent question the traditional psychoanalytic claim to the

28. See also Schafer (1992, 45).

status of an empirical, inductive, objectively obser-
vational science. Constructivism and perspectivism
are theoretical positions on what we can and should
mean by "reality" or on the sense in which we
can "know" reality. In constructivism, the world
we claim to know objectively is not given directly
to perception and reason. Rather, reality is constructed according to rules; these rules, though
usually implicit, are ascertainable through critical
study, no matter whether they are known as such
to the subject or not. People follow these rules in
observing or making observable whatever it is that
they go on to say is in the real world. Broadly
viewed, these rules are pretty much the same among
members of the same culture and historical period,
although the selection, comprehension, and application of the rules are more or less individualized.
Hence the cultural diversity within conformity, or
the conformity within diversity, that we generally
acknowledge and more or less accept. The result
is not reality plain but a perspective on reality or,
more exactly, *reality by means of a perspective.*[29]

In all of this, what can we find of Schafer's views on truth? If
psychoanalytic interpretations are simply narratives or stories,
what becomes of their truth? Are they, as it were, true stories?
In what sense?

29. See Schafer (1992, 177–78). Schafer continues by expressing his
view in more traditional language: "Instead of the terms *constructivism,
perspectivism,* and *narration* or *storyline,* often other words or phrases are
used to grapple with the same issues of knowledge of reality or how to
arrive at the sense of an answer; these include *paradigms, models of the
mind, leading metaphors,* or just plain *theory.*"

In contrast to the early Schafer, who hedges this point, the later Schafer is clear that psychoanalytic narratives may, indeed, be true: "In the sense used here, narratives are not made-up stories (fictitious in the established sense) with beginnings, middles, and endings. Narrating, giving an account, presenting a version, developing a storyline, telling: These terms and others like them make up the core vocabulary of the narrational approach" (1992, xiv):

> It is especially important to emphasize that narrative is not an alternative to truth or reality; rather, it is the mode in which, inevitably, truth and reality are presented. We have only versions of the true and the real. Narratively unmediated, definitive access to truth and reality cannot be demonstrated. In this respect, therefore, there can be no absolute foundation on which any observer or thinker stands; each must choose his or her narrative or version. Further, each narrative presupposes or establishes a context, and the sentences of any one account attain full significance only within their context and through more or less systematic or consistent use of the language appropriate to the purpose. (1992, xiv–xv)

Schafer took essentially this view not only at the late stage of *Retelling A Life,* but also at the earlier stage of *The Analytic Attitude:*

> It must be asked next whether these histories comprise a set of new personal myths. To assert that they are myths is equivalent to saying that a history of any kind is a myth. This nihilistic (or pretentious?) conclusion does not follow from the preceding discussion. . . . What does follow is that it

is in the nature of historical accounts to be subject to challenge, revision, and extension in the
light of new questions and the new data that they
establish or bring to the foreground. That no history is the single and final one does not mean that
each history is a mythic creation which is exempt
from the rules of verification, coherence, consistency, and (for the time being) completeness. In
this sense, the psychoanalytic life histories are versions of the truth. . . . They are new, never before
possible versions of the truth and therefore new
truths. (1983, 206)

Indeed, Schafer makes essentially the same point when, as
we have seen, he denies that just any narrative is possible—that
one has complete freedom in choosing narratives:

[It is not being proposed] that any account is as
acceptable as any other. [What is being proposed
is] this—when we speak of true and false accounts
of actions, we are positioning ourselves in a matrix
of narratives that are always open to examination
as to their precritical assumptions and values and
as to their usefulness in one or another project.
Some versions of S.M.'s [a sadomasochist's] conduct, such as that he is totally permissive, would
depart so far from the conventions and uses of
social or clinical discourse that they would founder
from the start, except perhaps if they were being
developed with obvious irony. Of them we say that
they are false, inadequate, or illogical in any comprehensive discourse. Some accounts will be judged
to be better or closer to the truth than others on
the basis that they show a higher degree of consis-

tency, coherence, comprehensiveness, and common sense than the others. But in the complex instances that concern us the most, we cannot count on incontestable proofs of superiority, and we resort to, or submit to, rhetorical, ethical, and esthetic persuasiveness to decide what is better or best. Such, at any rate, is the account being used here of the way narratives of action are constructed and used. (1992, 56)[30]

Schafer, then, is persuaded that truth is possible in his narrational world.[31] One question that immediately arises is, How do we establish truth in the case of psychoanalytic interpretations? what are the criteria of validation? Schafer has some things to say about this too: "To speak of the unreliable narrator, one must have some conception of a reliable narrator, that is, of validity; and yet the trend of my argument suggests that there is no single definitive account to be achieved. Validity, it seems, can only be achieved within a system that is viewed as such and that appears, after careful consideration, to have the virtues of coherence, consistency, comprehensiveness, and common sense" (1983, 236).[32]

Schafer continues in a way that suggests that he counts therapeutic efficacy as a criterion of validity. Thus, the "in-

30. See also Schafer (1983, 203).

31. Of course, it is truth understood in a particular way—as an account that is consistent, coherent, comprehensive, and commonsensical. As Schafer puts it later, "Analytic case summaries purport to say what is true of the individual when they should say what is true according to the details of the different investigations that have been carried out within each analysis" (1983, 204).

32. He also has some ideas about what is an unacceptable criterion: "We cannot depend uncritically on convention and consensual validation in making claims about what is real or true" (1992, 55).

creased possibility of change" is an aim of the project and "an important criterion of its progress" (1983, 236), as is the re-allocation of activity and passivity in the analysand's life. The accounts must also "withstand further tough and searching questions" (1983, 236).

Schafer uses language suggestive of the "hermeneutic circle" when he claims that we cannot get outside of our narratives, as it were, to verify interpretations: "In another respect, I am only restating Freud's criteria for the verification of reconstructions: Verification is established by an accumulation of indirect or implicit responses, *the kind of responses that become evidence only upon interpretation, further analytic dialogue, and further interpretation*" (1992, 176). And so classic "constructions" that are not directly corroborated by memory may be "required for the coherence, followability, and further development of the analytic life histories, and ideally they will withstand the challenge posed by alternative interpretations."

If Schafer is convinced that psychoanalytic interpretations may be true in an unproblematic sense, he seems also to adopt a coherence theory of truth. Narrative, as Schafer says, is not an alternative to truth or reality, but rather the mode in which they are presented. And so when we speak of true or false accounts, we are positioning ourselves within a matrix of narratives. Schafer speaks of accounts being false in a comprehensive discourse and of some accounts being closer to the truth on the ground that they demonstrate a higher degree of coherence, consistency and common sense. Validity, he says, can be achieved only within a system. And so Schafer suggests that we cannot get outside our narrative accounts: evidence becomes evidence only upon further interpretation and dialogue.

Yet in a small piece responding to Richard Geha, Schafer suggests that he does not want altogether to abandon the role of correspondence in understanding the truth, if doing so would mean "the collapse of the distinction between history and art" (1984, 364). Schafer is troubled by Geha's "unqualified reliance on coherence, even while granting . . . both the epistemological difficulties associated with the usual positivistic notion of correspondence and the indispensability of criteria of coherence in assessing historical narratives" (366).

At the least, Schafer argues, criteria of correspondence "must refer or correspond to stable, communally recognized elements of a text and their interrelations. . . . Also, criteria of coherence imply consistency with similar elements of other historical texts, and the idea of 'other historical texts' implies the partial regulation of historical discourse by criteria of correspondence" (366–67).

For instance, though one may say that a text exists only in the minds of its readers, we can surely check Geha's references to R. G. Collingwood to determine whether they are—what? Just coherent? No, Schafer answers, the material "must also be portrayed reliably and accurately. It must observe conventions. The account must fall within a tradition or challenge a tradition" (367).

While some may charge Schafer with not following his arguments to their logical conclusion, he "would emphasize that [he has] repeatedly insisted that we cannot do without a conception of reality, even though we can attend to reality only by means of one or another version or vision of it" (368). "If we are to speak of perception at all . . . then we must presuppose not only a perceiver but also a perceived" (369). This is Schafer's central point: In order even to carry out Geha's recommended rhetorical analysis, "we would have to rely on some of the very convictions that are being challenged (e.g., that there is a past, that we can more or less agree on evidence, that we can in many respects recognize error, that we share a common language, etc.)" (370).

In short, at "the present time, the humanistic disciplines

seem to be in considerable disarray owing to the absence of authoritative answers to the deeply challenging questions about reality . . . raised over the past century. . . . There *are* grounds for radical doubt" (368). Nevertheless, some things can be said: "All discourse presupposes at least the limited version of correspondence I have sketched. . . . We are not required to repudiate totally some kind of correspondence, even if that correspondence is only general, provisional, conventional, situation-bound, or discipline-bound" (370).

"The problem of reality or correspondence," then, "remains with us. If we continue to wrestle with it rather than settle it too quickly, we can at least hope to gain more perspective on the limits under which we operate in this realm of discourse" (370).

HERBERT FINGARETTE

In "Meaning and Being" (1963), Herbert Fingarette proposes a "meaning-reorganization" view of psychoanalytic interpretation as opposed to a "hidden reality" view. In so doing, Fingarette conceives of his task as dealing with the "ontological interpretations of psychoanalysis and their implications, not with the question as to whether psychoanalysis is valid—a point which is here assumed" (18).

The hidden reality view, as Fingarette describes it, is the view that the psychoanalyst "uncovers for the patient what had been present but invisible. . . . The door hiding the hidden past is opened; or the veil is ripped from the disguised present. What was in the shadow is now itself unchanged in essence, but it is illuminated. This way of thinking about the processes in question I shall call the 'hidden reality' view. Put in ontological terms, the repressed is a continuously existent, potent, but hidden reality" (19).

This way of speaking is, of course, metaphorical. And Fingarette contrasts Freud's hidden reality metaphors with a different set of metaphors that conveys the essence of the meaning-reorganization view when one is talking about unconscious ideas, repression, and insight:

> "The therapeutic insight does not show the patient what he is or was; it *changes* him into someone *new*." "The therapist does not present information; he presents options." "Insight in its main function does not reveal unknown events of the past but helps us to see known past events in a new way." "The phrase 'unconscious process' does not refer directly to a spatio-temporal process." "Insight into an unconscious wish is like noticing suddenly a well-formed 'ship' in the cloud instead of a poorly formed 'rabbit.' On the other hand, insight is not like discovering an animal which has been hiding in the bushes." "Insight does not reveal a hidden, past reality; it is a reorganization of the meaning of present experience, a present reorientation toward both future *and* past." (20)

Fingarette offers several analogies to enable us to understand the meaning-reorganization view. Take the case of a person carefully reading a poem; though he understands all of the words, he does not appreciate the poem. A friend then suggests to the person "an over-all organization or unifying meaning-scheme which had not occurred to him. Suddenly, [the poem] 'clicks'" (21). The point is that the "words, without some unifying scheme of meanings, are not a poem. A poem is an experience which is generated only as there is also brought to bear some unifying scheme by the one who interprets" (21).

A therapeutic example enables Fingarette to distinguish more sharply the meaning-reorganization and the hidden reality views. In the example, a woman comes to a therapy session with a headache that she developed after her employer offered her an extra week's vacation. The therapist's interpretation is that the patient feels indebted to her boss and resents his kindness as threatening her typical intense efforts to maintain her independence. Indeed, the patient's desire to be independent is really an overreaction to a severe temptation she feels to give in to strong, unconscious dependency needs that she finds unacceptable. The headache begins to disappear.

The patient's old meaning-scheme, focusing on generosity and friendship, did not make sense of her headache; such a response is "not a part of the 'game' of being befriended." But "frustration, fearful temptation, and resentment are meaning-structures in experience which 'imply' or meaningfully lead to the possibility of unpleasant affect" (29). Thus, the headache becomes meaningful in terms of that scheme.

But what has the therapist done in offering the interpretation? Has the therapist revealed past but hidden realities, feelings or thought processes of a hidden kind that were actually operating at the time of the boss's offer? The hidden reality interpretation of psychoanalysis implies an affirmative answer. The meaning-reorganization view implies the contrary: that there were neither temporal occurrences of feelings of anger or resentment, nor any unobservable space-time event that one could call a "wish to be dependent." The therapist does indeed help point out certain past events, but these events were observable and observed. His object is to furnish new descriptions, new meanings now for the events that were described or conceived differently then (28).

Indeed, Freud's justification for using the concept of the unconscious is that it enables us to achieve a gain in meaning. This success, Freud claims, gives us an "incontrovertible" proof of the existence of what was assumed. "But what," Fingarette asks, "has been provided with an 'incontrovertible proof'? Have we proved the assumption that all these processes actually occurred in secret at the former time? Or is it that the patient's acceptance and use of the language of hidden wishes makes it possible for her to see herself in a different light now and, as a result, to act differently hereafter? Have we not . . . *now provided* a new meaning for the past?" (30).

To further help explain the difference between the hidden reality and the meaning-reorganization view, Fingarette uses the example of our seeing the pictures of a wedding we did not know about versus a judge's pronouncing that two persons have been in a common-law marriage as of a certain date in the past:

> The news pictures, in the first analogy, *reproduce* what we did not see. The judge's pronouncement in court *does not reproduce anything;* it is neither a replica nor a making public of what was secret. . . . The judge's pronouncement is a novel act, a *present* act; it is an *authoritative reconstrual* of the past, a reconstrual which is oriented toward influencing the future. The judge does not reveal a secret ceremony in the past; he *now establishes a new context for our present and future response* to the *known* events of the past" (34).

Whereas a wedding is "a relatively well-defined and local act in space and time" (34–35), a "common-law marriage is not an *act* at all. The phrase 'common-law marriage' . . . in truth . . . refers to the *absence* of a ceremony and to a complex set of events, all directly knowable in principle, all subjected to a retrospective review and to an authoritative reclassification with attendant reshuffling of individual events among the new categories" (35).

The same sort of thing happens when, in therapy, I come to see my behavior toward my little brother in the past in terms of the meaning-scheme "jealous aggression toward brother" rather than the scheme "well-meaning help of brother." It is not that I remember feeling hatred and jealousy of him—"I could not truly recall such feelings because I felt no feelings at the time" (35)—although I may recall other things about our relationship. But when therapy reveals the more appropriate meaning-scheme, "everything hangs together in a new way—and a much more unified, meaningful way" (35). Again, it is not that I "discover unfelt feelings; I reinterpret the feelings I felt (and this may lead me to have new feelings and responses now)" (35). In short, "the acceptance of a therapeutic interpretation consists in reconstructing present experience (including memories and expectations) in a more coherent manner; it is not a discovery of secret occurrences of the past" (40).

To further explain his meaning, Fingarette introduces some metaphors: "I move from one lookout point to another, although I look at the very same landscape. I travel from east to west in a land where I had always traveled north and south. How strange and new! How familiar!" (36).

Fingarette proceeds to ask the crucial question: "Are we here denying the truth of the proposition 'unconscious motives really existed in the past and function in the present?'" (36). The answer, says Fingarette, is, "Not at all" (36):

> We have consistently accepted the truth of the fundamental psychoanalytic propositions in our analyses. But we are now asking, "What do these statements mean?" Under what conditions are they legitimately used? We consider whether "an unconscious wish existed in the past" means that an "invisible" duplicate of a "visible" something has been discovered to have secretly coexisted with other events in the past. Or we consider an alterna-

tive: Does it not mean that the relevant events were not secret but that we could not, would not see part of their meaning? Does it not mean that the known or rememberable events of the past, along with their feelings and thoughts, can now be construed within a pattern of meanings which makes more of a unity than the meaning patterns we had formerly used? (36)

In short, "theories within which we interpret our true statements are in no sense challenges to the truth of those statements" (36–37). On Fingarette's conceptualization of the nature of psychoanalytic interpretations, how then does psychoanalysis work? Like the reader of a poem whose meaning may be mysterious, the patient "'reads' . . . the bits and pieces of his life," and then the therapist "suggests a meaning-scheme in terms of which to reorganize and unify the patient's experience" (21).

Now concepts, according to Fingarette, "not only 'reflect' and report our experience; as meanings, not merely as verbalistic structures, they are *constitutive* of experience" (22).[33] Moreover, in human experience, meaning-structure is not only constitutive of the experience-content, but also "efficacious with regard to the course of that content's transformations" (22). Thus, "it is easy to see that the therapist's effective introduction of a different meaning-scheme from that formerly used by the patient is a way of *directly* acting upon, a way of reorganiz-

33. Fingarette is thus postmodern in his conception of language and reality. See also (1963, 50): "The therapist may well be loyal to the Reality Principle, but reality in this context is defined to a great extent by social structure, language, ideology, and esthetic tradition as well as by physical environment."

ing the current experience rather than a way of revealing the truth about a hidden past" (23).

To change the metaphor,

> therapeutic interventions are analogous to tempo-
> rary digressions in a game where we turn our at-
> tention to the rules, strategy, or data instead of to
> the making of moves in the game. . . . We can
> "clarify" and "confront," i.e., we can focus on the
> meaning-scheme (the rules of the game) presently
> being used, clarifying the patient's actual use of it
> and its proper use. . . . [Or] we may give "interpre-
> tations" and develop "constructions," i.e., we can
> construct a new meaning-scheme (or set of rules)
> and thereafter play the game of life in a basically
> new way. . . . A therapeutic interpretation . . . is . . .
> a suggestion that a new conception of one's life
> may be worth trying, a new "game" played. . . . It
> involves the hint that the structure of experience
> will be more unified, i.e., that there will be fewer
> meaningless gaps if this new scheme can become
> the very frame of one's being (25).

Indeed, a symptom is essentially a "quasi-autonomous system of meanings, one which is not itself meaningfully linked
to the main fabric of meanings" (38). And so,

> insight therapy may now be viewed as the attempt
> to provide integrating meanings where before we
> had the "disconnected and unintelligible." It is the
> attempt to reweave instead of putting what Freud
> called a "patch on the spot where there was a rent."
> Insight therapy is the attempt to elucidate "all the

enigmatic products of life." The therapist and patient seek schemes which not only make sense of the symptom-behavior but also tie it into the main, integrated body of meanings constituting the ego. There is achieved thus . . . "a gain in meaning." (38)

Interestingly, although Fingarette proposes the meaning-reorganization language in his ontological interpretation of therapy, he recommends against use of that language within therapy: "I think there are good reasons to suppose that it is usually better to present insight psychotherapy as an attempt to *discover* what is present but hidden in one's life rather than as a task of *making* a new world for oneself by 'creative choice,' by the mobilization of will and purpose" (57).

To present therapy as a search for a hidden reality, Fingarette suggests, "sets in the clearest possible contrast the appropriate, nonneurotic background behavior of passivity and undirectedness, and the neurotically motivated single-mindedness, the dogged and unjustified willfulness, of the neurotic symptom and especially of the transference" (57). "Neurosis is precisely the disease of uncontrollable 'willfulness'" (58), and so it would be a mistake to use meanings that focus attention on the concepts of "choice" and "will." Openness is the more important part of the deliberative process—and the part least cultivated in the neurotic. Whereas neurotic passivity is defensive pseudo-passivity—passivity "in the sense of rigidly avoiding something"—"therapeutic passivity is openness" (58).

Fingarette turns to the question of whether, on the meaning-reorganization view, insight therapy depends on suggestion and influence: "Does it imply that the therapist imposes his will, his values, his interpretation of things upon the patient? Is it a disguised form of retraining or reconditioning rather than a discovery of objective truth?" (39). Indeed, if the acceptance of a therapeutic interpretation "consists in reconstructing present experience . . . in a more coherent manner," "what then becomes of the truth-value, the objectivity of psychoanalytic therapeutic insights" (40)? "It is easy to jump to the conclusion that, except in a crudely pragmatic sense, objectivity is impossible and that therapy is only a form of 'suggestion.' If, somehow or other, the patient can be enticed to accept a proffered therapeutic interpretation, then all is as well as can be, for there is no 'real' meaning or event which was the historical basis for the therapeutic interpretation" (40). He continues, "Are therapeutic interpretations valid merely because they are accepted and used by the patient, or must they in some sense be true, objectively grounded, in accord with a reality independent of what the patient may find useful to believe at any moment?" (40).

To respond to this problem, Fingarette goes through the kinds of evidence that would be taken to support an interpretation, concluding, "It should be evident that, according to the 'meaning-reorganization' view, *precisely the same sort of evidence* would be essential to confirm a therapeutic insight" (42) as to confirm an interpretation on the hidden reality view: "We now see that both views require with equal force and in the same way that psychoanalytic propositions be ultimately linked in complex ways to the behavioral. But neither view calls for confirmation by reference to a single, past event. This ultimate linkage, the 'meaning-reorganization' view reveals, is a matter of creative ingenuity as well as objective inquiry" (45).

With regard to the objectivity of interpretations, Fingarette further notes that "according to the 'meaning-reorganization' view, it is precisely because the neurotic is not objective, cannot freely explore, test, and check his isolated meaning-schemes against the data and other meanings of his experience that he is called neurotic. . . . It is the neurotic, in short, who is 'subjective'. . . . [And] the point of therapy is to establish the capacity for objectivity and to be objective. The *essence* of insight psychotherapy is the rejection of partial-ity [*sic*] in relating of facts one to another in meaningful ways" (43).

The objectivity of psychoanalytic interpretations is not gainsaid by the fact that the "world is multimeaninged" (46). Indeed, it was one of Freud's fundamental insights that all behavior is overdetermined—"has an unspecifiable number of meanings" (46). Even though the world is multimeaninged, however, it "does not have *all* meanings. This would indeed be the end of objectivity. An act may have many meanings, but there are infinitely more meanings which it can be objectively shown not to have" (46).

Fingarette also addresses the question of whether the therapist "implant[s], willfully or unknowingly, values and beliefs, valid or not, in the patient." "Or is there some sense in which the acceptance of a new meaning-pattern in therapy is genuinely rational and voluntary, the free and responsible response of an autonomous agent?" (46).

Fingarette concludes that the latter is closer to the truth: "If I explain the rules [of a game] to a person, I 'influence' him, but I do not act counter to his autonomy; on the contrary, I increase his autonomy" (48). In essence, the therapist suggests a game the patient can play for himself, but does not play the game for him. In brief, "Insight therapy is . . . value-neutral and liberating in its results" (49).

Fingarette concludes this chapter by noting a critical ambiguity in the concept of meaning and linking to this ambiguity the fact that psychoanalysis is taken by some as a science, by others as a form of humanities: "The language of 'meaning' can function in scientific theory as a more generalized interpretation of the psychoanalytic language. . . . Or the language of meaning may function expressively, existentially, in the very coming to grips with life. The concept 'meaning' is, in short, a point of intersection from which one may move either into living or into theories about living" (63):

> This ambiguity in [psychoanalysis'] commitment to "Reality" was—and is—a generative source of the power of psychoanalysis. The Reality of the many dimensions of life's drama and the Reality of the many dimensions of science have, when juxtaposed, generated a high-tension equilibrium which has been the basis of the psychological revolution of our age. Psychoanalysis in particular laid the basis for a *systematic* contemporary perspective on the life of the spirit. Like its great cousin-syntheses of other times and places, it infected men's minds while receiving their scorn. (68)

ROBERT STEELE

In "Psychoanalysis and Hermeneutics" (1979), Robert Steele elaborates the ways in which psychoanalysis is a hermeneutic discipline. In the course of his discussion, he claims that "psychoanalysis through language constructs meaningful life histories and does not provide causal explanations" (1979, 408).[34] Freud, of course, viewed his reconstructions as causal explanations, but for Steele psychoanalysis provides, not causal explanations, but "reasonable interpretations that help make the past intelligible" (406). More particularly,"psychoanalytic case histories are narratives linking the life of the individual to a general historical scheme. This scheme does not provide causes for a life, but a framework of general story elements, supplied

34. See also Steele (1979, 408): "For analyses and case studies do not disclose facts about objects, they construct life stories. To understand a story we do not quantify it, we participate in it and interpret it."

by psychoanalysis, which can be used in the reconstruction of individual life histories" (405).

Why, then, are psychoanalytic interpretations often cast in causal form? For Steele, when the analysand "no longer understands himself and therefore can no longer communicate as a partner in full control of his meanings" (396), the analyst changes his view of the analysand and considers him as an *object*. (Part of the patient's own self is then "as foreign to him as any object" [396].) The analyst then turns to analytic theory and to his previous analytic experience to help him understand: "In the theory he finds naturalistic and historical explanations in a causal objective language . . . that aid him in explaining the otherwise incomprehensible activities of the analysand" (396). Crucially, however, the "quasi-naturalistic phase serves the hermeneutic interest" (396):

> Causal explanation . . . serves understanding, it is not an end in itself. Quasi-naturalistic explanations treat symptoms and dreams as objects to be observed and interpreted, but their explanation in terms of an interpretation to the client serves to transform them from the objective to the subjective. For analyst and analysand it brings such phenomena into the human sphere of meaning and intention. It facilitates the dialogue and builds greater mutual understanding which can be used when communication breaks down again. (396)

Now Steele, most importantly, sees interpretations not only as meaning-providing stories, but also, in effect, as creating the reality they are describing. Holding, with Wolfgang Loch, that truth in analysis is not the correct statement of a historical fact, but "the construction of something that makes sense," Steele asserts that "reality is not given, but created and recreated. . . .

New truth is constructed within the ever expanding circles of psychoanalytical dialogue" (398). Thus, "reality comes to reside in the ever expanding circle of meaning between analysand and analyst" (402).

For example, on whether causes in particular preexist the interpretations that reveal them, Steele is clear: "Freud . . . is not finding causes but creating them. Establishing 'causality retrospectively' is not discovery, it is *post hoc* interpretation" (406). Similarly, "the meaning of [the] unconscious background is constituted by depth hermeneutics in the act of interpretation that makes the unknown, known. Interpretation does not reveal something real" (405). Steele expands upon this theme by noting a disanalogy in Freud's example of solving a jigsaw puzzle and interpreting a dream. Unlike a jigsaw puzzle, the "original text of the dream—its solution, the latent meaning— exists solely as a product of interpretation. . . . There simply is not a master with which to compare one's analytic puzzle solutions" (404).

But how does one adjudicate among different psychoanalytic interpretations so conceived? For Steele, once an analyst proposes an interpretation, "he finds out if it is correct by telling it to the analysand. In hermeneutics and psychoanalysis *'one of the main control mechanisms is the "answers" which the texts* [analysand] *themselves provide'* " (402).[35] Steele elaborates: "The first and last line of defence is evidence from the psychoanalytic situation. Correctness here must be evaluated by the hermeneutic methods which constitute psychoanalytic checking procedures: the articulation of the parts with the whole, the arrival at shared meanings between analyst and analysand, and the maximal freeing from distortions of the analysand's life story" (405). Finally, "the end to either the interpretation of a

35. Citing Radnitzky (1973, 213).

dream, or . . . the analysis as a whole, comes when analyst and analysand overcome doubt" (403).

Serge Viderman

In "The Analytic Space: Meaning and Problems" (1979), Serge Viderman presents his version of hermeneutic psychoanalysis. Viderman dwells at some length on the role of language in the analytic field. He claims, for example, that the drives of the unconscious cannot be understood without the medium of language, which "structures and modifies them in the very process" (1979, 261). Indeed, Viderman goes even further: the "existence of the drive in its most archaic representation . . . is linked to the speech of the analyst who, by giving a name and form to it, is not so much discovering it as he is creating it" (261).

In the same way, Viderman urges that "speech provides a denomination that unifies and concretizes [the most archaic experiences] in a totally original way and in a form that exists nowhere in the unconscious of the patient, or anywhere else but in the analytic space through the language that provides it with form" (262). Given the gap between some manifest content and the construct of interpretive speech, we can see that the interpretive activity is "in this sense . . . an original creation" (262).

Viderman gives some examples of concrete interpretations. Melanie Klein, for example, observed a child patient cover some marbles in a goblet so that they would not roll out and interpreted the marbles as representing children in the belly of the patient's mother. This interpretation could not, according to Viderman, "lay claim to any other truth than the one created for it in the analytic space by the speech which formulate[d] it" (263).

Similarly, in the case of the Wolf Man, Freud inferred the

existence of the primal scene from the patient's dream: "In order to discover it in the dream, he first had to imagine it: that he invented it and the term for it should not startle us if I have been sufficiently clear in my explanations. He imagined it, then, as pre-existing both the dream and the associations" (269). The interpretation, reached by a very circuitous path, is saved from being absurd, Viderman claims, once we recognize the "fragility of the hypothesis of a real, historical event experienced by the patient. . . . This is one of the advantages of the coherence we regain when we no longer feel so strictly bound to retrace, stroke by stroke, a history nowhere to be found" (269). The primal scene, in short, *"could not be discovered but only imagined"* (270).

Viderman's central example is an interpretation from his own practice. The patient dreams of picking some flowers and offering his father a bouquet of six roses. While the patient stressed the positive nature of the gift to his father, Viderman, wanting to illuminate the thorns hidden in the roses, said to the patient, "Six roses or cirrhosis?"[36] About this interpretation Viderman says, "I hope one can clearly see here how useless it would be to ask who was right and what was the true meaning of the dream. . . . [The connection] was *invented* by phonetic similarity and was more in the mind of the analyst than in that of the patient. In the instant before it was uttered, it was nowhere. After it was uttered, several possible perspectives were opened up" (265). If Viderman's appraisal of the proximity of unconscious negative feelings was correct, and the state of the transference "allowed the interpretation to be ac-

36. In French, "six roses" and "cirrhosis" are phonetically close enough to pass for homonyms. Note that the patient's father had died as a result of alcoholism.

cepted and integrated," then "it *became true* through a dynamic process which created it; it is not as if it were true per se, that is, outside the situation in which it was uttered" (265).[37] In a word, one "cannot say that this interpretation [was] *either* true *or* false, for it [could not] be contained in an alternative binary proposition of truth or untruth" (266).

WOLFGANG LOCH

In "Some Comments on the Subject of Psychoanalysis and Truth" (1977), Wolfgang Loch examines the relationship of psychoanalysis to truth. He sees the task of psychoanalysis as both the search for historical truth and the development of sense out of a dyadic relationship (1977, 221). The latter, indeed, he sees as a second form of truth: "We are confronted with two notions of truth: truth understood as the correct statement, the historical fact—only in need of discovery to be brought to the surface; and truth as the emergent, the construction of something that makes sense and that therefore permits one to rely on it and to continue living" (220-21).[38] Loch links this second notion to a pragmatic theory of truth (232) and sees it as

37. Though Viderman speaks of the correctness of the appraisal of unconscious hostility to the father, he seems committed to the view that such hostility did not bring about the "six roses" image in the dream ("The connection was more in the mind of the analyst than that of the patient. In the instant before it was uttered, it was nowhere" [1979, 265]).

38. See also Loch (1977, 227): "Fantasies or recollections do not represent discovered truths of a historical character but are attempts to create a sense, a significance, in order to go on existing. I believe . . . that interpretations in the form of reconstructions have, in essence, the very same character and task"; (1977, 232): "I personally believe that an understanding of truth as something that is sustaining me, that permits me to go on living, is completely legitimate. As I mentioned earlier, this is a definition in the Hebrew tradition."

unmistakably the more important for psychoanalysis: "Psychoanalysis does not discover truth understood as a correspondence
between facts of the past and propositions in the form of interpretations concerning this past. Rather, it *constructs truth* in
the service of self-coherence for the present and for the future,
on the basis of mutual agreement" (238).

At times Loch concedes that historical truth plays some role
in psychoanalysis, but it is plainly secondary, and its presence
does not diminish the importance of truth as sense: "Thus, we
may say that truth in its scientific sense cannot be what analysts
are really concerned with. And this opinion is not invalidated
if we concede with Freud that there are 'fragments of historical
truth' in all the productions of the patient and also in the analyst's constructions" (228). Indeed, because interpretations may
contain a "kernel of truth," they may restore a patient's confidence in his own perceptions (238). "On the whole, however,
analytical material does not give a veridical picture of the past
and therefore does not contain 'scientific truth-values'" (239).

Although Loch speaks often of interpretations as not giving
a veridical picture of the past, his claim is not restricted to
efforts to reconstruct the patient's remote history. Even interpretations about current phenomena, such as dreams, aim for
truth as sense and not correspondence. Thus Loch claims that
psychoanalytic procedure "*constructs truth* in the service of self-
coherence for the present and for the future" not only for such
things as "past traumatic events," but also for "interpretations
of the ego's defense-operations" (238).

Loch's concept of sense as truth has implications for the
aims of therapy: "Psychoanalytic interpretations—insofar as
they are predominantly arrived at to make sense—are not so
much concerned with meaning comprehended as a fixed sig-
nification (truth in a scientific perspective), but are meant to
open possibilities. They enable the patient to discover and con-

struct new meanings" (245–46).[39] Psychoanalysis helps people "to discover new truth in the sense of the freedom to construct, to invent, new thoughts and new meanings and significations" (247). Finally, "the subject now knows by experience that it is the search for sense, for reasons, that is the very foundation for living as an actor" (248).

DONALD SPENCE

In *Narrative Truth and Historical Truth* (1982a), Donald Spence elaborates and defends a conception of psychoanalysis as achieving, in its interpretations and constructions, primarily narrative truth as opposed to historical truth:

> The linguistic and narrative aspects of an interpretation may well have priority over its historical truth, and we are making the somewhat heretical claim that an interpretation is effective because it gives the awkward happening a kind of linguistic and narrative closure, not because it can account for it in a purely causal sense. An interpretation satisfies because we are able to contain an unfinished piece of reality in a meaningful sentence; that is part of what we mean by finding its narrative home. The sentence acquires additional meaning when it meshes with other parts of the patient's life; it acquires narrative force by virtue of these

39. For the idea of "sense as truth," see also, e.g., Loch (1977, 230) ("the introduction of reasons that make sense and are thus true"); (1977, 231) ("The *coherence* that the person cannot escape looking for builds meaning and sense—that is, creates *truth*"); (1977, 240) ("I believe it is warranted to equate sense and truth for this psychoanalytic work of ours"); (1977, 243) ("This search for sense as truth is the main task we must fulfill").

connections, and adds narrative understanding to what is already known and understood. The power of language is such that simply putting something into words gives it a certain kind of authenticity; finding a narrative home for these words amplifies and expands this truth. (138)

Narrative truth, in other words, is prior to historical truth, yet interpretations that do not reveal historical truth may nevertheless be therapeutic.

According to Spence, it may not impair the effectiveness of an interpretation that it "does not grow out of the material," for "its historical truth may be less important than its narrative truth" (150).[40] In essence, we "are primarily interested in the effect [an interpretation] produces rather than its past credentials," and so we should "give up our concern for historical accuracy" (276).

Spence likens the distinction between historical truth and narrative truth to that between reconstruction and construction (288)[41] and suggests that "narrative truth cannot be validated by appeal to historical fact. On the contrary, it speaks to a different domain, a domain that only comes alive within the analytic situation" (292). And so an interpretation, rather "than representing a piece of the past . . . is more likely a creation of the present . . . that can take on any number of meanings depending on the surrounding context" (267). In short, "in making

40. As the block quotation above suggests, Spence distinguishes, more particularly, between two forms of narrative truth: "The idea of narrative truth can be seen to have two forms: a weak form, defined as finding a verbal expression for the anomalous event, and a strong form, defined as fitting the expression into the patient's life story" (1982a, 165). That both of these forms of narrative truth might provide comfort and "narrative closure" to the patient seems clear. See below.

41. See also Spence (1982a, 165).

a formal interpretation, we exchange one kind of truth—historical truth—for the truth of being coherent and sayable—narrative truth. Language gives us this power" (173).

For Spence, interpretations may, over time, acquire narrative truth; they may become true:[42] "Once we shift to the idea that we can create truth by statement—the concept of becoming true—we have left the domain of archeology and opened up new and dangerous doors. . . . The interpretation . . . can bring an idea into being for the first time. Once stated, it becomes partially true; as it is repeated and extended, it becomes familiar; and as its familiarity adds to its plausibility, it becomes completely true" (177). Furthermore, "an entirely imaginary interpretation may achieve a certain truth status in the analytic space" (171).

Indeed, Edward Glover's famous distinction between "inexact" and "apparently exact" interpretations loses some of its force. Glover suggested that inexact interpretations provide patients with mere fantasies and thus with defensive substitutes that might do more harm than good, but Spence is not convinced: "An interpretation may be inexact in the sense that it does not correspond to a piece of the past, but to the extent that it is creative and allows a new theme to emerge, it becomes a positive factor in the treatment and not necessarily a resistance" (173).

Adjudicating among different interpretations is, of course, always a concern for the psychoanalyst and for the psychoanalytic theorist, and Spence assesses Michael Sherwood's dual criteria of adequacy and accuracy. Criteria of adequacy include self-consistency, coherence, and comprehensiveness; these Spence identifies with narrative truth (180). But ade-

42. See, e.g., Spence (1982a, 166–71). Compare the concept of "becoming the past" (1982a, 175).

quacy, or narrative truth, is not a good gauge of accuracy, or historical truth: "For if narrative suitability is used to justify the truth value of a particular construction, then we begin to see that the criteria of adequacy (narrative truth) may sometimes be a poor substitute for the criteria of accuracy (historical truth) because an almost infinite number of items can be accommodated in any particular chronology" (183). Indeed, Sherwood's two sets of criteria may conflict, and "on occasion, the need for narrative fit may be controlling and the constructions that are needed to make the narrative coherent and comprehensive may later be accepted as true" (181).

Spence is convinced that Freud's archeological model, through which he tried to escape ambiguity and answer the charge of suggestion (265), is inadequate. As an alternative to that model, with its emphasis on historical truth, Spence proposes that we consider an interpretation as an *aesthetic experience* and a *pragmatic statement*.

The artistic model makes very clear that truth is somewhat beside the point: "Once we have moved into an aesthetic domain, it becomes less important to ask about the historical truth of the interpretation, just as we would hardly think of asking about the historical 'truth' of a painting" (269).[43] On the other hand, we do

> ask about another kind of truth when faced with
> a painting—something we would call its artistic

43. On the other hand, perhaps we do ask about the "historical truth" of a *representational* painting. In the same way, Sharpe (see below) claims that there is no correct way to play a Beethoven sonata; truth here, he claims, is also beside the point. Yet Beethoven's musical pieces have markings indicating the way they are to be played. Perhaps there are a number of ways of playing them that conform to these markings. But there are just as obviously wrong ways to play them—at least if we think that the composer's intent is significant.

truth. . . . The notion of artistic truth means that not just any painting or interpretation will qualify; it must conform to certain artistic or clinical standards. But so long as these are satisfied, it becomes an object of beauty without regard to how faithfully it represents the scene in question. (270)

Construing interpretations in this way makes room for "Viderman's notion that interpretations are essentially creative (in the best artistic sense) and for his hypothesis that a number of different interpretations might be provided for any particular clinical event" (270).

Spence's example of a pragmatic statement is the politician's claim to the electorate, "I am going to win next Tuesday." This claim, according to Spence, is neither true nor false "because we have no grounds for checking its truth value; rather, it is an instrument for bringing about a certain course of action" (271). Spence claims that a psychoanalytic interpretation can be understood in the same way: "It is, first of all, a means to an end, uttered in the expectation that it will lead to additional, clarifying material. Its truth . . . lies more in the present and future than in the past: it may become true for the first time just by being said" (271).[44]

To elucidate the notion of an interpretation as a pragmatic statement, Spence introduces John Searle's discussion of the three commitments a newspaper reporter makes when he writes a factual article: first, to the truth of the statements in the story; second, to his ability to give evidence for the truth of the statements; and third, to his belief in their truth (272). A nov-

---

44. Spence is clear that historical accuracy and pragmatic effectiveness are distinct. See Spence (1982a, 272).

elist, by contrast, is pretending to make these claims but can actually perform none of them (272).

The analyst is in an intermediate position:

> In making an interpretation, . . . [the analyst] is also pretending to perform certain kinds of speech acts, but in a slightly different manner. We would say that he shares with the reporter a commitment to a belief in the proposition he is putting forward but that he is less committed to its truth—as we will see, the truth may actually be indefinable—and he is often unable to provide supporting evidence. The interpretation, then, can be defined by a claim to a *belief* in the proposition and nothing more. . . . Put another way, we would say that the analyst commits himself to a belief in his formulation but not necessarily to a belief in its referent. (273)

Spence's conceptualization focuses on the interpretation as a speech act that is designed to "make something happen." Moreover, it focuses on the interpretation as something whose relation to historical truth—and so the analyst's commitment to its truth—is less than robust: "The analyst, in contrast to the novelist, commits himself to a belief in his hypothesis and is inclined to use it in a pragmatic fashion, as a way of making something happen. He is less committed to a belief in its truth value —either because he has no clear way of knowing whether or not it actually occurred or because he is proposing something that has no clear correspondence with an event in the patient's life."

Spence suggests at points that analysts are not committed to the truth of their interpretations only in the sense that they are not sure they are true (the analyst "has no clear way of knowing whether or not it actually occurred"). This suggestion is uncontroversial—but also very uninteresting. At most points, however, Spence seems to be making the more truly controversial and interesting claim that interpretations have "no clear correspondence with . . . event[s] in the patient's life." As his discussion above continues, "The Viderman [interpretation] . . . cannot be said to correspond to a particular happening, and thus we can hardly ask questions about its historical truth. The more appropriate question concerns what might be called its artistic truth, its significance as a kind of creative endeavor, a putting-together of known facts about the patient in a new form that carries a high probability of making something happen in the analytic space" (275).

Similarly, Spence's discussion of the relation of interpretations as aesthetic and pragmatic statements to truth implies the more radical position:

> Thinking about interpretations in this manner, we see that questions about their historical truth are either impossible to answer—as in the case of creative utterances—or relatively unimportant. If we think about them as pragmatic statements, we realize that they are designed to produce results rather than to document the past; they are designed primarily to bring about a change in belief. The more creative they are, the harder to document, because to the extent that they represent truly artistic productions, they have never happened before in just that form (think of [the interpretation] *six roses or cirrhosis*) and, therefore, they have no more provable correspondence with reality than a painting or a piece of music. Once we conceive of interpretations as artistic creations that have the potential of pro-

ducing an aesthetic response, we are . . . even less interested in the truth of the particular parts. (276)

Interpretations, in short, do not have a "provable correspondence with reality"; it is no more possible to answer questions about their historical truth than to answer whether the fictional Romeo was fond of his first teacher.

If Spence is right about all of this, why are interpretations therapeutic? Freud, of course, subscribed to the "tally theory" (Grünbaum 1984, 8): interpretations are effective because they are true.[45] But if we must cease to see interpretations as either true or false, the tally theory cannot be right. Spence, indeed, calls the theory "something of a straw man" (290), and essentially denies its truth.

But what, then, substitutes for it? Spence finds many reasons for thinking that interpretations, as he has construed them, can be therapeutic. For one, an interpretation allows the analyst to "make certain kinds of experience accessible to the patient; once expressed in words, they can be integrated into other parts of the patient's life story and linked up with other parts of our theory" (173). For another, an interpretation may "open up new possibilities, . . . bring separate ideas together in a new and potentially evocative combination. Its fate will be determined

45. See also Grünbaum (1988) (Freud committed to tally theory, in particular to two principles: psychoanalysis alone can yield correct insight into unconscious pathogens; the patient's correct insight into the etiology of his condition and the unconscious dynamics of his character is causally necessary for the therapeutic conquest of his neurosis. Although Freud strayed some from this thesis toward the end of his career, he generally held to it; he seemed undeterred by the fact that other therapies produced symptomatic relief or that spontaneous remissions occurred); Cioffi (1988, 61) (Freud did not subscribe to the tally argument, and it is a bad argument anyway, since, even if psychoanalysis does achieve success, it may do so as a result of things other than the truth of interpretations).

by how the patient responds and by what new associations come to mind" (178). Indeed, interpretations "lend meaning to otherwise disconnected pieces of the patient's life. The very process [of interpretation] . . . enables the patient gradually to see his life as continuous, coherent, and, therefore, meaningful" (280).

Spence also focuses on the comfort that understanding may provide: "Part of the appeal of the interpretation lies in the fact that we almost always prefer the known to the unknown" (141). Thus, an interpretation "may bring about a positive effect not because it corresponds to a specific piece of the past but because it appears to relate the known to the unknown, to provide explanation in the place of uncertainty" (141).[46] Spence suggests that this decrease in uncertainty may have further positive effects: interpretations give the patient "explanation in place of uncertainty, and they sometimes lead to further recall. Putting a construction in the proper context often gives it a reality that is so compelling that we quickly assume, along with Freud, that we have uncovered a piece of the past" (187).

The satisfaction of tying things together—indeed, the thrill of discovery—may be therapeutic in itself:

> There is satisfaction in seeing a tangled life reduced to a relatively small number of organizing principles; satisfaction in seeing a previous explanation (e.g., the primal scene) come to life again in new circumstances; and finally, satisfaction in finding correspondence between events that are separated in time and space. There is no doubting the aes-

46. See also (1982a, 143) ("Once again we have exchanged the uncertainty and mystery of the clinical happening for a plausible and compelling explanation—and who would prefer the first to the second?"); (1982a, 167) ("Finding a single event to explain a train of bewildering and apparently happenstance occurrences can, as we pointed out earlier, be enormously satisfying and provide great psychological support").

thetic value of these different satisfactions. Even though they should not be confused with the historical truth of the resulting interpretations, they should not be dismissed as having no significance in their own right. And we may come to find that it is the excitement of the discovery, in finding an explanation or in participating in its unfolding, that accounts for its therapeutic effect much more than the substantive nature of the reasoning. In other words, it is the interpretation as a creative act—as a piece of narrative truth—that takes precedence. (163–64)

Spence speculates on how interpretations may achieve their effect, analogizing again to the arts: "If an interpretation is seen as an artistic product, we might argue further that it achieves its effect through something analogous to the well-known *suspension of disbelief.* An interpretation may produce the desired result because the patient, supported by a belief in the analyst and reinforced by the power of the transference, may allow himself to suspend disbelief in the literal meaning of a given interpretation and thereby make himself accessible to its artistic and rhetorical surround" (289).

ROBERT SHARPE

Freud conceived of his procedure as an "explanation of visible phenomena through a concealed mechanism" (Sharpe 1988). In "Mirrors, Lamps, Organisms and Texts" (1988), Robert Sharpe suggests that, although a hermeneutic conception of Freudian procedure differs from Freud's own, Freud's *practice* was interpretative. Sharpe describes interpretations in terms of four characteristics, of which the first—that interpretations are not fully controlled by the facts—is most important here.

Freud believed that judgments about the mind were always determinate—true or false regardless of our capacity to discover the facts. Yet the multiplicity of possible interpretations of mental phenomena pushes interpretive theorists toward a nonrealist indeterminacy. Sharpe distinguishes two different senses of indeterminacy: "On the one hand there is the case which allows that there is a right answer though we may be never able to tell what it is. . . . Indeterminacy proper, however, takes the view that no truth as to the matter exists independently of what we have available to us" (1988, 190).

Sharpe cites Schafer as an example of a theorist for whom the multiplicity of interpretations spells interpretations' indeterminacy. Schafer believes that "any analytic situation can be matched by a multiplicity of interpretations of which no single one is true" (189).[47] "The interpretation," in other words, "is underdetermined" (189). In the same way, there are many ways to play a Beethoven sonata; it hardly makes sense to ask which is true.

To illustrate his indeterminacy thesis, Sharpe gives the example of a woman who smashes "by accident" a vase—a gift from her husband whom she has just discovered in adultery. Under certain conditions, we can feel fairly comfortable concluding that the smashing was motivated, albeit unconsciously—for example, the woman "eyed it with some chagrin before and she is usually careful" (190). But if the signs are less clearcut, "it is reasonable to conclude that there is no answer as to whether the accident was or was not motivated." Judgments in these cases may be indeterminate in either of two ways: "They will certainly be indeterminate . . . in the sense that there

47. Citing Schafer (1980, 80–83).

is no underlying pattern of mental events with which their judgement corresponds or fails to correspond and they may be indeterminate in the sense that no correct answer exists to a question about their truth" (191).

Sharpe's principal aim in this article is to raise and answer two problems for an interpretive or narrative approach: first, "how can we reconcile [the narrative] approach with the causal form which analyses commonly take?" And, second, "how can the conquering of [say] compulsive rituals simply depend upon the mere exchange of one story for another, particularly if the choice between many of these stories is arbitrary" (193)? Surely we need to alter the causal origins of the neurotic's behavior, which seems to require a single correct narrative that recapitulates these origins. If we are free to form what narratives we like, then the impression of compulsion is illusion; "Whether or not he is free is narrative-relative and by choosing another narrative he can view his actions as free" (194). "There is no reason why he should not take up his bed and walk" (194).

To the first question Sharpe responds that a trauma has causal force "because the person who suffers it describes the occurrence in a certain way" (199). To change his patient, then, the analyst "must reveal the possibility of so describing the original event that it loses its causal force" (199). Sharpe seems to be suggesting here that the analyst must give the patient an alternative causal account to diminish the force of the patient's own view of the relevant causation. Thus, the narrative must take a causal form—but it is still a narrative.

To the problem of the unfreedom of the neurotic Sharpe responds that the necessity the compulsive feels is "relative to a particular mode of narrative. A neurotic cannot see that other accounts of his behaviour are possible. It is as though he or she can only arrange the facts of the past in one particular way" (199). Redescription thus can empower the neurotic to refrain from some neurotic ritual that he previously could not avoid: "The causal force of these events depends upon the descriptions the sufferer gives of these. We may neutralize them by getting him to see them in another way" (200).

Of course this view and the indeterminacy thesis itself mean that Freud's tally thesis is false. If interpretations are indeterminate—if "no sense can be attached to which out of a range of alternatives is true" (195)—then the therapeutic force of the analysis cannot depend on its being correct. Similarly, if therapy works by helping people to see themselves differently, it need not necessarily tell them the truth about themselves to be effective.

Sharpe concedes that the effectiveness of therapy is not a matter of the truth of interpretations, but of the placebo effect, and has endeavored to give a rationale for this effect. A little thought, he argues, suggests that truth is not critical to effectiveness, and that we should not be troubled that analysis seems to work as a placebo: "There is, after all, no special reason to suppose that an ideological or religious conversion that enables a man to make sense of his life, that recognizes as important what he feels to be important, which only demands of him those things which he can achieve, which gives him the moderate self-esteem and the mutual support of people he admires, is of necessity a conversion to a set of true doctrines" (196). Successful therapy does not, then, require that pathogens in the patient's life be identified with any degree of precision. It merely requires that "the narrative which replaces the original redresses the emphases placed upon the pathogen and it can do this simply by relegating to comparative insignificance a sector of the analysand's past which contains that experience" (196).

The influence of different narratives on people's self-conceptions, indeed, can be profound: "When somebody is offered a Freudian narrative of his life, by changing his picture of himself we may also change his behaviour so that we create an identity in the course of trying to describe it" (196). If this is so, there is a sense in which "interpretations may converge on determinacy and that is through the acceptance of the patient. . . . [N]o gap need occur between the accuracy of an analysis and its acceptance by the patient" (197).

3

The Models

The eight hermeneutic thinkers I have presented often speak the same language—use the same words and concepts, images and analogies. And, indeed, some commentators take them to be holding essentially the same position.[1] Yet this is a mistake. There are at least five possible views that these hermeneutic thinkers may be holding.[2] I organize these five views around the hermeneuts' position on the truth of psychoanalytic interpretations. Although a theory's position on truth may be orthogonal to its status as a hermeneutic theory, there is value to this organization, which the reader will appreciate when I come to critique the views in terms of the argument from patient rejection.

1. See below.

2. Other commentators make other distinctions among the hermeneuts. See, e.g., Freeman (1985) (hermeneuts who take the position that psychoanalytic interpretations do not refer to a reality beyond themselves because they despair of ever finding the reality beyond versus those who do so because they are relativists); Moore (1989) (very ambitious hermeneuts versus ambitious or dualist hermeneuts versus modest hermeneuts; among the middle group, metaphysically dualist hermeneuts versus philosophical hermeneuts versus linguistically dualist hermeneuts); Phillips (1991) (hermeneuts who say there is a methodology distinctive to the human sciences versus hermeneuts who emphasize the presence of a multiplicity of incommensurable discourses); and Rubovits-Seitz (1986) (hermeneuts who concern themselves with the problem of validation versus those who contend that objective knowledge and validity are impossible versus those who see natural science and hermeneutic approaches as mediating each other).

In presenting the five models, I briefly describe them and then offer reasons for thinking one or more of the eight hermeneuts might subscribe to any given one. Some use language suggestive of more than one of the models, and no effort is made to arrive at a definitive reading of any of these hermeneutic thinkers. Part of the reason for quoting from them so extensively is to establish how difficult classification is—and to put the reader in a position to come to her own preliminary conclusions about these thinkers.

The first model I call the clinical psychoanalysis model. On this model, psychoanalysis seeks after meanings, not causes, in the sense that it looks for conscious and unconscious purposes, wishes, and aims, and not neurophysiological antecedents of behavior. Psychoanalytic interpretations are true in an unproblematic way under a correspondence theory of truth.

The second model, which I call the story model, is at the opposite pole from the first. On this model, psychoanalysis seeks after meaning in the sense of meaningful stories that make sense of people's lives, rather than the actual mental states, conscious and unconscious, that underlie behavior. Psychoanalytic interpretations on this model do not purport to be true—perhaps they are neither true nor false.

The third model is the alternative metaphysics model. This model proposes a new metaphysical worldview underpinning psychoanalysis—new theories of reality, truth, and justification. On this model, psychoanalysis seeks after meaning in the sense of psychological antecedents of behavior, but the interpretations revealing those antecedents are true in a different sense of "true" than that found under the traditional correspondence theory; psychoanalytic interpretations are true only in the sense of "true" given, say, by a coherence theory.

On the fourth model, the metaphor model, psychoanalysis

seeks meaning in the sense of psychological antecedents of behavior, but the interpretations revealing those antecedents are
only metaphorically true.

Under the fifth model, which I call the interpretations-as-
literary-criticism model, psychoanalysis searches after meaning
in the way that critics search after the meaning of a novel; analysts are not looking for causes of behavior (as critics do not
look for causes of the scenes in the novel), but, in interpreting
behavior, they do discover truths—truths, in fact, about the
patient. These truths may be true in an unproblematic, traditional way, under a correspondence theory of truth.

THE CLINICAL PSYCHOANALYSIS MODEL

The clinical psychoanalysis model says that psychoanalysis is
hermeneutic in the sense that it is not a natural science concerned with uncovering the neurophysiological causes of behavior. Although Freud's metapsychology is indeed based on a
natural science model—an outdated one at that—we ought to
reject the metapsychology in favor of the clinical theory. The
clinical theory is hermeneutic—it looks for the meanings of
behavior in the sense of underlying aims, purposes, wishes, and
desires, both conscious and unconscious. These two theories in
psychoanalysis are not reducible to one another. They occupy
different realms of discourse.

The hermeneuts' emphasis on meaning, on the clinical psychoanalysis model, amounts to an emphasis on the psychological rather than the physical. Importantly, the psychological
states that interpretation uncovers are revealed as present in
an unproblematic way. To give an interpretation, for example,
that unconscious hostility motivated the accidental breaking of
the vase is to say that, at an unconscious level, one was feeling hostility, and this hostility caused one accidentally to break

the vase.[3] If true, the interpretation is true in a straightforward way: the statement corresponds to the facts of the world.[4]

George Klein and the early Schafer seem to be hermeneuts who fit the clinical psychoanalysis model.[5] Klein, as we have seen, distinguished between two psychoanalyses, the clinical theory, concerned with the analysand as a meaning-creating subject, and the metapsychological theory, concerned with the analysand as a natural object subject to the laws of physics. The clinical theory is primary, metapsychology being simply irrelevant to the clinical enterprise. The terms of the clinical theory are not reducible to those of the metapsychology. Nevertheless, the clinical theory, for Klein, is not beyond the possibility of verification and falsification; inferring from data to lawfulness is a matter crucial to the development of psychoanalysis.

Now the "fundamental intent of the [clinical] psychoanalytic enterprise," according to Klein, "[is] *unlocking meanings*" (1976a, 48). To interpret dreams or symptoms is to find "the

3. Actions motivated only unconsciously may still be said to be accidental, although they are accidental in a sense that is different from actions motivated on no level.

4. Theorists other than alternative metaphysicians do not generally talk about their theories of truth, so I am making an assumption when I say they subscribe to a correspondence theory of truth. I do so because that is the most traditional theory of truth, and I am supposing that anyone who does not explicitly question theories of truth simply accepts the traditional one. In any case, it does not affect the force of the argument from patient rejection if this is wrong; so long as the theorist subscribes to some reasonable theory of truth, the application of the argument to the different theories goes through.

5. Other theorists following Klein are Holt (1976) (the metapsychology of drive is most problematic; humans are meaning-processors); and Holzman (1976) (the metapsychology obstructs attention from the clinical theory; psychoanalysis is concerned with meaning). For an account of why various thinkers like Holt and Klein might have abandoned the metapsychology, see Aronson (1992).

distinctive meanings that behaviors acquire when interpreted in terms of sexual and aggressive wishes, conscious and unconscious events, displacements of aims, transference, unconscious fantasy, and related principles" (1976a, 43). Thus, the meaning of, say, a dream is the unconscious psychological states that underlie it. These are revealed in an unproblematic way.

While Klein's theory, in short, is distinctly hermeneutic in establishing a "separate realm" for clinical psychoanalysis and in seeing the focus there to be on meaning, his hermeneutics does not consist of a radical metaphysics—or of an effort to move beyond metaphysics altogether.

The early Schafer's hermeneutic psychoanalysis is quite close to Klein's. The early Schafer recommends abandoning the metapsychology inasmuch as it is problematically anthropomorphic and it "excludes meaning from the center of psychoanalytic theory" (1976, 199). The metapsychology speaks a language that "cannot be concerned with meaning" (89)—the two psychoanalyses occupy different realms of discourse. Thus, psychoanalysis should be seen as a form of humanities, not a natural science.

Meaning for the early Schafer "is the same as 'psychic reality'" (199). In explaining why a person becomes unable to see, for example, we base our explanation "on that which has found disguised expression in 'looking,' which is to say, the latent *meaning* of looking" (87). Looking takes on the significance of certain drive activities and gratifications and is dealt with as if it were those activities. In psychic reality, the early Schafer says, it *is* those activities. Once again, the meaning of an act is found in the unconscious psychological states that underlie it, and these are revealed in an unproblematic way.

The early Schafer's views on the truth of analytic interpretations suggest that he is not wholly comfortable with the idea that interpretations are true in a straightforward sense. He says, for example, that the emerging life history of the patient is "not a fiction but not simply factual either,"[6] "not fictive, [but] also not what one might call the absolute truth" (50). The most plausible interpretation of these claims in context, however, is that interpretations are not the whole truth—there is more to be found; and they are not the final truth—what has been found is subject to revision in light of what is later found.[7] The early Schafer's view is also unmistakably hermeneutic—and in the same way and for the same reasons as Klein's.

The Story Model

The story model says that psychoanalysis is a hermeneutic discipline in the sense that it seeks after the meaning of people's behavior. The meaning of people's behavior does not consist (as it does in the clinical psychoanalysis model) of the psychological states, conscious and unconscious, that underlie their behavior, but rather it is a story that makes sense of that behavior—that gives it meaning. For example, to be told that one accidentally broke the vase because of unconscious anger at one's spouse is to be given a story that makes one's behavior intelligible; it is not to be given an account of an underlying cause of one's behavior.

Meaningful stories can be therapeutic inasmuch as uncertainty—still more, confusion—is psychologically debilitating. When the pieces of the puzzle fit together, one feels comforted. A gain in meaning, then, is a gain in well-being.

On the story model, psychoanalytic interpretations do not

6. Indeed, this claim is made in *The Analytic Attitude* (1983, 56), so that Schafer feels some ambivalence even at this later stage.

7. It is conceivable, however, that the early Schafer is tempted by the story model. See especially the personal communication that the early Schafer cites from Loewald.

purport to be true. At the least, truth is a matter of indifference; at the most, interpretations are but illusions. Somewhere in between, they are neither true nor false in the same way that statements about fictional characters are neither true nor false;[8] they are simply not the sorts of statements that can be true or false. To say, for example, that unconscious anger motivated the breaking of the vase no more purports to be true than saying that the fictional Romeo liked his first-grade teacher.

The story model is not confined to reconstructions of the remote past. It is true that here-and-now interpretations of the transference are currently regarded as a prominent part of psychoanalysis and that reconstructions of the remote past have receded in importance. It is also true that, because evidence about the past is less accessible, a story model may seem more compelling there. But even though some of the hermeneuts use language that suggests that stories are the only thing possible in the case of the remote past—recall Spence's phrase "historical truth"—all of them, as a careful reading of their language shows, consider the past to include the immediately past moment. Thus we can no more find the historical truth about the unconscious feelings underlying a current symptom than we can about the patient's early childhood.

In short, unlike the clinical psychoanalysis model—in which interpretations are true under a traditional correspondence theory of truth—on the story model, interpretations are not

8. Perhaps I should say, "*some* statements about fictional characters." For example, some statements may be true or false according to the rules of literary interpretation, e.g., "Romeo loved Juliet." It remains true, however, that the rules of literary interpretation preclude us from saying "Romeo loved Juliet *because* she reminded him of his first-grade teacher." It is these latter kinds of statements that interpretations on the story model arguably resemble.

true under any theory of truth. In this regard, the two models are at opposite extremes from each other.

Story model theorists may hold their position that interpretations do not purport to be true for a number of reasons. First, they may believe that it is in the nature of interpretations (as in statements about fictional characters) not to be true or false and that truth is in any case irrelevant to therapeutic efficacy. Psychoanalysis helps patients by making their behavior intelligible to them—and that is all there is to it.

Second, they may wish to protect psychoanalysis from the charge that it is unscientific, either in the sense that its statements are false scientifically or in the sense that they are nonfalsifiable. If psychoanalytic interpretations are neither true nor false, they cannot be false scientifically, and because they are part of a discipline that does not aspire to be scientific, their nonfalsifiability is unproblematic: if one is not trying to say true things, one cannot be faulted for saying things that are not true or things that cannot be proved to be true.

Third, story model theorists may hold their position about the truth of interpretations as a response to the problem of competing psychoanalytic interpretations.[9] That so many dynamic accounts of a patient's behavior are available makes perfect sense on the story model: the same behavior can be the subject of different stories, each told from its unique point of view. The commitment of story hermeneuts to the view that interpretations do not purport to be true makes perfect sense; if they were true, these truths might at times conflict.[10]

9. This problem, of course, is related to the last: it is especially embarrassing for a science to be faced with competing theories among which no means of adjudication exists.

10. But is it the case that the phenomenon of different interpretations of the same behavior drives one to the story model? Perhaps not. It is true

Fourth, Michael Moore has argued that hermeneutic theorists of all stripes—not just psychoanalytic hermeneuts—are committed to the project of ridding theory of metaphysics.[11] One prominent metaphysical question is the nature of truth; should we hold to a correspondence theory of truth, for example, or a coherence theory? The story model theorists may wish to escape the grasp of metaphysics by taking care that their

_____

that analysts will interpret the same material differently. For example, one analyst may relate a patient's anger to his feeling humiliated by a more powerful contemporary, while another will relate it to his feeling frustrated by not having his needs for closeness met. It is also true that analysts from different schools will give varying accounts of the same psychological phenomenon. A Kleinian, for example, may understand a child's feelings of depression to derive from his realization that the mother he hates is the same mother as the mother he loves; he feels guilty about his ambivalence. A Freudian, by contrast, may understand the child's depression to derive from his anger at his mother turned inward.

But cannot both interpretations and accounts be correct? The man is angry both because he is humiliated by his relative lack of power and because he is frustrated by his need for closeness being unmet. The child is depressed both because he feels guilty about the anger he realizes is directed at a loved one and because he turns that same anger inward. In the same way, a fire may be caused both by a match striking the carbon and by the presence of inflammable objects. After all, behavior, as Freud contended, is overdetermined: there may be many causes of the same behavior, all equally valid. If this is so, the supposed incompatibility of differing dynamic explanations and accounts of behavior need not drive us to the story model of psychodynamic explanation.

But this observation takes us only so far, and so the conclusion is too sweeping. First, the differing theories cannot in all details all be right. Moreover, even at the level of individual dynamic explanations, many will often be in fact incompatible. The problem, then, remains, at least as to many cases. The answer, of course, may be to determine means to establish that some of the accounts are false, not to declare that none purports to be true.

11. For a thoroughgoing exegesis and rejection of this project as misconceived, see Moore (1989).

interpretations not aspire to truth; if they did, all the metaphysical questions that truth raises would arguably remain. And so their interpretations may simply "further conversation" or "further dialogue," helping patients without raising the specter of futile metaphysical debate.

A number of the hermeneutic commentators I have discussed seem to adopt the story model. Sharpe believes that judgments about the mind are indeterminate in the sense that "no truth as to the matter exists independently of what we have available to us" (1988, 190). The question, for example, whether the woman's smashing of the vase was motivated at an unconscious level may be such that "there is no answer as to whether the accident was or was not motivated."

Indeed, judgments in these cases "will certainly be indeterminate . . . in the sense that there is no underlying pattern of mental events with which their judgment corresponds or fails to correspond and they may be indeterminate in the sense that no correct answer exists to a question about their truth" (191). Thus, an interpretation that the smashing was motivated is not uncovering a psychological state of unconscious hostility that played a role in the woman's accident.

If "no sense can be attached to which out of a range of alternatives is true" (195), then psychoanalytic interpretations are effective not *because* they are true, as Freud thought; they simply aren't true (or false). Sharpe is willing to concede that truth is not necessary for effectiveness; this is the placebo effect. But we should not be surprised that a story that makes sense of one's life and is reassuring in other ways would be therapeutic; an ideological or religious conversion may be enormously satisfying and helpful without being "a conversion to a set of true doctrines" (196).

Donald Spence also seems to subscribe to the story model, although his position is somewhat more equivocal. Spence is clear, first of all, that psychoanalytic interpretations do not purport to what he calls "historical truth." At least the "narrative aspects of an interpretation may . . . have priority over its historical truth" (1982a, 137)—its "historical truth may be less important than its narrative truth" (150). But Spence goes farther: interpretations are not designed "to document the past" (276), and so we should positively "give up our concern for historical accuracy" (276); the point is that interpretations do not represent or "correspond to a piece of the past" (173).

As an example of his claim that interpretations have "no clear correspondence with event[s] in the patient's life," Spence gives Serge Viderman's "six roses or cirrhosis" interpretation: the Viderman interpretation "cannot be said to correspond to a particular happening, and thus we can hardly ask questions about its historical truth" (275).

As an alternative to Freud's archeological model, Spence proposes that we think of interpretations as aesthetic and pragmatic statements. The artistic model makes clear that truth is at best beside the point: "We would hardly think of asking about the historical 'truth' of a painting" (269).[12] A pragmatic statement like "He is going to win the election next Tuesday" is also neither true nor false ("because we have no grounds for checking its truth value") (271). Thus in making an interpretation, the analyst believes the proposition he is putting forward but does not believe in its truth: "The analyst commits himself to a belief in his formulation but not necessarily to a belief in its referent" (273). It is instructive that Spence suggests that

12. See also Spence (1982a, 276) (to the extent that interpretations are "artistic productions, they have never happened before in just that form . . . and, therefore, they have no more provable correspondence with reality than a painting or a piece of music"); and (1982a, 276) (questions about historical truth are "impossible to answer" in the case of creative utterances).

the analyst pretends to believe in the proposition's truth (as a novelist does in hers), no doubt in order to induce the patient to believe in it.

It is a little vague how we are to understand the analyst's believing in the proposition without believing in its truth. Perhaps Spence means that analysts believe in their propositions in the sense that they think them useful for patients to hold: the analyst "commits himself to a belief in his hypothesis and is inclined to use it in a pragmatic fashion, as a way of making something happen. He is less committed to a belief in its truth value—either because he has no clear way of knowing whether or not it actually occurred or because he is proposing something that has no clear correspondence with an event in the patient's life" (275).

Indeed, throughout Spence's work runs the theme that interpretations are speech acts designed to make something happen. Thus, "if we think of [interpretations] as pragmatic statements, we realize that they are designed to produce results rather than to document the past; they are designed primarily to bring about a change in belief" (276). In other words, we "are primarily concerned in the effect [an interpretation] produces rather than in its past credentials" (276).[13]

Yet while Spence denies that interpretations are historically true, he insists that they may be "narratively true." But what does this mean? Spence says that narrative truth is the "truth of being coherent and sayable" (173). More precisely, he identifies two forms of narrative truth: "finding a verbal expression for [an] anomalous event, and . . . fitting the expression into the patient's life story" (165). Spence also identifies Sherwood's criteria of adequacy—consistency, coherence, and comprehensiveness—with narrative truth (180) and says that sometimes,

13. See also Spence (1982a, 173, 267, 271, 275, 292).

when narrative and historical truth conflict, the "need for narrative fit may be controlling" (181).[14]

Narrative truth is something interpretations may acquire over time. They may, that is, become true: "Once we shift to the idea that we can create truth by statement—the concept of becoming true—we have left the domain of archeology and opened up new and dangerous doors. . . . The interpretation . . . can bring an idea into being for the first time. Once stated, it becomes partially true; as it is repeated and extended, it becomes familiar; and as its familiarity adds to its plausibility, it becomes completely true" (177). In short, "an entirely imaginary interpretation may achieve a certain truth status in the analytic space" (171).

Given his views on the truth of interpretations, Spence must hold that interpretations are not, as Freud believed, effective because they are true (244). If we must cease to see interpretations as either true or false, the tally theory cannot be right. Interpretations are effective for other reasons: they may make certain kinds of experience accessible to the patient (173), "open up new possibilities" (178), lend meaning to disconnected pieces of life (247). Providing explanation in place of uncertainty can be very comforting (141, 167, 290). Indeed, even the thrill of discovery may play a therapeutic role (163–64). In essence, interpretations allow patients to see their lives as continuous, coherent, and meaningful (280). It is not surprising that they would be therapeutic.

Does Spence, then, subscribe to the story model? On one reading, all Spence's view amounts to is that we can never know whether interpretations are true. Thus, as noted, he says of an interpretation that we have "no grounds for checking its truth value" (271), "no clear way of knowing whether or not [the

14. See also Spence (1983, 270).

event it refers to] actually occurred" (275). On this view, analysts should give up caring about historical truth because it is beyond reach.[15]

This view may be thought of as a mild form of the story model: interpretations are stories in the sense that, for all we know, they are probably no more than stories. To say that given interpretations may not be true is fairly uncontroversial. But to accept that we should be happy in conceiving of interpretations as stories in this sense is problematic, as I shall argue below: interpretations must at least aim to be true for psychoanalysis to be viable. Still, this conception of the story model is not so problematic as the more extreme (and usual) form of the model.

The modest interpretation of Spence has some evidence, but there is considerably more evidence for a more robust interpretation of his views. Thus, "interpretations [are not] designed to document the past" (276), they do not "represent" or "correspond to a piece of the past" (267, 173, respectively), and they have "no more provable correspondence with reality than a painting" (276). In the same vein, interpretations propose things that "[have] no clear correspondence with an event in the patient's life," and "cannot be said to correspond to a particular happening" (275). Indeed, as noted above, "an entirely imaginary interpretation may achieve a certain truth status in the analytic space" (171). Through its resonance with other issues and its repetition and extension, an interpretation can become true (177)—which seems to mean that it can come to seem true, to be believed as true.[16]

15. Hence Spence's distinction in "Clinical Interpretation: Some Comments on the Nature of the Evidence" (1976) between the analyst's asking, when interpreting, "What could it be?" rather than "What is it?" We can never know what it is, so we might as well stop asking that, and ask the more modest question instead.

16. *Being* true, in other words, is equated with *seeming* true.

On the more robust interpretation of Spence's version of the story model, it is not just that interpretations may not be true. They are not true—do not correspond with reality. They are not even designed to be true. Perhaps they are not the sorts of things that can be true or false, just as artistic creations cannot be true or false. In any event, to say that unconscious hostility motivated the accidental breaking of the vase is not to refer to some unconscious psychological state that caused this result, but to tell a story in order to "make something happen" in the analytic space. Spence's view of the therapeutic efficacy of interpretations and of the kinds of reasons interpretations can be therapeutic strongly suggests that he subscribes to the story model: interpretations are effective not because they are true, as he explicitly concedes, but because they give patients meaning and comfort.

Spence himself has tried to evade the full implications of his theory in "Narrative Persuasion" (1983), in which he responds to Morris Eagle's charge that on his view "analysts simply go around making up stories" (1983, 469). But his response—that not just any meaning-scheme, however coherent, will do—is insufficient to remove him from the category of story theorists as I construe them. The "hard facts" (1983, 470), he says, should not be disregarded. In other words, one does not have complete freedom to tell any story one likes; but one still has a great deal of freedom.

Thus Spence asserts that because most of the hard facts will never be known, the analyst must make "as convincing a story as possible with the facts at his disposal and with his best guesses about what the facts might have been like." In other words, although narratives "must incorporate the known and partly known facts of the patient's life," the "facts are always inserted into a larger context, and this context must be supplied—it does not simply grow out of the evidence" (1983, 470).

Spence's response to Eagle is essentially to say that there are some constraints on the stories analysts may tell; the stories must at least incorporate the hard facts. Nevertheless, he seems to concede that in large measure the analyst's interpretations remain just stories.[17] Spence, in short, is classifiable as a story theorist, however much part of him resists the classification.

I want now briefly to show how Loch might also be understood as a story theorist. Loch sees psychoanalysis as both the search for historical truth and the development of sense out of a dyadic relationship. The latter he sees as a second form of truth—"truth as the emergent, the construction of something that makes sense and that therefore permits one to rely on it and to continue living" (1977, 221). Historical truth nevertheless plays some role in interpretations—there may be "fragments of historical truth" in the analyst's constructions (228). Interpretations, therefore, are not so much concerned with uncovering the truth, as with opening up possibilities (245–46).

Loch seems to mean by the "second form of truth" something that is useful and comforting to believe. Still, there is such a thing as truth on a correspondence theory. Given that there is such a thing, in his worldview, as an interpretation's corresponding to reality, interpretations are just stories to the extent that they do not so correspond; presumably it does not matter if interpretations are false in this way, so long as they have the second form of truth. Although for much of his discussion Loch appears to be saying that reconstructions attain only this second kind of truth, it becomes obvious later that he

17. In critiquing the story model below, I suggest an interpretation of it according to which interpretations are forward-looking rather than backward-looking: they give direction for the future, rather that insight about the past. Spence's language that interpretations are designed to "make something happen" may suggest this view. I consider this view more carefully below.

extends this view to interpretations of unconscious motives and the like as well. Loch, then, can be accurately interpreted as a story theorist.

Robert Steele also says things that suggest the story model, although his position is not entirely clear. Steele says that psychoanalytic case histories do "not provide causes for a life, but a framework of general story elements" (1979, 405); they "do not disclose facts about objects, they construct life stories" (408). Steele echoes Loch's view that truth is the "construction of something that makes sense. . . . Reality is not given, but created and recreated. . . . New truth is constructed within the ever expanding circles of psychoanalytical dialogue" (398). In brief, "interpretation does not reveal something real" (405).

This language appears to be saying that interpretations are mere stories: reality that is created is generally thought of as fantasy. The reality that "comes to reside in the ever expanding circle of meaning between analysand and analyst" (402) seems to be a vision of reality—a story—that analyst and analysand share, not the brute facts of the external world ("not 'truth' understood as the correct statement, the historical fact" [398]).[18]

18. But note that while Steele seems committed to the idea that interpretation does not reveal historical facts, some of his language is ambiguous. Thus, he speaks frequently of analysands increasing their "self-understanding" (1979, 395). See also (1979, 396, 398, 408). But one typically thinks of understanding as being of truths. Steele also speaks of free association as allowing the analyst to "uncover the wish, the thought, the desire that has been distorted by the censor, the agent of false consciousness" (1979, 398), and of the goal of interpretation's being "to make known to the analysand that part of himself which is unknown and yet influences his thoughts and actions" (1979, 401). Both of these locutions hint that interpretation uncovers the existence of unconscious mental phenomena that exert real effects on people's behavior. One might try to explain away such locutions. For example, phrases such as the above are meant to be understood in the context of the quasi-naturalistic moment

It is also possible that Steele is an alternative metaphysics hermeneut: to say that reality is created is to hold to some form of idealism. Finally, Steele may subscribe to the interpretations-as-literary-criticism model, which I discuss below. It remains plausible, however, to classify Steele as a story theorist.

Viderman may also hold the story model, although his position is unclear for the same reasons and in the same way as Steele's. Viderman speaks of the analyst as creating drives by giving them a name and form (1979, 261). Interpretations "create" not only drives (261), but also primal scenes (269), archaic unconscious experiences (262), and ordinary unconscious experiences (265); these items do not exist anywhere "but in the analytic space through the language that provides [them] with form" (262). And so an interpretation of, for example, unconscious anger's having motivated an act cannot "lay claim to any other truth than the one created for it in the analytic space by the speech which formulate[d] it" (263). One cannot say interpretations are "*either* true *or* false, for [they] cannot be contained in an alternative binary proposition of truth or untruth" (266).

Some of Viderman's language suggests the story view; but

---

of interpretation (see above), and they are ultimately to serve hermeneutic understanding. Alternatively, we should read these statements in light of Steele's other statements about interpretation's creating the phenomena it reveals; the wish that is uncovered is created by its uncovering, and the unknown part of the patient comes into being *by* being known. These explanations are perhaps possible. But it is perhaps likelier that Steele is somewhat ambivalent about his more radical positions, and this ambivalence shows itself in such seeming inconsistencies. Perhaps, then, we should classify Steele as a hermeneut who holds that interpretations conform to a traditional theory of truth (e.g., as a version of a clinical psychoanalysis hermeneut). Alternatively, he might be an alternative metaphysician, see below. But it remains possible that he is a story theorist.

some brings to mind a more moderate position. For example, language may create the drives in a particular form in the sense that drives are essentially unknowable and achieve symbolic form only when they are expressed in language. Similarly, Viderman's claim that the truth of an interpretation resides in the moment of its utterance may mean that it can be accepted by the patient only then, given the configuration of the transference at that time.

On the other hand, Viderman also gives indications of the story view. He believes that reconstructions of historical events are at best reconstructions of fantasies, at worst constructions designed "to make something happen." Yet he also seems to believe that interpretations about underlying unconscious events, e.g., fantasies, may not achieve historical truth; for example, the desire that mother not give birth to other children may not really be in the patient—may be imagined, created—and the unconscious hostility to father, while it may exist, is not presumed to be a cause of the "six roses" dream.

Like Steele, Viderman may be some form of alternative metaphysics theorist. On the other hand, he does not seem to be a simple idealist; he appears to leave no doubt that fantasies, unconscious motivations, and so on, can and do have an independent existence. Viderman may also be an interpretations-as-literary-criticism theorist, a possibility I consider below. But it remains true that it is plausible to think Viderman a story theorist.

A number of hermeneutic psychoanalysts, then, seem to subscribe to the story model.[19] I spend a good deal of time docu-

19. See also, for example, Morse (1982, 1017), both a clinician and a lawyer:

> Dynamic psychology is best understood, I believe, as a method of interpreting and giving meaning to behavior, rather than as a mechanistic, causal explanation of it. . . . Even if [dynamic psy-

menting this claim because the story model is most vulnerable to the argument from patient rejection. Later I give further reasons still for thinking that this is a real position—not just a straw man. The story view does exist.

The Alternative Metaphysics Model

The alternative metaphysics model says that psychoanalysis is hermeneutic in the sense that it adopts an alternative metaphysics to that underlying the traditional positivist metaphysics of those who see psychoanalysis as a natural science. Typically, alternative metaphysics theorists hold a postmodern vision of reality and our means of knowing it. Perception is always theory-laden—there is no unmediated access to reality. One always sees reality from a perspective—and of course there are always many such perspectives.

Alternative metaphysics theorists consequently tend to hold a coherence theory of justification. One is justified in believing

---

chology] is not a causal account, . . . the provision of meaning can be crucial in peoples' lives. It is often said, unfairly, that psychoanalysis is the modern secular religion and that analysts are the latter-day priests. Dynamic therapists are probably able to impart meaning authoritatively to skeptical modern patients because the therapists are trained in psychiatry or psychology, which are, in a sense, modern religions. For millennia, religions have had the vitally important effects of comforting people and of giving an account of and imparting meaning to their lives. This has been true even though the spiritual doctrines of the world's religions are not scientifically verifiable. Dynamic therapists give meaning to the lives of patients, and meaning counts. In short, dynamic therapy is "an interpretive story that provides meaning and may therefore be comforting to persons." (1982, 1017)

See also below for some therapists who have appropriated the concept of "narrative truth" to refer to fantasies of early childhood abuse.

something if it best fits with the other things one knows—if, together with this other knowledge, it forms the best theory of the part of the world one is studying. Alternative metaphysics theorists also tend to hold a coherence theory of truth:[20] to say that some proposition *p* is true is to say that it best fits into the best account of the part of the world one is studying. Alternative metaphysics theorists thus tend to be nonfoundationalists both epistemologically and metaphysically: there are no absolute foundations from which we can know things and none which, through correspondence, provide the criterion of truth.

In terms of the truth of interpretations, then, alternative metaphysics theorists tend to hold a position intermediate between clinical psychoanalysis theorists and story theorists. On this model, psychoanalysts do seek after meaning in the sense of psychological antecedents of behavior, but their interpretations revealing those antecedents are true only in a sense of "true" alternative to the traditional sense.

The later Schafer manifestly subscribes to the alternative metaphysics model of hermeneutic psychoanalysis.[21] He explicitly contrasts his worldview to the positivist worldview.[22] In Schafer's view, reality is always mediated by narration (1983, 257). Facts, in other words, are constructed. Schafer does not seem to mean by this that reality is a story—that facts are entirely created by us.[23] What Schafer rather seems to mean is

20. Other hermeneutic psychoanalysts propose other "alternative" theories of truth, some rather novel. See, e.g., Spezzano (1993) (relational view of truth); and Draeger (1983) (phenomenological approach to problem of truth in psychotherapy). For another postmodern analyst who has a nontraditional view of truth, see Horner (1995).

21. I shall call him simply Schafer, in contrast to the early Schafer, whom I call the early Schafer.

22. See, e.g., Schafer (1983, 184, 188, 191, 203, 212, 234, 238, 257, 284); Schafer (1992, 189).

23. The story theorists do seem to be taking this view. By contrast,

that we do not have access to facts in their unadulterated form; we bring something to perception. In essence, all seeing is "seeing as."[24]

For Schafer, in addition, multiple constructions are always possible; one must accept the "inevitability of alternative descriptions" (1992, xiv). As a result, one has some choice—but not unlimited choice—about which of many possible constructions to adopt. Schafer, then, holds constructivism and perspectivism—"theoretical positions on what we can and should mean by 'reality' or on the sense in which we can 'know' reality" (177)—as crucial. His position has both ontological and epistemological implications. And it is patently a form of nonfoundationalism (xiv-xv).

Schafer's position also encompasses a view about the nature of truth. First, he decisively rejects the story model: "Narrative is not an alternative to truth or reality" (xiv)—it is the mode in which they are presented. Indeed, to assert that psychoanalytic histories "comprise a set of new personal myths . . . is equiva-

---

even the "second reality" of unconscious psychological processes is, on Schafer's view, to be understood as real. See above.

24. While the idea that reality is "constructed" may seem to suggest, as noted, that it is created out of whole cloth, Schafer's view is rather that we bring something to everything we perceive. Consider the concept of abuse. Whether we perceive certain behavior as abusive depends on a host of factors, including the context of the act, the relation of the parties, the parties' intentions and feelings, and so forth. What we perceive as abuse today may not have been so perceived fifty years ago. To say that a judgment of abuse may require interpretation, however, is not to say that there is no fact of the matter about whether abuse occurred. Without a doubt there is a fact of the matter, although spelling out *when*, given the other facts (e.g., the parties' intentions and so on), we would make that interpretive judgment may be difficult to say. Another clear example of the concept of a constructed fact is that of male domination, whose existence is much more visible to our eyes than to the eyes of someone, say, in the nineteenth century.

lent to saying that a history of any kind is a myth. This nihilistic (or pretentious?) conclusion does not follow from the preceding discussion" (1983, 206). Although his language in *A New Language for Psychoanalysis* at times intimates that he is struggling with the story view,[25] by the time of *The Analytic Attitude* and *Retelling a Life*, Schafer has no doubt that psychoanalytic interpretations may be true in an unproblematic sense.

It is a little unclear, however, in what unproblematic sense of "truth" interpretations are true. Throughout *The Analytic Attitude* and *Retelling a Life*, as I argued above, Schafer seems to be working with a coherence theory of truth. Yet he shows some resistance to this theory in "Misconceiving Historiography and Psychoanalysis as Art" (1984, 364), as I also showed. One wonders whether Schafer is not misconstruing the coherence theory to require a collapse of the distinction between history and art;[26] I do not believe that it does require such a collapse. It is possible, on the other hand, that while Schafer insists we need some element of correspondence for our views of reality and truth to be plausible, we are meant to understand this notion of correspondence in coherence-type terms: "We are not required to repudiate totally some kind of correspondence, even if that correspondence is only general, provisional, conventional, situation-bound, or discipline-bound" (1984, 370).

Schafer, in conclusion, is without doubt an alternative metaphysics hermeneut, except that he has some resistance to unqualifiedly accepting a coherence theory of truth. Nonetheless, whether he holds a correspondence theory, a coherence theory, or some mixed theory of truth, Schafer does believe that psychoanalytic interpretations are true in an unproblematic sense. The interpretation that unconscious anger motivated

25. See above, especially the personal communication from Loewald.
26. Conceivably it does so in the hands of Geha, whom Schafer is here criticizing.

the breaking of the vase means what it says: one was experiencing anger at an unconscious level, and that anger contributed to the apparent accident.

Fingarette, another hermeneut who subscribes to the alternative metaphysics model, at times uses language reminiscent of Schafer's. Thus, he says that new concepts "not only 'reflect' and report our experience; as meanings, not merely as verbalistic structure, they are *constitutive* of experience."[27] Moreover, Fingarette, like Schafer, sees the world as "multimeaninged"— though it does not have "*all* meanings" (1963, 46).

Most important, Fingarette explicitly conceives of his task as metaphysical: in contrasting his meaning-reorganization view with the hidden reality view, Fingarette is dealing with "ontological interpretations of psychoanalysis and their implications, not with the question as to whether psychoanalysis is valid—a point which is here assumed" (18).

Fingarette's meaning-reorganization view is, admittedly, somewhat difficult to grasp. Recall his example of the patient's developing a headache in response to her boss's offer of an extra week of vacation, which the analyst interprets as resulting from her unconscious, defended-against dependency needs causing her to resent his generosity. In offering this interpretation, Fingarette says, the analyst is not revealing past, but hidden realities. Rather, his object "is to provide new descriptions, new meanings *now* for the events which were described or conceived differently *then*" (28).

Or again, in coming to see my behavior toward my little brother in the past in terms of the meaning-scheme "jealous aggression toward brother" rather than "well-meaning help of brother," it is not that I remember feeling hatred and jealousy of him—"I could not truly *recall* such feelings, for I *felt* no

27. See Fingarette (1963, 154). See also Fingarette (1963, 50).

such feelings at the time" (35). I do not discover unfelt feelings, but "I reinterpret the feelings I felt" (35). "The acceptance of a therapeutic interpretation consists in reconstructing present experience (including memories and expectations) in a more coherent manner; it is not a discovery of secret occurrences of the past" (40).

But it is a little difficult to understand fully Fingarette's suggestion as an ontological suggestion. To see oneself now as having been motivated by jealousy of one's brother then appears to imply that one really was feeling jealous then but did not know it. Yet Fingarette seems to reject this interpretation— there were no conscious feelings of jealousy then, and there were no hidden feelings of that kind either.

Even if we insist that the only alternative to the "hidden reality" view is that one *was* consciously feeling jealous then— one just did not know it—our problem remains. For "feeling-jealous-without-knowing-it" is surely a very different conscious experience from feeling jealous and knowing it. Yet what does this difference consist in?

The analogy to common-law marriage is not as helpful as Fingarette would like. One could know everything (else) there was to know about a couple without knowing they were married at common law. Discovering their common-law marriage is not like discovering something hidden behind some bushes— or discovering the pictures of a marriage ceremony one had not seen. But the common-law marriage is an additional fact about the couple—the fact that the other facts we know amount, in law, to a certain kind of relationship between the partners, a relationship that entails other rights and duties. The facts, in other words, have this additional significance.

But this analogy is unhelpful in the case of the older sister's jealousy of her brother: to say that all the facts we know about the sister have the significance that she was jealous of her brother is not to say that these facts have some practical, legal significance, with its own attendant consequences. It seems to say that something else in the subject was going on, as opposed to being a tag for further duties and entitlements that others may or will bestow.

Because of this difficulty, it may be tempting to see Fingarette as in essence adopting the story model, not the alternative metaphysics model. Consider Fingarette's contention that "insight does not reveal a hidden, past reality [but] is a re-organization of the meaning of present experience, a present reorientation toward both future *and* past" (20). Or consider his analogy again to the common-law marriage: "The judge's pronouncement is a novel act, a *present* act; it is an *authoritative reconstrual* of the past, a reconstrual which is oriented toward influencing the future. The judge does not reveal a secret ceremony in the past; *he now establishes a new context for our present and future response* to the *known* events of the past" (34).

Now the "reconstruals" and "reclassifications" Fingarette speaks of may simply be new stories one tells that are therapeutically helpful.[28] They are not, after all, accounts of hidden realities, and they are not cases of correctly renaming events one misconstrued in the past. (Recall that one wasn't feeling

28. There is also evidence that Fingarette holds to the view that interpretations give guidance for the future, instead of accounts of the past. ("The therapeutic insight does not show the patient what he is or was; it *changes* him into someone *new*" ([963, 20]. "The patient's acceptance and use of the language of hidden wishes makes it possible for her to see herself in a different light now and, as a result, to act differently hereafter" [1963, 30]. By interpreting, "we can construct a new meaning-scheme (or set of rules) and thereafter play the game of life in a basically new way. . . . A therapeutic interpretation . . . is . . . a suggestion that a new conception of one's life may be worth trying, a new 'game' played" [1963, 25]. I consider this view in more detail below.

jealousy then on a conscious level.) If the reconstruals do not refer to hidden or evident feelings, what do they refer to?[29]

The problem here, however, may be the fuzziness of Fingarette's ontological proposal, not his commitment to the story model. In fact, he explicitly rejects the view that interpretations do not purport to be true. He is not "denying the truth of the proposition 'unconscious motives really existed in the past and function in the present'" (36), and so he need not be saying that interpretations are mere stories that do not refer to reality.

More important, Fingarette is sensitive to the charge of suggestion—that psychoanalysis is "a disguised form of retraining or reconditioning rather than a discovery of objective truth" (1963, 39)—and insists that "the point of therapy is to establish the capacity for objectivity and to be objective" (43). He is eager to respond to the question, "What . . . becomes of the truth-value, the objectivity of psychoanalytic therapeutic insights?" (40), implying that interpretations must "in some sense be true, objectively grounded, in accord with a reality independent of what the patient may find useful to believe at any moment" (40). His main strategy is to point out that the same sort of evidence is essential to confirm interpretations on the meaning-reorganization view as on the hidden reality view. This strategy leaves many questions unanswered and establishes only that the theories of justification, not the theories of truth, would be the same on the two views.

But Fingarette does say that "neither view calls for confirmation by reference to a single, past event" (45). I infer from this language that Fingarette shies away from a correspondence

29. Perhaps Fingarette simply objects to the idea of some hidden feelings going on in the patient—as if there were a little person in his head feeling these other feelings. He may mean there are feelings the patient is actually feeling, whose significance he does not appreciate—hidden in that sense—but not a wholly other feeling hiding somewhere in his brain.

theory of truth and would probably be more comfortable with a coherence theory. But because he is not explicit on this point, one can only speculate.

In any event, Fingarette is plainly proposing an alternative ontological conception of psychoanalysis. And although his theory of truth is unclear, he certainly believes that psychoanalytic interpretations may be true in an unproblematic way. I therefore believe that Fingarette is an example of a theorist who subscribes to the alternative metaphysics model of hermeneutic psychoanalysis.[30]

THE METAPHOR MODEL

The metaphor model says that psychoanalysis is hermeneutic in the sense that it offers patients stories or narratives that are

---

30. Another example of an alternative metaphysician is Richard Geha. Geha's "fictionalism" seems to amount to the view that all reality is created by our minds. That is, he seems to be an idealist rejecting realism. At the same time, he does not reject the concept of truth. Indeed, he explicitly adopts a coherence theory. Nevertheless, there are indications that he collapses the distinction between fictions in the sense of "realities created by the mind" and in the sense of distortions. He seems, for example—at least at times—to think the classic transference story is wrong simply because there is no reality to distort. (At other times, by contrast, he seems to allow that the transference can be understood to be a distortion on a coherence theory.) Similarly, Geha is unwilling to say that a story that one was suckled by a mechanical cow is wrong; it may be simply that we think it wrong because we privilege one kind of story. In short, if everything is a story, there is no such thing as a "mere story." A failure to distinguish between stories as products of our minds and stories as distortions or falsehoods threatens to make Geha a story theorist—as he has clearly been read by others—and a suitable target of my critique. On the other hand, he may want to make this distinction and is merely being sloppy. In my view, the likeliest view is that Geha is an idealist who holds a coherence theory of truth and is therefore an alternative metaphysician in my schema.

true only metaphorically, not in the way that a natural scientific statement about causal antecedents of an event is true. The hermeneuts' names for psychoanalytic interpretations—stories, narratives—hint at this view. Fiction and drama are true in the sense of speaking to one's experience. And so psychoanalytic interpretations help one understand oneself better in the way that metaphors do.

On this model, then, psychoanalysis does seek after meaning in the sense of psychological antecedents of behavior, but the interpretations revealing those antecedents are only metaphorically true. To say that one's unconscious hostility motivated the accidental breaking of the vase is to say that it is as if one were experiencing that psychological state and it had the effect of causing one to break the vase. In the same way, to say that the plant's wanting sunlight caused it to move in the direction of the sun is to say that it is as if the plant had those wants and they caused this movement: it is to speak in metaphor. But metaphors can be helpful, and so both statements may be useful.

None of the hermeneutic thinkers I have discussed here explicitly takes this view, but it may be the best reading of some of them. In particular, all of the hermeneuts I have classified as story theorists may actually hold this somewhat less stark view: if psychoanalytic interpretations are stories, they are nevertheless stories that may teach us things about ourselves. Even if we do not achieve truth in any of its conventional senses, we do achieve it in this metaphorical sense.

Thus Spence, for example, may mean by his contrast between historical truth and narrative truth a contrast between truth (under any conventional theory) and metaphorical truth.[31]

31. Similarly, Loch's second kind of truth may be metaphoric truth—although he seems in fact to mean that a statement true in the second way is useful more than metaphorically true.

Later I will argue that it is implausible to think that narrative truth, for Spence, could be truth on a coherence theory, while historical truth is truth on a correspondence theory; one cannot tenably hold both a coherence and a correspondence theory as to the truth of statements about the same kinds of entities. But it is perfectly acceptable to do so with a metaphoric theory and a correspondence theory; one might reasonably hold that some statements are only metaphorically true, even while one generally holds a correspondence theory of truth. Everyone who believes that metaphors can sometimes speak the truth holds a mixed view in this way.

Perhaps, however, the more correct thing to say is that, although none of the theorists I have discussed subscribes to the metaphor model, some of them ought to.[32] Whether the meta-

32. In fact, it seems unlikely that at the time of *Narrative Truth and Historical Truth* Spence held the metaphor model. Consider that in his later book, *The Freudian Metaphor* (1987)—which may, as the title implies, hold the metaphor view—Spence seems to use "narrative" and "historical truth" in the same way as in his earlier book and seems to differentiate narrative truth from metaphoric truth. That Spence may hold the metaphor view in this later book is clear from his argument. Spence argues here that much of what Freud proposed is a metaphor; in particular, the notion of the unconscious and unconscious motivation is metaphoric. Later Spence discusses four overarching metaphors of Freudianism: the scientific metaphor, the narrative metaphor, the legal metaphor, and the post-Freudian metaphor (there is chaos in the world). In discussing the metaphor of analysis as literature, he says that the metaphor is wrongheaded precisely because analysis does not take the position that "anything goes." "Certain interpretations are preferred over others," unlike literature, which "rests on the assumption that there are any number of ways of representing the world and that any of them will do, that we know nothing for certain, and that, in the last analysis, narrative truth carries the day" (199). Given that Spence held in *Narrative Truth and Historical Truth* that interpretations are analogous to "aesthetic statements" and that narrative truth indeed carries the day, this seems to be a clear change in position.

phor model is able to evade all the problems the story view faces we shall see below. In terms of its position on truth, then, the metaphor model is between the story model on the one hand, and the clinical psychoanalysis and alternative metaphysics models on the other.

The Interpretations-As-Literary-Criticism Model

The interpretations-as-literary-criticism model trades on the analogies to literature and literary criticism that we find in many of the hermeneuts. Thus Sharpe suggests that interpretations are underdetermined, analogizing to the various ways of playing a Beethoven sonata; Spence explicates interpretation in aesthetic terms and speaks of the truth interpretation achieves as narrative truth; Steele analogizes interpretation with storytelling ("Psychoanalytic case histories are narratives linking the life of the individual to a general historical scheme. This scheme does not provide causes for a life, but a framework of general story elements" [1979, 405]); and Schafer uses the language of narratives.

As it turns out, most of these hermeneuts seem not to adopt the interpretations-as-literary-criticism model, but their language leads one to it. And some others, as we shall see, may well adopt this model. The analogy to literary interpretation, in any case, is seductive in a number of ways. Most prominently, to interpret a piece of literature is to find its meaning, as opposed to causes in the author that brought it about. Moreover, many literary interpretations of the same short story, for example, may be possible, and each may be compelling in its own way.

The interpretations-as-literary-criticism model, then, says that psychoanalysis is hermeneutic in the sense that it seeks after meaning rather than causes, in the way the literary critic seeks after the meaning of a piece of art rather than the psychological states in the author that brought it about. Although the model bears a superficial similarity to the story model, the "literary critic" psychoanalysts do purport to reveal psychological truths about the patient. Psychoanalysts are telling patients stories that are meant to reveal things about the patient's unconscious wishes or desires, even though they are not explaining behavior in terms of those wishes and desires.

Thus, we may learn true things about patients by considering the meaning of such phenomena as dreams and other bits of behavior. The idea is that a piece of behavior may signify many things about us even if those things do not causally explain that behavior. In seeking the meaning of the dream image of six roses, for example, we may learn that the patient felt anger toward her father, without supposing that the anger caused the dream image. In this way, actions, dreams, and symptoms are very much like the creations of a novelist. The novelist's account of a humiliating encounter of her hero may have its source in a similar humiliation that the novelist herself suffered in the past. Yet the hero's reaction to the humiliation may have many shades of meaning that the novelist never entertained, consciously or unconsciously; her words signify much more than she consciously or unconsciously intended. On the interpretations-as-literary-criticism model, psychoanalysis is hermeneutic in seeking after meaning, not causes. This version of hermeneutic psychoanalysis offers a particular interpretation of the nature of *interpretation:* interpretation reveals unconscious mental states but does not suppose that they are the causes of the behavior interpreted. Nevertheless, these states are unproblematically real, and statements about them may be true in the most traditional sense of "truth."

Some of Viderman's language suggests the interpretations-as-literary-criticism model. Consider again what he says about his "six roses or cirrhosis?" interpretation: "I hope one can clearly see here how useless it would be to ask who was right [the patient or the analyst] and what was the true meaning of the dream. . . . [The connection] was *invented* by phonetic similarity and was more in the mind of the analyst than in that of the patient. In the instant before it was uttered, it was nowhere. After it was uttered, several possible perspectives were opened up" (1979, 265).

Now on one reading, Viderman is saying that the interpretation is a story that does not purport to be true, and he is subscribing to the story model. Indeed, he says that the interpretation only becomes true "through the dynamic process which created it; it is not as if it were true per se, that is, outside the situation in which it was uttered" (265). But Viderman also suggests that, in giving the interpretation, he is making an appraisal that unconscious negative feelings are proximate (265). By interpreting the dream—a creative act, like art interpretation, that takes place "more in the mind of the analyst than in that of the patient" (265)—Viderman is uncovering unconscious states which, though not to be supposed causes of the dream image, are real. On this view, it is perhaps the claim that the unconscious negative feelings had a role in producing the dream image which "becomes true"—that is, true only within the interaction between analyst and patient.[33]

33. See also Viderman's example of Klein's interpretation of the child's play. The interpretation can lay claim only to the truth "created for it in the analytic space by the speech which formulate[d] it" (1979, 263). Once again, perhaps the interpretation reveals something true about the patient—she has unconscious fears about the safety of the babies in mother's belly—but is true only as a supposed cause of the play "in the analytic space." On this interpretation of Viderman, it is a little hard to know what to do with his idea that the primal scene inferred from the Wolf Man's dream itself *"could not be discovered but only imagined"* (1979, 270). Viderman is suggesting that there may well not have been a primal

Steele, too, uses language that points to the interpretations-as-literary-criticism model. For instance, noting a disanalogy in Freud's example of solving a jigsaw puzzle and interpreting a dream, Steele says that, unlike the jigsaw puzzle, the "original text of the dream—its solution, the latent meaning—exists solely as a product of interpretation. . . . There simply is not a master with which to compare one's analytic puzzle solutions" (1979, 404). Steele may be saying only that, when we ˙nterpret a dream, we are not finding the underlying psychological states which caused the dream (the "master"), although he may allow that we do uncover states that are real ("interpretation . . . makes the unknown, known" [405]).[34]

In short, Viderman and Steele may subscribe to the interpretations-as-literary-criticism model, although there is perhaps

---

scene that the Wolf Man witnessed. Is he then saying the interpretation is only a story as on the story model? Perhaps. Alternatively, he may be taking the interpretation-as-literary-criticism model if he believes the Wolf Man had real fantasies about the primal scene revealed by the interpretation. How we should finally interpret Viderman—as a story theorist or an interpretations-as-literary-criticism theorist—is not at all clear. As in the case of the other theorists I have considered, I leave for others the task of arriving at a definitive interpretation.

34. To complicate the picture further, note that the sentence following the one just quoted in the text is, "Interpretation does not reveal something real" (1979, 405). Other of Steele's statements are equivocal in this way as well. Thus he says, "Reality is not given, but created and recreated. . . . New truth is constructed within the ever expanding circles of psychoanalytical dialogue" (1979, 398). Steele may mean that the act of interpretation is creative, the way art interpretation is, but that it may reveal new truths about the patient nonetheless, just not causal truths (the interpretations-as-literary-criticism model). Alternatively, Steele may mean that analytic interpretations create new realities for patients— are stories that make their lives meaningful (the story model). Finally, Steele may mean that the world is a function of our ideas (the alternative metaphysics model taking the form of idealism).

better evidence that they are story theorists. In terms of its position on truth, the interpretations-as-literary-criticism model allows that interpretations may be true in an unproblematic way but denies that they reveal causal truths.

Concluding Remarks on the Models of the Hermeneuts

It appears that there are at least five strains of hermeneutic psychoanalysis. When hermeneuts in theorizing about psychoanalysis say that "psychoanalysis seeks after meaning, not causes," they seem to mean a number of things. The clinical psychoanalysis theorists mean simply that psychoanalysts are interested in the aims, purposes, and wishes underlying behavior, not in its neurophysiological antecedents. At the opposite end of the spectrum, the story theorists mean that psychoanalysts simply tell stories that give meaning to patients' lives. The alternative metaphysics theorists agree that psychoanalysts are interested in actual aims, purposes, and wishes, but they propose a radically new metaphysical understanding of knowledge, truth, and reality. The metaphor theorists suggest that analysts uncover metaphoric truths about patients when they interpret behavior. Finally, the interpretations-as-literary-criticism theorists maintain that interpretation yields noncausal truths about patients' underlying psychological states.

Hermeneuts who adopt the various models also, importantly, hold differing theories about the truth of psychoanalytic interpretations. The clinical psychoanalysis and interpretations-as-literary-criticism theorists believe that interpretations are true in the most traditional sense; they may well subscribe to a correspondence theory of truth. The alternative metaphysics theorists hold that interpretations are true under an alternative conception of truth—perhaps a coherence theory. The metaphor theorists deem that interpretations are true only in the most tenuous sense, that is, metaphorically. And the story theorists imply that interpretations are not true at all under any conventional meaning of "truth."[35]

Are these five models really so disparate, however? Could they not all be seen as actually the same? There may be no difference between the story model and the alternative metaphysics model—two I most strongly contrast. To say that a coherence theory of truth is correct, that is, just is to say that accounts of things are nothing but stories.

This objection is misconceived. First, story theorists, unlike alternative metaphysicians, tend to believe in some concept of truth (what kind does not matter) that interpretations do not purport to attain—although they may purport to attain to a lesser kind. This means that for the story theorist interpretations may be false. Alternative metaphysicians, by contrast, require that interpretations purport to be possibly true, albeit on a coherence theory of truth. Second, coherence theorists of

35. Perhaps a helpful way of thinking about the distinctions among the hermeneutic theorists is to ponder the difference between novels and docudramas on the one hand, and biographies and documentaries on the other. Those writing novels and docudramas may employ facts but are essentially seeking after an aesthetic experience. On the other hand, those writing biographies and documentaries know that they must use interpretation and that views other than their own are plausible, but they try to explain what actually happened. Their product is in the form of a narrative, not a law of nature, but they still accept criteria of historical accuracy. Aligned with the writers of novels and docudramas are the hermeneuts who think narratives are only stories to be judged by their beneficial effects (the story theorists). Aligned with the writers of biographies and documentaries are all the other hermeneuts, who believe that their narratives must meet criteria of historical truth—although there may be several narratives that may be true to the facts. In terms of this schema, it is the story theorists who hold the most radical view, and it is they who are most vulnerable to the argument from patient rejection.

truth unarguably make a distinction between story and history. There are true and false accounts, however much their truth or falsity is a matter of coherence of the elements of the account. Thus, not all accounts are mere stories—some of them are true stories. Finally, if alternative metaphysicians do not make a distinction between story and history and thus the alternative metaphysics and story models are actually the same, the arguments directed against the latter apply also to the former. The five models really do differ from each other, then, most importantly for us in their positions on the truth of interpretations.

Other themes run through the work of these thinkers. A number struggle with the problem that interpretations seem to be straightforward causal explanations of behavior; how can we square this with the theorists' radical visions of the nature of interpretation? Thus Steele speaks of the quasi-causal moment of interpretation in psychoanalysis—a moment that ultimately serves the hermeneutic interest. Fingarette explains that it is therapeutic for patients to believe that they are, with their analysts, uncovering "hidden realities"—even though they are not actually doing that. And Sharpe intimates that analysts must give patients alternative causal accounts to diminish the force of the patient's own pathologic view of the relevant causation.

Many of the theorists also propose criteria for validating psychoanalytic interpretations, and these require scrutiny in their own right. In addition, most have a position on whether Freud's tally thesis is correct—as indeed they must, if they believe that interpretations do not purport to be true. Finally, other important themes that run through all these hermeneuts deserve scrutiny. Space requires me, however, to leave that exercise for another time.

One final task remains in this chapter: to explore how my own practices of textual interpretation here replicate some of the very issues I am concerned with vis-à-vis hermeneutic psychoanalysis. I noted earlier that I am not attempting to provide a definitive interpretation of the eight hermeneutic thinkers. Then what am I trying to do? Am I claiming to accurately portray the views of these thinkers, or am I only telling stories about what they have said, making no claim to have portrayed their views accurately? Am I setting up straw men to make my arguments easier to formulate and more convincing to the reader? I answer this latter question in the Appendix, but the general question remains: How shall we understand what I am doing here?

Further, my discussion here raises important questions about the way in which my claims about these thinkers are true. When I classify the eight thinkers, do I mean that there is a correspondence, a "fact of the matter," about which box each fits into, or is my judgment a judgment of coherence? Should we think the five models really exist independently of my articulation of them in this book and, if so, did they exist before I articulated them? Or am I just trying to explain the basic issues in a way that can be understood and usefully applied? And in general, given that the positions of these thinkers were articulated long before I constructed my categories for describing them, what does it mean to claim that I have given an accurate (or adequate) account of their thought? Can we learn something from this about what analyst and patient are doing in forging contemporary interpretations of events that occurred long ago?

Finally, if these categories are my creation, what if some of the thinkers I classify appear to make inconsistent or contradictory claims—claims that do not cohere with each other—because of the way I have framed my ad hoc categories? Isn't there always a danger that I am forcing these thinkers into boxes that are convenient for me but fit the complexities of their thought badly? When I construct my categories, am I under a duty to make the thinkers look their best and most consistent, or am I entitled to choose explanatory categories that make them look inconsistent—even foolish—if this allows the reader to understand my argument more clearly?

In sum, in describing and classifying the various hermeneutic thinkers in this chapter I am raising many of the key issues in hermeneutic practice. My treatment may also have similarities to what analyst and patient are doing together in formulating interpretations. Perhaps I should be said to be delineating heuristic accounts based on concepts that were not articulated at the time the events they explain took place. These heuristics *are* claims to truth, but only truth of a particular sort. As heuristics, they are good enough for the purpose at hand, although they might in some other respects or for some other purposes be thought inadequate.

I do want to reiterate, then, that I have made only suggestions as to how to classify the eight hermeneuts in terms of my five-part schema. Although I hope not to have distorted, I do not pretend to have given a definitive reading of any of them. Most of them have written extensively, and I do not canvas all of their writings. I do not draw on the intellectual tradition in the context of which these hermeneuts write. I leave for others the task of explicating the hermeneutic psychoanalysts. I shall have accomplished my goal if readers are left with some sense of these hermeneuts' positions and if they are persuaded that my five models are viable readings of hermeneutic psychoanalysis.

In this connection, one final point bears mentioning: these hermeneuts often use very similar language, yet they also frequently seem to be saying quite different things—making quite different points. A number of the hermeneuts considered could be classified in any number of the five models I have proposed. Commentators in fact have read them in totally diverse ways. For example, Era Loewenstein (1991, 9-10) sees all of the hermeneuts as alternative metaphysics theorists, while Morris Eagle (1980, 1984) sees them all as story theorists; and Mark Freeman (1985), for example, reads Schafer as essentially a story theorist. The hermeneuts must bear some blame for the difficulty commentators have in interpreting them; one wishes that the hermeneuts would take greater care in the future to explicate their views clearly.

4

The Plausibility of the Story Model of Hermeneutic Psychoanalysis

I want to evaluate the five visions of hermeneutic analysis primarily in terms of the argument from patient rejection; each vision may have additional weaknesses and strengths that I do not discuss. The story model is most vulnerable to the argument, and I devote the most attention to it. The other versions of hermeneutic psychoanalysis are less vulnerable to the argument or possibly vulnerable to it only in a different form.[1] Thus, in the course of discussing the models of hermeneutic psychoanalysis, I identify a strong and a weak version of the argument from patient rejection. Later I return to the weak version to evaluate just how compelling it is. I also identify an alternative, more sophisticated variant of the strong version and evaluate that. Most of the versions of hermeneutic psychoanalysis are susceptible to one form of the argument or another; but only the strong, nonsophisticated version of the argument allows a knockdown argument against the model subject to it, namely, the story model.

The essential structure of the argument from patient rejection of the story model of hermeneutic psychoanalysis runs as follows:

1. The interpretations-as-literary-criticism model is in a somewhat different genus than the others, inasmuch as its problems do not derive from its position on the truth of psychoanalytic interpretations. Still, its position on whether interpretations reveal causal truths is at issue, so that the structure of the argument against this model shares some features with the structure of the argument against the other models.

1. Patients will not accept a version of psychoanalysis that holds out to them stories that do not purport to be possibly true;[2] as an empirical matter, that is, patients will reject a psychoanalysis so understood;

2. Patients ought not to accept a psychoanalysis so understood; it is normatively undesirable to believe interpretations that do not purport to be possibly true;

3. Psychoanalysts ought not to secure their patients' acceptance of psychoanalysis by lying to them about the truth-status of their interpretations; placebos may be acceptable in some contexts, but not here;

4. Alternative understandings of the story model of psychoanalysis under which the interpretations' truth-status seems not to be an issue at best radically alter the nature of psychoanalysis, at worst are subject to the same objection as the story model itself.

There are, then, empirical and normative components of the argument from patient rejection of the story model. As we shall see, there is also a definitional component of this argument that applies to some of the versions of the story model and of the other models. The propositions in the argument are fairly straightforward, although there are some subtleties. Yet they do require argument to be convincing.

Before turning to each of these propositions in detail, I

2. I put the matter this way because, although story theorists contemplate offering patients interpretations that are not true—either they are false or they are not the kinds of statements that could be true—it can nevertheless not be a condition of accepting a statement that it be true; it simply has to purport to be possibly true.

wish to enter some caveats about my view of analysis, lest the reader draw some wrong conclusions. Although I focus here on the truth or falsehood of interpretations, the reader should not conclude that I believe that analysis works only via insight offered by interpretations.[3] Working through, for example, is as important as or more important than the original insight—as are many other facets of the analytic situation as well, such as the sense of being heard.

Similarly, although I focus on the truth or falsehood of interpretations, I do not have in mind that analysis is largely a matter of reconstruction of the historical past. Truth matters, it is true, in the courtroom, where often we try to reconstruct past events. But in the courtroom no less than in analysis, it may be important not only whether, say, a rape occurred, but also how the injured party feels about and constructs the event. I care as much or more about the feelings and constructions as about the occurrence, and there is as much a truth or falsity about them as about the occurrence. Indeed, the story theorists are all clear on this. Wherever interpretations may be true or false, my argument obtains.

Additionally, I speak often of the analyst's interpretation of the patient's material. But the analyst's narrative is *of* the patient's narrative. In the same way, the literary critic interprets the piece of literature, which is itself an interpretation. Although the analyst proffers interpretations, they are arguably not her creation alone. Neither is she the sole arbiter of their truth. The interpretations are perhaps a joint product of analyst and analysand. The analyst is not the final authority.

Finally, to speak to the first and penultimate points further, it is not the analyst's sole job to provide insight. Indeed, one might argue that the transfer of meaning ("truth") from analyst

3. See also below.

to patient is not the analytic goal at all; analyzing the patient's desire for meaning is. That is, analysis questions the desire to receive meaning from the analyst. Yet, while I agree that analyzing the patient's desire for meaning is an important analytic goal and that providing insight is not the analyst's sole job, I do believe that such provision is an important goal of analysis. So long as this is so, then my argument in this book that the insights offered must be real insights is a significant critique of certain versions of hermeneutic psychoanalysis.

As an Empirical Matter, Patients Will Reject Mere Stories

Patients will not subscribe to a vision of psychoanalysis under which psychoanalytic interpretations are mere stories that do not purport to be possibly true. The idea is that people wish to understand themselves—to know the truth about why they feel and do such and such. They will not be satisfied with stories that make sense of their behavior unless they might be true. Told that the stories will endow their lives with meaning, patients will respond that fairy tales are not appropriate at their age; they want the facts and will seek to endow their lives with meaning in light of the facts.

In saying that patients want interpretations that purport to be possibly true, I do not mean to imply, as I have noted, that they want interpretations for only that reason: interpretations may furnish not only insight, but also meaning and comfort. Through a well-timed interpretation, the patient will feel empathically understood; and she may want her analyst to give her that feeling. And of course, as I mentioned above, there is more to analysis than interpretation. Patients, then, are looking for more than truth. Moreover, what they are looking for and what they think they are looking for may be different; and what they are looking for at the beginning of analysis may be different from what they are looking for as it progresses. Nevertheless, in terms of interpretations, patients will reject those that do only those things enumerated above: a right-thinking patient will not be satisfied with comfort and meaning in the absence of the possibility of truth.

The claim that patients will reject hermeneutic psychoanalysis under the story model for these kinds of reasons is clearly empirical.[4] And I do not have empirical evidence for the claim, let alone tests that establish its truth. I believe nonetheless that the claim is intuitively plausible, and I will present some examples to strengthen its plausibility.

Imagine this scenario: a woman walks from her living room to the kitchen with some purpose in mind but forgets midway why she was going there. Her friends in the living room help her try to reconstruct why she went to the kitchen: a television commercial had just advertised coffee, and she may have wished to have some; a few hours had passed since dinner, and she may have wanted a snack; the movie on television flashed letters on the screen, and she may have needed her glasses to read them; or she had mentioned earlier in the evening wanting to call her mother, and she may have gone into the kitchen to make the call. All of these explanations are consistent with the evidence; and of course her guests did not cite the many other explanations possible because the evidence ruled them out.

Now the woman's friends, here, are trying to provide an explanation for her act; they are trying, as I said, to reconstruct

4. And of course, there is likely to be variation among patients. We must ask who the patient is who will reject hermeneutic psychoanalysis. Is the patient well informed about analysis generally? Is he well motivated? Is he very acquiescent? My claim, in essence, is that, on average, patients will reject a psychoanalysis that offers them interpretations that do not purport to be possibly true. I give my reasons for thinking this below.

her reason for going to the kitchen. That is why the accounts aim for consistency with the facts. The woman, I suggest, is interested in her friends' accounts only insofar as they are an attempt to supply such an explanation. She wants to know the reason she so acted and will be interested in their accounts only to the degree they purport to answer her question.

The woman's lapse of memory, needless to say, might occasion a very different activity—a parlor game in which the woman's friends make up the most interesting or amusing or aesthetically pleasing story they can about her act. This story might well interest, amuse, or aesthetically please the woman, as it might anyone else in the room; but it would hardly recommend itself to her as a basis for understanding or governing her life. It would not tell her about herself. Why should she, then, care about such a story anymore than anyone else?

Consider another case. A man who suffers an accident wholly loses his memory, and nothing seems to restore it. A detective, aided by psychologists, discovers a number of things about the man: he knows several foreign languages, likes novelty, and has friends named Tom, Dick, and Jane. Various hypotheses can explain these facts. For example, he is an interpreter, he likes the novelty of new interpreting assignments, and he has friends named Tom, Dick, and Jane who interpret for the European Economic Community. Or he is someone who travels a lot and has friends named Tom, Dick, and Jane who recently took a tour he might have been on. (Plastic surgery following his accident prevents the various possible friends from recognizing him.)

I contend that the man will not be satisfied to hear these two interesting stories about his identity, even if they make sense of and give meaning to his life, unless the stories might be true. If told by the investigator that these stories are mere stories, and that he, the investigator, does not believe "their referents," the man will be left cold. He wants to know what his identity might actually be, and if the evidence is not persuasive, he will choose an identity and goals on other grounds. He will surely not assume the identity that a novelist thinks makes for the best story out of the data uncovered by the investigator.[5]

The woman who went to the kitchen and the man who lost his memory might have to be satisfied with a less-than-certain story. They might never learn the truth. Still, the enterprise is to find the truth. Each is looking for an explanation of his or her situation, and those aiding them in their search are purporting to give such an explanation. Although each of these people may have to be satisfied with a less-than-certain story, they need not and will not be satisfied by stories that make no claim to possible truth. Why would such stories matter to them at all?

I do not deny that understanding can comfort. People feel more secure when they have a sense of what they are about: where they came from, why they are here now, where they are going. Uncertainty can be very threatening and debilitating. But to achieve this sense of security, people must believe that the stories they are told do or might reveal the truth about them. Unless the stories purport to be possibly true, the people will have no reason to believe them; and it is only belief in the stories that will bring comfort. To give meaning to one's life, then, a story must make a claim to possible truth.

In short, although a story of this kind can comfort even if it is not true, one must think it *might* be true. To the extent that

5. Of course, if there is no way for the man to recover the truth about his identity—or something that might be the truth—he may consider the novelist's story; fantasy has its uses. No doubt he will also take into account other factors, such as values he holds important. In that case, however, the enterprise is not to discover who he is, but to decide who he will become. See below for the interpretations-as-giving-meaning-for-the-future reading of the story model.

analysts inform patients of the true nature of their enterprise, patients will reject psychoanalysis so understood.

As a Normative Matter, Patients Should Reject Mere Stories

It is true not only that patients will be unsatisfied with mere stories that do not purport to be possibly true, but also that they *ought* not to be satisfied with such stories.[6]

The reason is not hard to find: it is normatively desirable to believe statements only if they are or might be true.[7] To take the simplest case, it is normatively undesirable to believe things that are false because they lead one away from the good of knowing the truth. Knowledge—justified belief in true things—is a good both intrinsically and instrumentally: it gives one the satisfaction of having an enlarged understanding of the world, and it enables one to make decisions cognizant of their consequences in the world.

If it is normatively undesirable to believe things that are

6. I am not suggesting that analyst and patient must negotiate the treatment as if each were on the witness stand. That would destroy much of the playfulness and opportunity for discovery of the clinical encounter. Still, each must be committed to the effort to find the truth, although it may often be impossible to do so. A regime under which the truth of interpretations is not even a concern seems problematic.

7. One might think that certain beliefs could prove useful without being true and that in that case it might be normatively acceptable to hold them. A voice instructor, for example, might tell a pupil that it is useful to believe he is hanging from a hook as he sings; that way, his diaphragm will be maximally extended and he will sing better. But I believe it is misleading to imply that this is a matter of *believing* useful but false things—which would be something of a shame. Rather, one is doing other things incident to apparently holding the belief—here, picturing it, imagining it is true, trying to hold one's body as it would be were the statement true. See below for the imagine-and-react view.

false, it is also normatively undesirable to believe things that one knows or believes to be false. I have suggested that it is a good to believe true things, and so it must be a bad to believe false things. And one has a duty to try to avoid the bad. Indeed, it might not even be conceptually possible to believe a proposition one thinks is false; to believe some proposition p may just be to believe it is or might be true. But assuming that one can induce oneself to hold beliefs one believes to be false, one ought not to do so.

The analysis becomes more complicated when the proposition in question is not clearly false but simply does not purport to be possibly true. Yet I suggest that it is still normatively undesirable to believe such a proposition and that one has a duty not to believe it if one thinks it is of this kind. In essence, if something does not at least claim to be possibly true, one has no more grounds for believing it than if it positively claimed to be false.

Imagine a schoolteacher who tells his class that he does not claim that there might be life on the moon but offers it up to them only as an interesting story. Should students believe that there is life on the moon and mark True if the statement appeared on a true/false exam? I think not. They have no reason to think the proposition true, and one should strive to believe only things that are or might be true, for the reasons given above.

Indeed, one should not even believe *as true* something that only might be true, especially if it is not claimed to be true. Imagine the same teacher telling his class that Columbus might or might not have discovered America, and that he, the teacher, does not claim that he did. Here, too, I suggest that the students should not believe that Columbus discovered America and mark True when that statement appears on their true/false exam. Once again, they have no reason to think the proposition true, and one should strive to believe things as true only when they purport to be true.

If a proposition is not the sort of proposition that could be true—if it is neither true nor false—then one should also not believe it. To believe that the fictional Romeo liked his first-grade teacher is not only to suffer the detriments of believing something that is neither true nor false, but is also to suffer from confusion about the possibility of truth in such a case. And so once again, if one thinks a proposition is of this kind, one has a duty to avoid believing it.[8]

If psychoanalytic interpretations are mere stories, then, it is not only empirically likely that patients will reject the interpretations, but they positively ought to do so.

Does the Analysis Change with Different Examples?

I started my critique of the story model by suggesting that patients would not be satisfied with mere stories about themselves; they would want to know the truth or at least something purporting to be the truth, not simply something that gave meaning to their lives. To establish this claim, I posed the examples of the woman who wants to know why she went into

8. Perhaps this claim is less clear than I am making out. To believe a falsehood is something of a shame. To believe something that is neither true nor false is not to believe a falsehood; what one believes is no more false than it is true. Perhaps believing something that is neither true nor false is more like making some arcane metaphysical mistake than like being seriously deceived. My own view is as I present it in the text—it is always a shame to believe something that is not possibly true—but I recognize that the cases of falsehoods and statements that are neither true nor false should arguably be kept separate—and that different conclusions should arguably be drawn in these cases.

the kitchen, and the man who wants to know who he is. Mere stories would leave them cold—they want to know the truth about themselves, even if they realize they may not ascertain it. But these examples may load the dice against the story model. After all, the woman who left the living room to make her way to the kitchen at one point had a reason in mind for doing so. And the man who lost his identity at one time had one. Moreover, just as the woman at one time knew why she was going to the kitchen, so the man at one time knew who he was.

In these cases, then, at least two things are striking. First, there are definite answers to the questions What reason did the woman have for going into the kitchen?[9] and What was the man's identity? Second, both the woman and the man knew the answers to these questions at one time. Thus, when they ask now for the answers, they have in mind that there are answers; and they have a simple way of validating the answers: they may recover the appropriate memories. In these circumstances, to be satisfied with a mere story seems to be to give up the game too easily: one will (and should) want to know the truth.

But there may be other cases in which patients would be satisfied with stories, on the theory that that is all that it is possible to get. If psychoanalytic interpretations are like these cases, then patients arguably will not reject hermeneutic psychoanalysis on the story model.

I posit the case of a man who never consciously entertained a reason for going to the kitchen but simply found himself on the way there. Is there a truth of the matter about why he was going to the kitchen? He certainly never knew it if there was; and so he could never recover a memory of it. We at least know

9. I omit here complications about unconscious motivation and self-deception; I am assuming, that is, that the reason the woman had in mind was her actual reason. The case of unconscious motivation is discussed in the case of the example of the vase, below.

what it would be to be right in the case of the woman; we have clear methods of validation. In the case of this second man, we do not.

Even the case of a man finding himself on the way to the kitchen without ever having formulated a reason for doing so is not as hard a case as one might imagine. The man may remain convinced that, at some subterranean level, he did have a reason for going; his behavior was not simply haphazard, and perhaps, with effort, he could convince himself that he had recovered the reason (although he would not strictly be remembering it).

Consider, then, the more difficult case discussed earlier: that of the woman who learns that her husband is having an affair and shortly thereafter accidentally breaks a vase he had given her as a gift. Did hostility motivate the breaking at an unconscious level? Or what about the case raised by Spence in which a patient recalls that he refused to wear glasses as an adolescent? The question is why. No doubt he will be able to recover some of the reasons he told himself at the time that he did not wear his glasses. But what were his true reasons?

In these two examples, neither the two subjects nor anyone else once knew the truth of the matter and then simply forgot it. And so no simple restoration of a memory will validate our proposed answers. We can venture various answers in the two cases but can never be sure that we are right. To speak here of narratives or stories arguably makes a great deal of sense: we can construct plausible stories about what was going on in the people's conscious and unconscious minds in the two cases, but to say that we could ever explain their actions by a simple causal account seems farfetched.

The Los Angeles riots of 1992 may provide an appropriate analogy to the two cases. In attempting to understand the riots, one person might talk about poverty, another about the decline in family values and the weakening of the country's moral fabric, and another about urges to violence in human genes. Others might use frank metaphors, bringing out the narrative aspect of the explanations even more clearly; for instance, one person might say the Rodney King verdict was like a match touching off kindling soaked in gasoline, while another might say the verdict was like a slap in the face of an enraged person. No one believes that we will ever be able to identify the complex causes of the riots. All we can do is tell stories, more or less plausible, to try to understand the meaning of the event.

The interpreting of mental phenomena seems a lot closer to my later examples of the woman breaking the vase and the L.A. riots than to the earlier ones of the woman going to the kitchen and the man losing his identity.[10] If so, the language of narratives and stories may be more apt. Trying to understand a particular person's behavior is analogous to trying to understand a complex phenomenon like a riot, and not at all analogous to trying to find the cause of a car's mechanical failure. In the latter case, there is a clear answer and a way to establish that we have found it. In the former case, there is no clear answer and no clear way to establish that we have found it. All we can do is tell more or less plausible stories that endow the events with meaning.

I suggest, however, that this reasoning is insufficient to per-

10. To return to the example of the woman going to the kitchen, one can imagine a number of different questions she might ask: not only why she was going to the kitchen, but also, for example, why she forgot why she was going to the kitchen or, perhaps more generally, why she keeps forgetting things. The typical analytic question is closer to the second and third cases than to the first. But note that some psychoanalytic interpretation is designed to recover memories rather than establish complex underlying causes as in the second and third cases and the examples in the text. And this case then seems closer to my earlier examples than to the later ones, especially when the remembered event is not very remote in time.

suade one that patients will accept hermeneutic psychoanalysis on the story model. The difference between the earlier and the later examples is simply one of complexity: we know there is a truth and know when we know it in the earlier cases, but not in the later. Yet this is insufficient reason to deny that there is a truth in the later cases. If there is a truth in the later kinds of cases (and so in psychoanalytic interpretation), then patients will (and ought to) want to know it.

Thus, unless the man who found himself on the way to the kitchen was simply behaving haphazardly, he did have a reason for going there, even though he was never consciously aware of it. Similarly, the woman who broke the vase either felt unconscious hostility which contributed to her breaking of the vase or she did not. It may be extremely difficult ever to determine with certainty whether unconscious hostility had this causal role; but that is far from saying that there is no truth of the matter.

Even in the case of the Los Angeles riots, the accounts given are either true or false. It may be that any particular explanation omits some relevant facts—indeed, that doubtless is the case. But even metaphorical accounts either reveal or fail to reveal truths about the underlying causes of the riots; if none of the participants in the riot was angry over conditions before the Rodney King verdict and thus was not inflamed even more by the injustice of the verdict, then the metaphor of the slap to an already-enraged person is just plain wrong.[11]

In short, although these later examples at first glance seem to suggest that all we can get is stories—so that patients in the analytic situation hearing that they will get only stories will

11. Of course, the implicit explanatory claim may be false, and yet there may be merit to giving the explanation—we may, for example, learn some general truths about human nature that happen not to apply to the case in question. Below I consider the implications of this fact vis-à-vis the concept of interpretation in the psychoanalytic context.

be less resistant to accepting them—to say that all we can get is stories is ambiguous: it may mean that we must resign ourselves to never knowing the (whole) truth; or it may mean that there is no truth to be had. While the first may be true, the second has not been established. In particular, the examples do not show that one cannot get the truth—that there is no truth of the matter—but only that it may, at times, be hard to know the truth and to know that one knows it.

Moreover, even if we must resign ourselves to never getting the (whole) truth, there is no reason to resign ourselves to hearing mere stories from our analysts; we must care about the truth —as the story model implicitly denies—on pain of breaching the duty to believe only what purports to be possibly true. Analysts and patients alike must aim at finding the truth. The story model neglects at least this fact, making a virtue out of a defect (namely, our difficulty in achieving truth in complex cases).[12]

Most important, my more complex examples do not establish that there *is* no truth of the matter in these cases, so that patients have no choice but to accept stories. Yet what if story theorists could establish that there is no truth of the matter in the cases dealt with by psychoanalytic interpretations?

12. I say "at least," because this is the weakest reading of the story model. (Recall that I said above that Spence may hold only this weak view.) Although I suggest that the weak reading of the story model neglects the fact that interpretations must aim at the truth—patients must care about whether interpretations are true inasmuch as they are essentially asked to believe them—what is the significance of the fact that we often cannot get the truth? On one view, there is wisdom in not wanting the unattainable—so we content ourselves with stories. On another view, the wisdom lies in not losing sight of what one wants. It is this position that I stress here, for the reasons given above.

Must Patients Accept the Story Model If There Is No Truth of the Matter in the Case of Interpretations?

Suppose that the story theorists are able to establish that there is no truth of the matter in the cases dealt with by psychoanalytic interpretations.[13] I confess I find no arguments in their writing that do so; they give reasons for thinking that it is hard to find the truth, not impossible. Nevertheless, there may be some philosophical arguments that do establish that there is no truth of the matter.[14]

If there are such arguments, a disquieting possibility arises. Perhaps deferring to the sensibilities of patients who resist the story model is unsound. Arguing that we must abandon this conception of psychoanalysis because patients find it unacceptable may, in the end, be no more justifiable than arguing that we must abandon, say, idealism because the person on the street finds it unacceptable. A person may not like the notion that the apparently independent material world actually consists only of her ideas, but that does not make the notion false. If that is the way things are, she has no choice but to accept it.

If this is so, patients may simply be wrong to insist on explanation rather than accept stories; stories may be all that is possible. If explanation purporting to truth is beyond reach, patients may have no choice but to settle for stories.

13. This type of position seems more plausible to attribute to a Sharpe or Viderman, say, than to a Spence or Loch. See below.

14. In this event, the story model may have its own metaphysical underpinnings. Nevertheless, it is different from the alternative metaphysics model that I describe; theorists on that model believe that interpretations are true but subscribe to a different theory of truth. Interestingly, one motive for adopting the story model—namely, to avoid metaphysics—is undermined by this interpretation, for on this interpretation the story model makes use of a metaphysical argument.

A number of things may be said in response to this possibility. First, the fact that the person on the street finds a view like idealism implausible is a clear mark against the view—something its proponents must come to terms with—even if it is not dispositive. Simply to establish that the ordinary patient is likely to respond to the story model as the person on the street does to idealism is therefore important.

Second, the patient's reaction to the story model on this view is more justifiable than the person on the street's reaction to idealism, even supposing the story model and idealism are true. In the case of idealism, the person's naive view about what is the case—that there are physical objects independent of his perception—is frustrated. He does not want to believe that objects have a different kind of reality than he thought the case; but they do have a reality then.

The story theorists on this view, however, are saying something much more radical. They are saying that there is no fact of the matter about motivation because there is no fact—only stories we construct to make ourselves feel better. The patient, then, is not like the person on the street, who simply objects to the kind of world he occupies; the patient, rather, objects to being told about a world that is not referred to, in essence, at all. Unless the analyst's stories refer to things that have some kind of reality (even if only ideal), they are untruths about the patient—materially no better than lies. The patient may be right, then, to reject them—to wish not to engage in discourse about nothing, to be comforted by nothing.

This argument implicitly repeats one made earlier: patients not only will reject psychoanalytic interpretations that do not purport to be possibly true but should reject them. Statements referring to things about which there is no truth of the matter no more ought to be believed than statements that are simply false in the ordinary way. Thus, while patients may not like idealism, there is nothing wrong in believing in it. There is something wrong, on the other hand, in believing interpretations that do not purport to be possibly true.

Third, even if the story model just describes the way things are, it is false that patients have no choice but to accept psychoanalysis so construed. If idealism just describes the way things are, the person on the street must either come to terms with idealism, deceive himself about reality, or refuse to play, so to speak. Refusing to play in this case would amount to rejecting all discourse about and intercourse with the material world—perhaps out of petulance that the world frustrates one's expectations, perhaps out of a belief that the alternative is unwittingly to lie to oneself about the world.[15] But to reject all discourse about and intercourse with the material world would be to surrender to a kind of autism. That clearly is no choice.

The case is different with the story model on this view. Even if the story model describes the way things are, patients do have a choice about accepting it. The alternative to accepting the story model, or deceiving themselves, is to refuse to play—which is a viable option here. Patients can simply reject psychoanalytic discourse about unconscious motivation. The choice is not even between accepting the story model or foregoing therapy—they can simply ask for a different kind of therapy.[16]

15. The idea would be that it is psychologically impossible not to believe that the external world has an independent material existence as one lives one's life in this world.

16. For example, behavioral therapy does not involve coming to understand oneself—and therefore resigning oneself to mere stories. Even therapies that do work with psychic states do not always implicate a story model of this kind about therapeutic statements. For example, an abreaction kind of therapy may not value understanding or insight, but simply the release of emotions. Whereas some thoroughgoing hermeneuts believe that all knowledge involves the mere construction of stories that further discourse, others, as Moore has put it, are more "modest." The

Thus, patients can stick to their guns and claim that if the story model on this view is the sole correct view of psychoanalytic interpretation, they will have nothing to do with psychoanalytic interpretation. More important, the patients' disquietude about crediting mere stories may mean that they will not be helped by an analysis that tells stories in this way. Interpretations are therapeutic when they are believed, and these interpretations will not (and should not) command belief. The idea, then, is that psychoanalytic therapy becomes self-defeating if the story model is true. If so, the story theorists' claim that because the story model is true patients have no choice but to accept it is exactly backward: if the story model is true, patients have no choice but to reject it.[17]

Patients, in short, will be right to reject hermeneutic psychoanalysis on the story model. To say this is not to show that the story model on this view is wrong—in particular, that there is a truth of the matter when it comes to psychoanalytic interpretations. What it does show is that the story model on this view is a desperately unhappy vision of psychoanalysis if it is right—a vision that dooms its subject to nonexistence.

One qualification must be made here: if story theorists are radically hermeneutic about all human knowledge, then there is no truth of the matter about any statement, and everyday people are asked to credit all manner of statements that do

---

analysts we have considered may be very modest; they seem to take the view that, as to current psychic events, it is particularly motives, conscious or unconscious, about which analysis constructs narratives. If so, therapies that do not interpret conscious and unconscious states do not require the construction of stories. See below for the effect on the argument if all knowledge is narrative in the problematic sense.

17. That is, patients are not being in the least petulant when they reject hermeneutic psychoanalysis, but doing the only thing they can reasonably do: avoid a therapy that will not help them.

not purport to be possibly true. It may be normatively undesirable to believe things which do not purport to be possibly true, but if everything is of this kind, must we all simply cease believing? This radically hermeneutic view puts people to a cruel choice at best. In any event, one's self-deception in effect is so pervasive on this view that refusing to credit psychoanalytic interpretations accomplishes little, and perhaps patients would not and should not reject these interpretations. Psychoanalysis might not cease to exist on this radical view, but perhaps all discourse — including psychoanalytic discourse — should.

Is Deception a Viable Answer?

Patients, I have suggested, will reject psychoanalysis under the story model, for, although psychoanalytic stories might comfort them even if they are not true, patients must think they might be true. If story theorists are telling patients meaningful stories about their lives that do not purport to be true, they can comfort patients only insofar as they lie about what they are doing, if only by omission — only, that is, insofar as they create in their consumers the belief that they are doing more.[18] Thus psychoanalysis can avoid self-destruction only by becoming a therapy that heals by creating illusions.

Now critics external to psychoanalysis might believe that psychoanalysis heals by telling comforting stories — whatever psychoanalysts think they are doing. In the same way, critics

---

18. I do not mean to suggest that story analysts are currently guilty of conscious or bad-faith deception of their patients; they may not realize what their position commits them to, and they may not realize, as I argue, the obligation they are under to disclose their position to their patients. Nevertheless, failure to disclose after becoming aware of the obligation would, I think, violate a moral injunction for analysts not to deceive their patients.

external to religion might lodge the value of religious beliefs in the comfort they provide, while denying that those beliefs have anything to do with the way the world is. But self-respecting priests and analysts should not accept these characterizations of their practice. They should especially not accept them because to do anything else is to be deceptive: for priests to preach about the afterlife without believing that it exists or might exist, solely in order to make people feel better, is to tell a deliberate lie. Similarly, for analysts to put forward interpretations as explanations that purport to be possibly true is also (if only by omitting the correct characterization) to tell a deliberate lie.

The point, then, is not that psychoanalysts are expected to believe that their interpretations reveal true things about the unconscious because that is their faith, as it is priests' faith to believe in the afterlife—that would be to beg the question of what beliefs must characterize psychoanalysis. The point is rather that psychoanalysts are expected to believe that their interpretations possibly reveal true things about the unconscious (as priests believe in the afterlife) to the extent that they intentionally induce such belief in their patients.

My conclusion should not be surprising, given my argument above that believing a proposition that does not purport to be possibly true is normatively undesirable. Patients, of course, do not do wrong by believing such a proposition if they have no reason to be aware of its questionable truth-status. But if it is undesirable for them to believe it, it is undesirable for their analysts knowingly to induce them to believe it. More than that— it is wrong. Lying not only prevents people from acting with knowledge, but shows them disrespect as people.

If such a view is correct, story theorists cannot save the story model by recommending that analysts intentionally induce false beliefs in their patients. They must fully disclose to patients that their interpretations are mere stories; to disclose nothing is implicitly to hold the interpretations out as true and worthy of patients' belief. But once the disclosure is made, patients, as I argued above, will (and should) refuse to participate in psychoanalysis.

But perhaps I am being overly moralistic—even rigid—in denouncing the deception required on this view. If holding certain false beliefs will immeasurably improve the lives of patients, perhaps it is justified to induce these beliefs in the patients.[19] The requisite deception is, as it were, relatively trivial, and the benefits are great. Very few people believe that lying is never justified; and the lie here is fairly venial. The point is that if lying to patients will permit them to hold false beliefs that are curative, perhaps the lying is justified. On this interpretation, of course, psychoanalytic interpretations are in the nature of placebos, and to the extent that placebos are justified, so perhaps is inducing belief in the interpretations. But are placebos justified?[20] The question has resulted in a hardfought, protracted debate among medical ethicists, and I do not intend to enter the fray. I will say only that some strongly believe that lying to patients is never justified by expected therapeutic benefit, inasmuch as it trenches on patients' autonomy and shows them insufficient respect as people. Others believe that

19. In what follows, I implicitly criticize my argument above that it is normatively undesirable to believe—and induce belief—in propositions that do not purport to be possibly true. Perhaps if the benefits are great, the deception and self-deception are justified. I ultimately reject this argument in this case. See below.

20. I am concerned with the case in which placebos are used clinically: the doctor prescribes an inert substance in the hope that it will produce therapeutic benefit. Placebos are also used experimentally in randomized trials in order to test the efficacy of medications. The issues here are somewhat different, and, because the subject is informed that he might receive a placebo as part of the experiment, the practice is much less morally suspect.

inducing belief in the curative powers of an inert agent is a trivial harm if the patients may benefit thereby. Moderates believe that placebos are justified only if the harm avoided is great and there is no reasonable alternative.

As I have said, I do not intend to discuss the morality of placebos in a general way. What I wish to do is point out the differences between ordinary placebos and the false beliefs that analysts must induce in their patients on this interpretation. In administering an ordinary placebo, a doctor tells her patient that the drug is effective and will relieve his symptoms, even though the doctor believes that the drug is inert. The false belief that the patient comes to hold, then, is that the drug is an effective treatment for his malady. In the psychoanalytic context, by contrast, the analyst's false communication to the patient occurs on a metalevel: she tells the patient that her interpretations are or might be true, when she believes that that is not the case. The patient, then, comes to hold the required false belief, namely, that the analyst's interpretations are or might be true. More important, he comes to believe all the false interpretations that his first false belief leads him to accept as true. Thus, the analyst's deception is compounded; her patient comes to believe many false beliefs as a result of her deception, not just one.[21]

21. But although the consequences of this kind of deception may be more global, they may also be more effective. It is true that the pill may actually cure the patient of some malady, but the false picture of himself that the analytic patient comes to hold may have more profound effects. But I suggest below other reasons for thinking that placebo-interpretations may not have the desired effect and are more problematic than placebo-pills even if they do. My arguments in this section are essentially utilitarian—will the benefits in fact outweigh the costs? There are also, of course, normative arguments that lying is prima facie wrong whatever the benefits, but I do not rehearse those arguments here. In any case, the law clearly levels sanctions against deception in many arenas, including the medical.

Indeed, the nature of the false beliefs differs fundamentally in the two cases. The physically ill patient comes to believe simply that a particular pill will work beneficial effects. The psychoanalytic patient, by contrast, comes to believe very many things about the kind of person he is. He may learn, for instance, that as a child he felt rejected by his parents, wished his younger siblings dead, and was very competitive; that as an adult he often feels abandoned by his friends, envies others their close relationships, and works hard and accomplishes much partly in order to triumph over others. Coming to a false picture of oneself—of the kind of person one is—is much more problematic than coming to believe something false about a pill. One's self-concept is deeply personal. It fundamentally affects how one feels about oneself, and therefore one's well-being. And it fundamentally affects how one perceives and acts in relation to others. Should one not hesitate to deceive someone about such fundamental and personal things? [22]

Yet suppose the patient is a mean, grudging person whom the analyst describes as a kind and generous person. Coming to hold these false beliefs about himself will no doubt affect how he feels about himself—he is likely to feel much happier. Perhaps more important, it may even fundamentally affect how he acts in relation to others—he may become more kind and generous. Is this not a desirable outcome, one that justifies the mild deception?

Other considerations, however, cut the other way. The person may continue to act in a mean and grudging way toward other people, yet be less cognizant that he is doing so and feel

22. Everyone, of course, is somewhat deceived about himself or herself—although causing more self-deception in a person may still be problematic. In the case of the analytic patient, the problem is even more severe because the patient, on this view, is brought to suffer serious and pervasive self-deception.

happier about himself as he does it. He then gets the benefits of feeling happier but incurs the losses of mistreating others and receiving, perhaps, a response in kind. In any case, the others certainly suffer losses. And he will be less likely to feel bad about what he is doing and motivated to change and thus less likely to become a better person who is treated with affection and respect by others. In the long run, everyone loses.

Moreover, one may wonder whether the patient is in fact likely to feel happier. Perhaps he unconsciously senses what kind of person he is and at some deep level does not believe the analyst. In that case he loses the benefit of feeling better about himself and also feels betrayed by the person he senses is lying to him.

Of course, I am telling a story about an analyst who conveys only good news to his patient. In fact, the narratives that analysts tell patients are quite complex, as people are; people have some good in them and some bad, and they interact with each other in complicated ways. But the basic points I have made through my simplistic story remain valid. Patients may feel better as a result of the story they are told,[23] and they may therefore act better. On the other hand, they may act no better at all and be disabled from realizing that as a result of the false story.[24] Finally, the patient may sense his analyst's deception and therefore not only not feel better, but feel worse because betrayed.

I suspect, in fact, that people care deeply about holding more

23. In this case, they will feel better not because of the rosy picture the analyst paints, but for other reasons (e.g., they nevertheless like the complex person who is described, they feel understood by their analyst, etc.).

24. In the same way as that described above, the patient is disabled not because he holds a simplistic, rosy picture of himself, but because the picture he does hold interferes with his ability to see clearly how he affects others.

or less accurate views about themselves. We find most pitiable the people who are significantly deceived about what they are like; and people are most chagrined to learn that they have been operating under self-deception of this kind. Thus, if the patient senses or discovers his doctor's deception, he will feel betrayed not only because the doctor has breached his trust, but also because he has breached his trust about a matter about which the patient cares so deeply.

Any time a doctor administers a placebo the patient may rightly feel he has been treated as less than a full adult who can accept and make the best of the truth about himself and the world. When the doctor induces in the patient illusory beliefs about his very nature—about the kind of person he is—this is even more the case; at best the patient may feel treated like a child who must be protected from the truth. Because trust is even more important in the psychoanalytic relationship than in other medical relationships, analysts should not trifle with it.

APPLYING THE ARGUMENT IN THE TROUBLING CASE OF APPARENT MEMORIES OF EARLY SEXUAL ABUSE

A number of story analysts and commentators discussing analysts' views invoke the example of apparently recovered memories of early sexual abuse to illustrate the notion of narrative truth as opposed to historical truth. Some of these commentators seem to say that, for purposes of therapy though not for the law, it suffices that these memories should be narratively true. (I quote from several of these commentators in the appendix.)

Would patients reject a form of analysis which suggested that they believe—for therapeutic purposes—that they were molested by members of their immediate family, when this claim was only "narratively" true—that is, did not purport to correspond to historical reality? The question answers itself. If ever there were a case in which patients would reject such an analysis, this is it.

The patient might well doubt that holding such a belief would be therapeutically beneficial. And, indeed, the therapeutic benefits of believing manufactured memories of sexual abuse are at best highly questionable; although such memories may give patients an "answer" for their pain and dysfunction and may temporarily organize them, they are also likely to *cause* them considerable pain and suffering. In addition, such beliefs will wreak havoc on the patient's relationship with her family members. Even if such beliefs were therapeutically beneficial to the patient—a dubious proposition at best—their harmful effects on other family members, particularly the accused, would and should lead all right-minded patients to reject outright the proposition that they should believe them.

Patients, then, both empirically will and normatively ought to reject a treatment that offers such interpretations. This example is intermediate between the examples of the woman going to the kitchen and the man losing his identity on the one hand, and the Los Angeles riots on the other. Although we may know what kind of evidence would establish, definitively, the facts of the alleged abuse, we may not have access to it. There may be no witnesses, and memory is notoriously fallible. It remains the case that patients will not want to believe they have been abused—even if it makes sense of their lives and speaks to some feeling of violation they had as a child—unless they really were, literally, abused. We may not be able to give them a definitive answer; but patients will not be content to be told that their belief in their abuse achieves narrative truth; they will at least want more.

What if there is no truth of the matter as to their abuse? Will patients be content then to arrive at solely narrative truth? This is a particularly unlikely case for saying there is no fact of the matter available: either the father raped his daughter or he did not. Even in cases in which there are some lingering interpretive issues—for example, was his looking at his daughter in that leering way abusive?—there are facts that the patient will want to know and will interpret as best she can. If for some reason we should believe that there are no facts at all in a case (even a rape case), the patient will decidedly not want to imagine that there are; there are few things she will want to believe less.

Finally, to fully retrace the steps of my argument, deception is not a viable answer here. It is antecedently unlikely that misleading patients about matters like this would in fact be therapeutic, but even if it were, as noted, this is a placebo with an immense cost to others. In addition there are all the dignitary costs associated with lying to someone, particularly about such an important matter.

No doubt most therapists, even those who believe that the narrative truth of memories like these is enough, inform their patients that memory is fallible and that their memories may be only narratively true. Some may not. Evidence of therapists who encourage such memories and are quick to credit them exists; perhaps they believe, without good reason, that the memories are true; perhaps they believe they are therapeutic or that casting doubt on them is antitherapeutic or that the memories are true in the most important sense (the child felt uncomfortable around the father). Notwithstanding these reasons, it is patently wrong for therapists to mislead patients about the veridicality of their recovered memories.

But if most therapists these days do inform their patients that their beliefs might be false, then in practice patients may generally be asked only to believe that the memories might be true. There is, of course, nothing wrong with this, if indeed the memories might be true. This tack of therapists is in itself of interest, inasmuch as it implies that they think it important to stress to patients the uncertainty of their interpretations when error is potentially so consequential. One might wish them to do so in all cases.

More important, the example of early child abuse totally undercuts the premise of the story model—that we should be content with narrative truth. Far from being content with narrative truth, we should rail against it, striving to achieve historical truth. Of course we may have to live with the uncertainty of never knowing what really happened. But making of this a virtue—holding that providing stories is a satisfactory way of doing psychoanalysis—is a view that the example of early sexual abuse belies.

I discuss this example in detail because, from the standpoint of current law and public policy, the issue is quite salient and is a principal source of the current controversies about the underlying theory of psychoanalysis. When we think of the advantages and disadvantages of a view like Spence's, we must count his and others' affirming of the importance of narrative truth in the arena of early memories of sexual abuse as a clear demerit. To the extent that there are therapists who are encouraging such memories—and, because of their narrative virtues, affirming them for patients as real—we face a significant public policy problem. Thus, the question of childhood memories, whether repressed or invented, is an excellent case of the argument from patient rejection that forms the centerpiece of this book. Obviously, if the story model of hermeneutic psychoanalysis in some way justifies or excuses—or even just enables—the implantation of false memories of sexual abuse, that is a strong argument against it. In sum, the story model is untenable—unless it can be reinterpreted.

The story model seems doomed to failure unless we can reinterpret hermeneutic psychoanalysis on this model in a way that renders it more acceptable to patients and analysts. I suggest three such reinterpretations; two ask patients to act *as if* interpretations are true, while the third says that interpretations give meaning for the future, instead of being reconstructions of the past.

The As-If Views

On the as-if versions of the story model of psychoanalysis, psychoanalysis concedes that patients want causal explanations of their behavior—not mere stories—and it offers patients such explanations. The hitch is, it does not offer them as truths; it asks patients to act as if they are true. The analyst here tells the patient no lies: she does not say her interpretations are or might be true, but that it is helpful therapeutically to act as if they are true. And so, on this view, analysis claims to have uncovered not truths about the unconscious but statements about it that are useful to patients if they accept them, and it informs patients of that fact.

The question is whether such a conception of psychoanalysis should be acceptable to patients. The analyst's charge to the patient to act as if the interpretation is true is ambiguous. On one plausible view of what this means (and why it would be helpful), the patient must come actually to believe the interpretation; and thus the analyst must hope to deceive him on some level. On another plausible view, the patient must merely imagine that the interpretation is true and thus need not believe it; but this view depends on a debased conception of psychoanalysis.[25] As-if views thus require the analyst to either still somewhat deceive the patient—even though she is seemingly forthright with him—or else propose an unacceptable conception of analysis.

The Belief Version of the As-If View   On the first version of the as-if view, the analyst asks the patient to act as if her interpretation is true on the ground that this will help the patient. It is clear, on one theory, why such acting-as-if would be therapeutic: if the patient accepts the interpretation as true, he feels more self-assured, in greater control—derives many of the benefits that actual self-knowledge gives. But "accepting the interpretation as true" here means believing it; that is why one gains these benefits. Whatever the precise theory of why such belief is therapeutic, on this view, clearly the belief itself is therapeutic.

The idea that beliefs can be therapeutic is not novel: placebos can work, for example, if one believes they will work. But then, of course, one must hold that belief. And so the analyst's asking the patient to act as if her interpretation is true is analogous to a doctor's telling a patient a pill is inert, but that it will be therapeutic if he acts as if it is therapeutic. To the extent that the patient believes that the substance is inactive, it will simply not work; its working depends on his faith that it will work. He must at least suspend his disbelief in its efficacy. Pla-

25. There are actually three natural readings of the "act-as-if" view. Consider an analyst's charge to act as if her interpretation that one is an envious kind of person were true. One may act as if the interpretation that one is envious were true—i.e., believe it. One may act as if one believed one was an envious person—i.e., pretend one believes it, imagine it to be true. Or one may act as if one were an envious kind of person—i.e., act enviously. The first two correspond to the two possibilities in the text; I ignore the third as not being a particularly plausible interpretation in our context.

cebos are effective because of the suggestion of efficacy; and so patients must be receptive to that suggestion. If they are, the placebo will induce hope, and hope can be powerfully curative.

In the same way, on this theory, for the man to benefit from acting as if he has learned his true identity, he must on some level come to believe he has. If he credits, instead, the analyst's statement that the identity is not truly his, he will not be helped. He will continue to feel angry about his fate, scared of the future, and generally lost. Similarly, for religious belief to be comforting, on this view, one must come on some level to believe it to be true.

I am suggesting, then, that one natural way to read the as-if theory is that it requires belief. For one thing, this seems a completely plausible interpretation of the actual words used; when analysts ask their patients to act as if interpretations are true, this is a ready way for patients to understand their instruction. More important, such acting-as-if is most easily understood to be therapeutic via the benefits of felt insight: the appearance of increased knowledge (and thus control), the comfort and self-assurance that belief may provide.

Yet if acting as if an interpretation is true works through belief, the analyst must hope on some level to deceive the patient; the analyst's informing the patient that her interpretation is not true does not cure her interaction with him of an intent to deceive. She does offer the patient her true view of the world, but she must hope that he will reject it—she must hope to induce a false belief in him. In any case, that is the way the prescription will be curative on this view. Thus, though the analyst does not actually lie to the patient on this view, she must still hope to deceive him; the deception is carried out with his collusion, as it were, but it is still deception.

Is this view any more acceptable than the view on which the analyst deceives the patient about the truth-status of her interpretations? There, it is true, the analyst tells outright lies to the patient, whereas here she informs him of her true beliefs. But while informing him of her true beliefs, she hopes he comes to accept false beliefs—and more important, she asks him to be the instrument of his own deception. But asking someone self-consciously to deceive himself is to ask him both to do a wrong—the very wrong the analyst is trying to avoid—and to do a wrong to himself. Although this posture shows him the respect of allowing him to choose whether the deception is in his interests, it demeans him by asking him to demean himself. In the end, frank deception is probably the worse of the two positions—but this alternative is not much better.

My conclusion should not be in the least surprising. Above I argued that patients would not and should not believe interpretations that do not purport to be possibly true; and that is what analysts are implicitly asking patients to do here. This case, nevertheless, presents some interesting twists of its own. By using the "act-as-if" locution, the analyst may mislead patients into thinking that they are not transgressing the proscription against believing untrue beliefs; they may not fully realize that such acting-as-if just is believing. Thus they are deceived not only about the subject of the analyst's interpretations, but also about their own mental state in acting as if they are true.

Even if patients do realize that acting-as-if is just believing, the analyst may tempt them, by offers of therapeutic benefit, to transgress the prohibition against believing the untrue. Left to their own devices, patients might refuse to participate. The analyst's mantle of authority serves, so to speak, to corrupt them. We have seen that informing patients of the actual status of interpretations is probably preferable to lying to them outright. But perhaps in informing them of the actual status of interpretations while asking them simultaneously to act as if they are true the analyst takes away with one hand what she has given with the other.

The Imagine-and-React Version of the As-If View   The second version of the act-as-if view, while not open to the charge of inducing deception in patients, offers a debased conception of psychoanalysis—indeed, on one view, perhaps a completely unrecognizable version of psychoanalysis. This as-if view, unlike the first, does not lodge the therapeutic benefit of acting as if an interpretation is true in believing it. And it does seem evident as a general matter that one need not on some level believe some proposition *p* in order to derive benefit from acting as if it is true. Thus the view does not require any deception.

Consider the benefit of watching a sad movie. One does suspend disbelief when one watches a sad movie; one acts as if it is true that, for example, a helpless child is being abandoned— and one therefore cries—even though one knows very well that not only is there no real abandonment, there is not even a real child. One can act as if the child is being abandoned without believing, on some level, that she really is being abandoned; and this can be most therapeutic.

To "act as if the child is being abandoned" in this sense is simply to imagine the child's being abandoned; and one may derive benefit from this without subscribing to any false beliefs. Similarly, one may believe religious teachings to be false but still derive benefit from practicing the religion, because, say, one enjoys listening to the music in the service or imagining the bliss of heaven.[26] In just this way, the man who adopts the

26. Earlier, indeed, I spoke of priests inducing parishioners to hold religious beliefs that they themselves did not hold, and of the value of religious faith turning on the beliefs one holds. But in analogizing to religion I may be overstressing the importance of beliefs. As my colleague Ronald

new identity might feel pleasure in acting as he imagines one with that identity would act. Even placebos might work their benefit not because the patient powerfully believes in them, but because, say, the very act of taking the pills is pleasurable.

In these cases, the therapy lies in engaging in activities — reacting to the scene, practicing the religion, or assuming the identity — that are sometimes incident to the beliefs. In the same way, the activities that accompany acting as if an interpretation is true might also be therapeutic regardless of whether one believes it true. An analytic interpretation that the patient unconsciously feels rejected by his mother, for example, might lead the patient who acts as if the interpretation is true to feel a good deal of sorrow — and to derive benefit from that. Alternatively, the patient might derive benefit from imagining angry conversations with his mother. Both can happen even if the patient's mother does not hate him, and he does not believe she hates him.[27] On this view, acting as if an interpretation is true

---

Garet has pointed out, for example, some religions may be more about "faith, hope, and love" than about any beliefs that p is or is not the case. Hope and love are certainly not well formulated in terms of any set of beliefs, and even faith may be more a performance (accepting God into one's life) than a belief. My example in the text of appreciating the music in the religious service may thus seem to trivialize the benefits of religion that come from noncognitive means. The religion analogy may also suggest that, in the psychoanalytic context, experiences (say, of imagining-and-reacting) may be more important than the beliefs one comes to hold. But see below for the claim that holding beliefs is essential, conceptually, to psychoanalysis.

27. One may feel unconvinced of this claim; the patient must surely tap into some (unconscious) feelings of rejection by his mother in order to be able to have cathartic experiences of this kind. Thus, he must believe the interpretation on some level. I think that this objection is fairly compelling. But it may be false; he may have unconscious feelings of rejection by someone else altogether, or he may have feelings of sorrow of some other

is *associated* with activities that are therapeutic. It in no way requires false belief.

Indeed, we may conceive such acting-as-if as leading to the traditional analytic benefit of insight. On this interpretation, the exercises in imagining and reacting are helpful precisely because they lead to greater self-understanding. Thus, the patient who feels sorrow and anger when he imagines feeling rejected by his mother may not simply be releasing pent-up feelings, but gaining understanding about himself—about how his mind works. Coming to understand himself as someone who may feel this sorrow and anger may be the ultimate value of the exercise.

Although this conception of analysis does seem invulnerable to the charge that it requires patients to be deceived, is it acceptable? First, as a positive matter, analysts do not seem to practice as if they are asking patients to consider possibilities and react—or at least to consider possibilities they know to be untrue and react. Analysts seem rather to be asking patients to regard their interpretations as a prelude to believing them if they seem compelling. In other words, this version of analysis seems descriptively inaccurate. At the least, if analysts are to reap the benefits of a conception of their practice that does not require deception, they must alter how they conceptualize their practice, what they tell their patients about this practice, and how they practice.

Second, even if analysts alter their conceptualizations and behavior in these ways, we should understand clearly that such reconceptualization of analysis is nothing less than radical. (Indeed, after I have discussed the other versions of hermeneutic

---

kind. In any case, it is worth assuming that the objection is false to see where the argument leads.

psychoanalysis, I shall have some things to say about the nature of psychoanalysis as a conceptual matter.)

On the pure imagine-and-react view, analysis has ceased to value insight.[28] The reactions the patient experiences in imagining-and-reacting may be beneficial in being cathartic—as in watching sad movies—or, more trivially, in simply being pleasurable—as in enjoying the music in a religious service. I shall have to deal later with the question of whether analysts should be prepared to see their therapy in this way.

On the version of analysis as imagining-and-reacting-that-leads-to-insight, at least analysis pursues its traditional goal. The result, however, may be somewhat incoherent. Why should analysts be better at interpreting the products of imagining-and-reacting than the traditional analytic products, such as dreams and symptoms? Indeed, imagining-and-reacting is simply a more focused and controlled kind of free association—one of the most fruitful sites of traditional analytic exploration. Any reasons we have for denying that analysts reveal truths

---

28. The reader will appreciate that, under the first as-if theory (the patient must actually come to believe the analyst's interpretations, even though she has told him they are not true), analysis values only apparent self-understanding. But even the view that analysis gives patients only apparent self-understanding may be more committed to the traditional analytic conception of therapeutic benefit than this view. In acquiring alternate self-conceptions, for example, the patient thinks about himself differently and in ways that might be quite productive. He feels the gratification of seeming to understand himself better. He feels empowered to better predict and control his state of mind. Finally, he is committed to seeking understanding and may in the process actually acquire it. Although the patient's self-understanding is only apparent—is a kind of sham understanding—this view at least seems to honor the paradigmatic commitment of analysis to the principle of self-understanding. Of course, it may well be preferable to depart from the commitments of analysis than only to appear to practice them.

when they interpret dreams and symptoms should apply equally to the products of imagining-and-reacting.[29]

Perhaps this charge of incoherence, however, is poorly taken. When the analyst interprets a dream or symptom, she generally draws inferences from some manifest content to some latent content—to unconscious processes underlying the visible phenomena. And stories may be all that is available here. By contrast, when the analyst "interprets" imagining-and-reacting, she need not draw any inferences; the analyst merely instructs the patient to observe how he is acting as he imagines-and-reacts and to come to appreciate himself as someone who can so act. Analyst and patient need not be confined to a world of stories here.

My response to this argument is twofold. First, I am not convinced that the contrast drawn between interpreting in the two cases is as distinct as it appears. A traditional, depth interpretation may enable a patient to recover a once-unconscious thought or feeling. In that case, why can he not know the truth about himself here just as on the imagine-and-react view?— in both cases he simply observes himself feeling or thinking a certain way. If so, story theorists must allow that some analytic interpretations lead to true insights about oneself: the interpretations, as it were, are retrospectively converted from being mere stories to being truths.

Second, one expects that analysts will be tempted to treat imagining-and-reacting as if it were free association and not confine themselves to bringing patients to observe what they are now unproblematically feeling. To the extent that they do not go beyond the manifest, psychoanalysis ceases to be a depth

29. To the extent that story theorists do deny that imagining-and-reacting can lead to insight, this version of the as-if view drops out of the picture; insight ceases to be a possibility on any versions of this view.

psychology at all: to avoid being confined to a world of stories amounts to being confined to a world of the obvious.

If these arguments are compelling, all as-if versions of the story model of hermeneutic psychoanalysis should arguably be rejected. On the first version, the analyst must continue to hope to induce a false belief in the patient even as she tells him that the belief is false; only by holding the belief does the patient benefit. The pure imagining-and-reacting version at least radically changes the nature of analysis; analysis is likened to— and may be no more beneficial than—listening to music in a religious service. The imagine-and-react view on which the practice leads to insight is not particularly coherent. The self-respecting analyst and patient should arguably reject all such as-if conceptions of psychoanalysis.

Interpretations as Giving Meaning for the Future, Not Reconstructing the Past

A second way to save the story model does not require psychoanalysts to deceive their patients. Perhaps the stories analysts tell patients are not so much backward-looking as forward-looking: they afford comfort not by giving understanding, but by giving direction. Recall the woman who went to the kitchen and the man who lost his memory. On having their questions answered, the woman now has a goal in the kitchen, and the man knows how to live his life. Of course, the stories do have a backward-looking component; we want the goals to be consistent with what we know about the people's past because then they are less likely to be discrepant with what we do not know about their past. But the enterprise is to give purpose for the future, not understanding of the past.

A number of the hermeneutic theorists I have considered

seem, at times, to embrace a view of this kind. For example, Fingarette, although not a story theorist, is wont to see interpretations as means of giving patients direction in their lives — pointing the way they should go, instead of telling them where they have been.[30] Similarly, Spence sometimes speaks of an interpretation's relation to the present and the future rather than to the past.[31] And Sharpe speaks of interpretations as at times constituting a person's identity; they tell him what he is, and then that is what he becomes.[32]

Is this conception of psychoanalysis plausible? Once again, it does not seem accurate as a descriptive matter. As now practiced, psychoanalysis strikes one as being focused on the past and on influences from the past, not on goals for the future. Patients may discuss their goals with their analysts and come to form new goals — but this seems a small part of analytic work.

Now some analysts might claim that helping patients to set goals may not look like what they are doing, but that is what they are in fact doing; they help patients reconceive their future

30. See, e.g., Fingarette (1963, 20): " 'The therapeutic insight does not show the patient what he is or was; it *changes* him into someone *new*.' 'The therapist does not present information; he presents options'. . . . 'Insight does not reveal a hidden, past reality; it is a reorganization of the meaning of present experience, a present reorientation toward both future *and* past.' " Thus Fingarette may be an alternative metaphysics hermeneut who also proposes an interpretations-as-giving-meaning-for-the-future conceptualization of the psychoanalytic process.

31. See, e.g., Spence (1982a, 271) (an interpretation's "truth . . . lies more in the present and future than in the past: it may become true for the first time just by being said"; (1982a, 173) (an interpretation's "fit with the present may be more relevant for the treatment than its correspondence with the past").

32. See, e.g., Sharpe (1988, 196): "When somebody is offered a Freudian narrative of his life, by changing his picture of himself we may also change his behaviour so that we create an identity in the course of trying to describe it."

by reconceiving their past. In other words, they tell stories that set goals, instead of frankly and explicitly setting the goals themselves. Given that there is some genuine focus on the past anyway (however slight), the appearance of focusing on the past is completely understandable.

I have three responses to this conception of psychoanalysis. First, if analysts are primarily setting goals for the future instead of reconstructing the past, they ought to be explicit about that with their patients. In other words, if the stories analysts tell in fact have quite different constraints and aims than they appear to have, patients ought to know that—unless, again, it is acceptable to treat by creating illusions. Truth-in-advertising, so to speak, requires analysts to be frank with their patients.

This objection is important beyond simply suggesting that analysts ought to be explicit about what they are doing. The alternative is not that patients will simply be in the dark; it is that they will be misled into accepting interpretations as true statements about the past. We have already seen that that is a normatively undesirable outcome.

Second, is telling stories about the patient's past really a sensible way to set goals for her future? When the woman going to the kitchen asks why she was going there, she is asking for a backward-looking explanation. As suggested, she could formulate a quite different question for herself—"Why shall I go to the kitchen?" But then the inquiry, one expects, would look quite different, as would the considerations. The woman might advert to her past. But she would also regard more directly what was best for the future: what she thinks is sensible, right, and good. Goal-setting, in short, does not seem most sensibly approached exclusively by telling stories about someone's past.

Finally, one wonders if analysts would really wish to accept the role of telling patients how they should live. If we conceive of analysts as helping patients understand how their

minds work, we do not cast them in the role of gurus who pre-
scribe answers to personal, moral questions about the way their
patients should lead their lives. One wonders if analysts are
especially qualified to adopt this role—and whether they would
want to.

One might object that analysts are not prescribing the goals
themselves but simply helping patients explore options when
they tell stories. Yet analysts do offer an interpretation—the
best they can come up with—at any given time; the conception of analysis underlying this objection does not match the
reality of analytic practice. Moreover, even if analysts did offer
a range of interpretations, to do so at least limits the possibilities. To avoid being cast in the role of one who prescribes for
the good life, analysts would have to cease to offer interpretations, asking patients themselves to suggest possible futures,
which they would then explore together.

Thus, the view that interpretations give meaning for the
future, while not as problematic perhaps as the as-if views,
leaves something to be desired. It does not seem descriptively
accurate, and if it is true nonetheless, analysts should be more
explicit about that. Appearing to interpret the past also seems
an ineffective—at least an incomplete—way of determining
what to do about the future. And casting analysts in a normative, prescriptive role also seems problematic. Certainly analysts should be concerned about how patients conceive of their
futures; an orientation toward the future is an important part
of analysis.[33] But just as certainly it is not the sole—or even the
main—objective.

33. Thus, I do not want to suggest that psychoanalysis as traditionally
conceived is indifferent to the patient's future; the analyst reconstructs
the patient's past in order to give help for the future. Still, this new interpretation of analysis does alter its nature into a procedure concerned
exclusively with setting goals for the future—the traditional and this new
view manifestly diverge.

The story model must finally be rejected. Patients will not and should not be willing to accept stories in place of explanations; it is normatively undesirable to believe what does not purport to be possibly true. Psychoanalysts might, of course, conceal from patients the true nature of their enterprise, but the administering of placebos, questionable in any case, becomes even more so when patients are radically deceived about their very selves. Psychoanalysts can avoid lying to their patients but will then be practicing a therapy that looks very different from analysis as we know it today. Thus, the story model may force analysts to rethink radically the theory and practice of psychoanalysis. To the extent that analysts wish to preserve psychoanalysis as we know it, at least in its basic outlines, they must reject the story model.[34]

34. As readers read on, they will appreciate that the two "nonbelief" alternative interpretations of the story model are actually subject to what I shall call the weak version of the argument from patient rejection. After spelling out the nature of that version in application to some of the subsequent theories, I return to it to tease apart and evaluate its features.

5

The Plausibility of the Other Models
of Hermeneutic Psychoanalysis

THE PLAUSIBILITY OF THE CLINICAL PSYCHOANALYSIS
AND ALTERNATIVE METAPHYSICS MODELS

The clinical psychoanalysis model and the alternative meta-physics model escape the criticism that applies to the story model. They are not subject to the argument from patient rejection—at least in the form in which I have presented it. The reason is that neither model asks patients to believe interpretations that do not purport to be possibly true.

On the clinical psychoanalysis model, psychoanalysts give interpretations that refer to psychological states, conscious and unconscious, that help explain behavior, and they eschew interpretations that refer to neurophysiological antecedents of behavior. But the interpretations referring to these psychological states are true in a straightforward way. Thus there is no reason for patients not to believe them, and analysis is able to do its traditional work through belief.

On the alternative metaphysics model, psychoanalysts also give interpretations that refer to psychological states, conscious and unconscious, that underlie behavior. The innovation is that our background understanding of the world and how we know it is different from the positivist worldview. These theorists, for example, tend to be nonfoundationalists both epistemo-logically and metaphysically: there are no absolute foundations upon which we can base knowledge, and none which, through correspondence, provide the criterion of truth.

Table 5.1

	Analyst Believes Interpretations True in Correspondence Sense	Analyst Believes Interpretations True in Coherence Sense	Analyst Wants Patient to Believe Interpretations True
Story Model	No	No	Yes
Clinical Psychoanalysis Model	Yes	No	Yes
Alternative Metaphysics Model	No	Yes	Yes

Thus alternative metaphysics theorists tend to hold a coherence theory of both justification and truth.[1] It is the coherence theory of truth that is most important from the point of view of the argument from patient rejection, for it means that psychoanalysts' interpretations, on this view, are true in an unproblematic way. They may be true in a different way from the traditional, but they are still true in an unproblematic way, and therefore patients need have no compunctions about believing them. Once again, analysis works in the ordinary way.

To summarize the similarities and dissimilarities among these three views on the vector with which my central argument is concerned, I schematically represent the criticism of the story model and the way in which clinical psychoanalysis and

1. The alternative metaphysics theorists I have discussed, Schafer and Fingarette, actually hold a more equivocal theory of truth. But the pure version of the alternative metaphysics model relies on a coherence theory of truth. My purposes in this section are best met by working with the pure version and glossing over the complexities in the theorists whose work I reviewed.

alternative metaphysics models escape that criticism (table 5.1). The problem with the story model is that the analyst wants the patient to believe interpretations that do not purport to be possibly true—and that she herself does not believe. By contrast, the clinical psychoanalyst and alternative metaphysician want the patient to believe her interpretations are true, just as she does; and they do purport to be true, albeit in very different ways.

Why does the story theorist want the patient to believe her interpretations are true even though she does not believe them to be true? Note first that the story theorist offers her patient interpretations as if they were true; she holds them out as being true.[2] One reason she does so is the traditional theory of psychoanalytic benefit: that it works via beliefs about oneself. A perhaps more important reason is that patients will reject interpretations that do not purport to be possibly true; it is empirically likely and normatively desirable that they do so. Thus, the story analyst wants patients to believe her interpretations are true when she does not because psychoanalysis as we know it will self-destruct otherwise.

Clinical psychoanalysis and alternative metaphysics analysts also want their patients to believe their interpretations are true for all these reasons; yet because they themselves believe the interpretations in an unproblematic way, they do not face the same dilemma. They hold different theories of truth, but those theories have long been respected and are likely to be worthy of belief.

In any case, I make no effort independently to evaluate these

2. Indeed, the very fact that story theorists propose that their stories must be consistent with the known facts suggests as much. Why should it matter whether the stories are consistent with what is known unless there is an effort to suggest to patients that they are also consistent with what is not known—that is, that they represent the truth and are to be believed?

theories; I leave that task to the philosophers. Schafer, as we have seen, worries about one disquieting possibility, namely, that a coherence theory of truth permits no distinction between stories and histories. If this is so, the alternative metaphysics model threatens to collapse into the story model, and all the criticisms that apply to that model follow. Yet I will take it on faith here that a well-conceived version of the coherence theory of truth is able to formulate a viable distinction between story and history, and so to withstand this criticism.

A somewhat variant argument against the alternative metaphysics model, with its coherence theory of truth, runs as follows. Patients will not be able to help believing interpretations are true in a correspondence sense, even if told that they are true only in a coherence sense. That is just the way that people who are untrained philosophically think; it is a brute fact of our psychology. Patients will and should reject a vision of psychoanalysis under which they will inevitably give credence to interpretations in an unwarranted way—that is, by believing them in a correspondence sense rather than in a coherence sense. Better to reject the interpretations than to fall into this self-deception.

This argument is flawed. First, if a coherence theory can preserve a viable distinction between story and history, I see no reason why patients should not be able to believe interpretations in the correct way. That is, I reject the claimed psychological "fact" that, given the way our minds work, we inevitably hold a correspondence theory. Second, it may not matter if patients believe that interpretations are true on a correspondence theory unless they are false on that theory. Coherence theorists generally think correspondence theories make no sense. The analysts who hold this view believe not that their interpretations are false in a correspondence sense, but that they are neither true nor false in that sense. Finally, if a coherence theory is true as respects psychoanalytic interpretations, it will also be true as respects all other statements; the alternative metaphysics model is a general model of the world, not just of the world of psychoanalysis. Therefore, if patients should refuse to believe psychoanalytic interpretations, they should also refuse to believe all statements whatever. We have much bigger problems than psychoanalysis if the claimed psychological fact is true and a coherence theory of truth is also true.[3]

The alternative metaphysicians, then, are invulnerable to the argument from patient rejection because they do not offer patients interpretations that do not purport to be possibly true; they offer them interpretations purporting to be true in a different sense of truth. And what could be wrong with that? Nothing is wrong with it if the only point of the argument is that patients do not want to be offered falsehoods. That is a very modest point—and one the alternative metaphysicians are immune from. But what about the more sophisticated point that patients do not want to be offered truths that are not worthy of the name truth? In other words, patients may want not only truth, but, more daringly, a particular version of truth, or at least they may reject certain versions. I will call this the sophisticated version of the strong form of the argument from patient rejection.[4]

Spence and Loch do in effect offer patients something they *call* truth. Surely it is not enough to merely say the word. One's theory of truth must itself be respectable. To say that the analyst's interpretation will sustain the patient, enable him to go on living, may not be enough—the patient may want some-

3. The reader will recognize that this is a variant of the argument explored under the story model's "no-fact-of-the-matter" version.

4. Below I discuss a weak form of the argument that may apply to the other theories.

thing that truly deserves the name truth. In the same way, he may want a more robust kind of truth if it makes sense and is available.

If this is right, it is but a short step to the notion that truth on a coherence theory may be as problematic to patients as truth viewed as "what will sustain one." If patients think that truth by coherence is not really truth, perhaps they will reject interpretations that achieve only truth of this kind. Below I shall examine an argument that if correspondence truth, say, is available, patients will want that. The argument now is that they will insist that correspondence truth (or some other acceptable theory of truth) be available.

Alternative metaphysicians hold other positions that bear on their theory of truth—for instance, that a multiplicity of interpretations may be true. And patients may say that any theory according to which multiple competing accounts may be true is not an acceptable theory of truth. Similarly, some think alternative metaphysics theories threaten to embrace relativism; and patients may say once again that "merely relative truth is not truth." The theorists' flirtation with subjectivism as opposed to objectivism leads to the same argument. In short, a more sophisticated version of the argument from patient rejection may be applied to the alternative metaphysics model: patients will reject psychoanalysis if it offers interpretations that achieve only truth of a kind that does not deserve the name. Indeed, critics have wondered whether philosophical hermeneutics in general does not lead to relativism, subjectivism, or other troubling "ism's" that distort a concept of truth.[5]

5. There are analogues to the alternative metaphysics model in the history of hermeneutics in general and critiques similar to the sophisticated version of the argument from patient rejection. (Of course the argument in the nonpsychoanalytic context is not that patients will reject the view, but that all right thinking people should.) The basic idea is that

The reader will appreciate the connection between the less sophisticated and the more sophisticated versions of the argument from patient rejection. On the former, patients reject nontruths; on the latter, they reject what, after reflection, amount to nontruths. Not surprisingly, then, the story model has been

---

the philosophical hermeneutic position, in all its various manifestations, is committed, say, to an implausible view of truth, or to a subjectivism or relativism that has as a consequence an implausible view of truth; as a result, it should be rejected. This critique has had currency in many of the disciplines studied in our universities that have taken a hermeneutic turn.

Doing full justice to this claim would take us too far afield. Nevertheless, the reader is referred to the following sources. For the history of these kinds of debates in the field of historiography, see Peter Novick, *That Noble Dream: The "Objectivity Question" and the American Historical Profession* (1988). See also Saul Friedlander, *Probing the Limits of Representation* (1992) (collecting essays about Nazi Germany and the limits of representation, many writers critiquing Hayden White's view that there is no difference between history and story). In the arena of philosophical hermeneutics in general, see the Habermas-Gadamer debate, which touches on issues of concern to us; on the debate, see McCarthy (1978, 187-93); Jay (1992, 102); Mendelson (1979); and How (1985). For an engagement with Gadamer, contrasting his answers to a series of questions with those of Habermas and Rorty (1979), see Georgia Warnke, *Gadamer: Hermeneutics, Tradition and Reason* (1987) (situating Gadamer between foundationalism and relativism and finding Rorty content with mere conversation that does not lead to knowledge; his account thus not only threatens to be subjectivistic and relativistic, but also dispenses with a notion of truth altogether). See also A. T. Nuyen (1992) (arguing that Rorty's position is not so close as he thinks to Gadamer's hermeneutics, and that it is vulgarly relativistic and at the same time, in a sense, conservative). For an account that takes on Warnke's version of Gadamer and Rorty, see Donald Rothberg (1986) (suggesting that the positions of the two philosophers are not so distinct as Warnke claims: Rorty's work seems to require, against his intentions, a concept of validity, and Gadamer's hermeneutics—although Gadamer is indeed concerned with truth—yields no coherent account of the nature of truth and so faces many of the same problems as Rorty's). See also Michael Moore (1989) (criticizing Gadamer on the ground that his view of all understanding as built on

offered and has come to be seen as hermeneutic; on this view, it is essentially no more guilty than other versions of hermeneutics of deforming the concept of the truth of interpretations.[6]

----

prejudgments or prejudices has the consequence that there is no question to be asked about the validity [correctness, truth] of an interpretation if the questioner seeks an interpretation's correspondence to something other than the interpreter's prejudices). For another thoughtful account and critique of Gadamer's theory of truth, see Hinman (1990). For other discussions of hermeneutics and relativism, see, e.g., Ingram (1984) (explicating Gadamer's hermeneutics as an attempt to provide an alternative to holistic relativism); Wellmer (1993) (discussing the antinomy of truth, namely, that while relativism appears to be inconsistent, absolutism seems to imply metaphysical assumptions. Two forms of solution exist: showing that absolutism need not be metaphysical—Putnam, Apel, and Habermas being examples; and showing that the critique of absolutism need not lead to relativism—of whom Rorty is the most noted proponent).

For the interested reader, these accounts will reveal connections between my subject and a subject that has engaged scholars in many bordering disciplines. Although most philosophical hermeneuts do not directly say that they reject the notion of truth, some, like Rorty, confine it to so narrow a sphere that it loses much of its meaning. Others adopt a theory of truth—or other views that have implications for their theory of truth—that has made for vigorous debate. As noted, critics have suggested that philosophical hermeneutics may lead to a relativism and subjectivism that distort a concept of truth. The debate in this arena has occurred among some of the foremost hermeneuts themselves—e.g., Habermas, Gadamer, and Rorty—and also in a burgeoning secondary literature. Hermeneutic psychoanalysis, then, is not unique in raising these kinds of problems. What is unique about it is its practical context, in which factors other than pure theory are important: the interactions of theory and practice—the efficacy of the practice given a new theory; the effects on our conceptualization of the practice given the new theory; and (what I have stressed most here), the views of ordinary people, and their commonsense reaction to the theory as it bears on their life.

6. In other words, it may be less surprising—supposing that story theorists do distort the hermeneutic view—that some story theorists have arrived at their version of hermeneutic psychoanalysis through *hermeneutics*. The idea would be that the difference between the classi-

The more sophisticated version of the argument from patient rejection, though it has some plausibility, is a much harder argument to make in this context than the more modest version, and I do not know that I support it myself. There are three responses to the argument. First, it is reasonable to suppose that patients will care about being offered falsehoods, but is it really reasonable to suppose that they will even care about their analysts' metaphysical theories of truth? How can we think that the average patient will have any views at all about theories of truth, relativism, or subjectivism? Analysts are surely under no obligation to inform their patients of something of so little concern to them, and even if they did inform them, patients would probably immediately dismiss what they were told from their minds. Only philosophers are preoccupied by metaphysical theories.

This response to the argument may be too facile, however. Perhaps the commonsense view of truth is a correspondence view, and most patients would want to know if their analysts departed from it. Patients could figure out quickly that their analysts' fancy metaphysical theories about truth, relativism, and subjectivism led to what, for them, was not a theory of truth at all. Thus they would want to know the theory; and once they knew it, they would reject a psychoanalysis based on it. If we can surmise that patients would care in this way,

_____

cally hermeneutic view on truth and the story theorists' acceptance of nontruths is not so great. The story theory, then, is less distorting than it might appear, which helps story theorists sound so much like other hermeneutic psychoanalysts. I myself would be prepared to accept this argument only if I were convinced that the classic hermeneutic view on truth is as deficient as some critics make out and as the more sophisticated strong argument supposes. See below.

then analysts would be under some obligation to inform their patients of their views.

This effort to defend the more sophisticated version is not wholly without merit. Yet surmising that patients will want to know this information and will react to it in the predicted way is much more difficult than surmising that patients will want to know truth. Who knows which theory of truth is more a matter of commonsense? Who knows whether people will see these alternative metaphysical conceptions as leading to unacceptable theories of truth? Who knows whether they will care to follow the argument through to that conclusion? One's intuitions about these matters, unlike intuitions about patients' desire for truth, are not very hardy. We are on much less solid empirical ground here, and the more sophisticated version appears problematic.

The second response turns on something discussed earlier. The alternative metaphysics model, unlike most versions of the story model, has a philosophical view of truth that presumably applies across the board. It is not that patients are offered falsehoods in a world in which there is such a thing as truth. They are offered truths of the only kind available. This is how the world is. Thus, they have no choice but to accept psychoanalytic interpretations; the cost to them, as to the person who rejects idealism, is to cease to discourse about anything. Patients can, of course, reject psychoanalysis for something like behavior therapy; but they have much bigger problems than psychoanalysis if they reject the notion of truth on which all of discourse depends.

This response is appealing. Yet perhaps it can be turned on itself: a theory of how the world is must be false if it is impossible to live in the world on that theory.[7]

7. Note the similarity between this general form of argument and Habermas's notion of the ideal speech situation (see, e.g., Habermas,

The third response to the more sophisticated version assumes essentially that patients will reject, say, a coherence theory of truth. But, the response goes, we must ask why they will do so. Presumably, the answer must be that that theory is an inadequate theory of truth. Yet we need reasons for thinking this is so. And once we have reasons, they are sufficient for rejection

---

1975): "The very act of participating in a discourse involves the supposition that genuine consensus is possible and that it can be distinguished from false consensus. If we did not suppose this, then the very meaning of discourse would be called into question. In attempting to come to a rational decision about truth claims, we must suppose that the outcome of our discussion will be (or at least can be) the result simply of the force of the better argument and not of accidental or systematic constraints on communication." See McCarthy (1978). Habermas is aware that actual situations of discourse rarely, if ever, approximate the purity of the ideal speech situation. But he insists that the ideal speech situation is an "unavoidable supposition" of discourse. Although it may be usually—perhaps even always—counterfactual, "it is made, and must be made, whenever we enter into discourse with the intention of arriving at rational agreement about truth claims; it is intrinsic to the very sense of doing so. . . . To state this in another way, in entering into discourse with the intention of settling a truth claim 'on its merits,' we suppose that we are capable of doing so, that the situation of discourse is such that only these merits will have force—that is, that we are in an ideal speech situation" (1978, 309).

Habermas's form of argument shares features with all forms of the strong version of the argument from patient rejection. In particular, its similarity to the nonsophisticated form of this argument is clear: in offering interpretations for belief and in accepting them, analysts and patients must be supposing that the interpretations purport to be possibly true. But Habermas's argument can also be applied in the context of the more sophisticated version of the argument: it is a supposition of discourse between analysts and patients that interpretations purport to be possibly true in a particular way. This, of course, is a much harder argument to make, but it is possible. Most important, it allows a response to the claim that patients have no choice but to accept interpretations on these terms, namely, that the very act of accepting an interpretation implies a radically different view.

of the theory, and we do not need to add that patients themselves will reject it. In other words, the substantive problems with the theory are a much more powerful reason to reject it than is patients' dislike of it. Of course, I have offered nothing in the way of a substantive, philosophical critique of this or any other theory of truth.

The less sophisticated version of the argument from patient rejection cannot be turned on itself in the same way. Patients have a plain and powerful reason to reject interpretations that do not purport to be possibly true: it is offensive to ask them to believe such things, if the belief is even conceptually possible. By contrast, they should reject interpretations that purport to be possibly true on an alternative version of truth only if that version of truth is problematic. Of course, it is possible that, in the commonsense view, this alternative version of truth is also somehow offensive or repulsive. But that is a much harder argument to make. (The likeliest scenario, in fact, is probably that there is no commonsense view of the nature of truth—common sense simply has no opinion on the matter.) If all of this is right, the more sophisticated version of the argument from patient rejection, although it has some modicum of plausibility, is not nearly so powerful as the less sophisticated version.

In conclusion, the clinical psychoanalysis and alternative metaphysics models escape the form of the argument from patient rejection that was so telling against the story model, although the alternative metaphysics model may be subject to a more sophisticated form of the argument. There may also be other criticisms of these models that I do not address. For example, one wonders about the payoff of the alternative metaphysics model in terms of our understanding of the theory and practice of psychoanalysis. I do not deny that it is a contribution to describe the correct (if it is correct) metaphysics behind psychoanalysis. Yet one wonders how great a contribution it is. Does discourse about the metaphysics have important implications for how we understand the theory and practice of psychoanalysis as such, or is it a bit of abstract philosophizing with few or no implications? I note below that exploration of this question would be a valuable contribution to the literature.

These models probably also have virtues that I leave unexplored. For example, George Klein, a clinical psychoanalysis theorist, may be right in saying that analysts should focus on the clinical theory and leave the metapsychology to the biologists. Schafer, an alternative metaphysics theorist, may be right to draw our attention to the pervasiveness of patients' self-narrations and to the role of analysts' retellings of these narrations within our theory of the psychoanalytic process. A more detailed exploration of these advantages and disadvantages must, however, be left for another time.

The Plausibility of the Metaphor Model

According to the metaphor model, psychoanalysis is hermeneutic in the sense that it offers patients stories or narratives that are true only metaphorically, not in the way that a natural scientific statement about causal antecedents of an event is true. In terms of its position on truth, then, the metaphor model lies between the story model on the one hand and the clinical psychoanalysis and alternative metaphysics models on the other: it does not deny that interpretations are true altogether, but it does hold that they are true only in a very special sense.[8]

8. The nature of metaphors has been discussed for twenty-five hundred years, and in what follows I do not enter the many debates that have animated this discussion; indeed, I rely on quite a crude and undeveloped notion of metaphor. Nevertheless, I discuss in this note some of the highlights of the debate. Many issues beyond the cognitive matters discussed here have been raised about metaphor. See, e.g., Monroe C. Beardsley

The question now is how the metaphor model fares in terms of the argument from patient rejection. To answer this, it will be useful to consider examples of other statements that are arguably true only metaphorically. Take the following three statements: the desk is solid and brown; the corporation de-

---

(1958); and Ted Cohen (1979). The questions of prime importance to us, however, are two: How do metaphors work? And what is the cognitive content of metaphors? In terms of their answers to these questions, metaphor theorists can be classified into four categories: (1) comparison-ists; (2) interactionists; (3) pragmatists; and (4) constructivists. For this classification schema, see Paul Davis (n.d.).

In answer to the question, How do metaphors work? comparisonists hold that metaphors are a word-based comparison or similarity between two objects that deviates from literal uses of language. At its crudest, metaphors are just similes with the "like" or "as" removed. In answer to the question, What is the cognitive content of metaphors? comparison-ists hold that the cognitive content of metaphors can be expressed as a paraphrase in literal language of the comparison being made. Apart from this literal paraphrase, a metaphoric statement either has no truth value or is false. Among comparisonists are numbered Aristotle (1984), Hobbes (1968), Locke (1721), and, in contemporary times, Paul Henle (1958). For objections to comparison theories, see, e.g., John R. Searle (1979); Black; Khatchadourian (1968); Lakoff and Johnson (1980). For a response to Searle, see, e.g., Levin (1993).

According to Max Black's original formulation, interactionists see metaphor as the interaction of a primary and secondary system of asso-ciated implications—i.e., commonplace beliefs—that generates a new perspective on some object. Thus, in answer to the first question, meta-phors work through the interaction of systems of associated implications that produces a new perspective on some object. "Interaction" has been unpacked in a variety of ways: as verbal opposition (Beardsley, 1958); as perspectival seeing (Aldrich, 1958; Hester, 1966); as gestalt-switching (Lakoff and Johnson, 1980a, 1980b; Lakoff, 1987); and as category mis-take (Goodman, 1968). (Note that some of these theorists have moved metaphor theory from the interactionist to the constructionist camp, al-though they still give an account of interaction.) In answer to the second question, What is the cognitive content of metaphors? interactionists fall into two camps, those who see metaphors as helping one discover already-

frauded its customers; and the plant's wants caused it to turn toward the sun.

In some sense all of these statements are only metaphorically true. The first fails to be literally true in that a physicist would tell quite another story about the desk: that it consists

---

existing categories (e.g., Khatchadourian, 1968; Warner, 1973) and those who see metaphors as generating new ones (e.g., Goodman, 1968; Lakoff and Johnson (1980a, 1980b); Ricoeur, 1978). Black says that the question, Can metaphorical statements be true? distorts the issue by focusing exclusively on "that special connection between statement and reality that we signal by the attribution of truth value" (1993, 38). Instead, he proposes that just as we talk about other familiar devices that show how things are—for example, maps, diagrams, and models—so we should talk about strong metaphors in terms of correctness and incorrectness so as to avoid the "violation of philosophical grammar" of trying "to assign either truth or falsity where it doesn't apply" (1993, 39).

John Searle (1979) has developed the most influential pragmatic theory of metaphor. For Searle, a speaker's utterance meaning and sentence meaning, while the same in literal uses of language, may be different when speakers use sentences metaphorically. Searle breaks understanding of metaphor into three steps and gives a series of guiding rules to explain how metaphors work. As for the cognitive content of metaphors, Searle claims that, although in theory all metaphorical expressions have literal paraphrases, in practice they do not (1979, 114). Further, metaphorical utterances always do more than their paraphrases could because they force the hearer to comprehend the metaphorical meaning through the utterance of words that literally mean something else. Thus, whatever cognitive content metaphors have that goes beyond a literal paraphrase is a function of how metaphors are used rather than any special "generative" quality of metaphorical "truth." See also, Davidson (1978), who makes this point even more emphatically. For responses, see Black (1979) and Goodman (1978).) A number of people have criticized Searle's theory. For criticisms of his theory of metaphor that are sympathetic with his theory of language use, see, e.g., Levin (1993); and Morgan (1993).

Andrew Ortony divides theories of metaphor into two categories: constructivist and nonconstructivist (1993, 2). Constructivism is "an approach in which any truly veridical epistemological access to reality is denied . . . [t]he central idea [of which] is that cognition is the result of

of atoms loosely linked in a way that gives the appearance of solidity and that its color is a function of its interaction with our sense organs. The second fails to be literally true because corporations are but legal fictions; in reality a group of people took steps, coordinated and uncoordinated, that resulted in the

---

mental *construction*. . . . The constructivist approach seems to entail an important role for metaphor in both language and thought, but it also tends to undermine the distinction between the metaphorical and literal" (1993, 1).

Lakoff and Johnson are an example of strong constructionists. For these theorists, conventional metaphors structure our very conceptual system. Language is metaphorically structured because of metaphorically structured concepts, which, in turn, metaphorically structure actions. For Lakoff and Johnson, the question, How do metaphors work? involves a shift from a question about words or sentences to one about conceptual frameworks. These concepts work systematically (1980, 7–9), coherently (1980, 41–45), and in accord with physical experience (1980, 19–21, 25). Similarly, the second question, What is the cognitive content of metaphors? has broader implications when asked of a constructionist theory than of other metaphor theories. Lakoff and Johnson find the traditional notion of truth too bound to what they call "the myth of objectivity" to be anything but misleading (1980, 186–88). Instead of embracing relativism, they propose an "experientialist synthesis" (see 1980, 192–93). For Lakoff and Johnson, then, as for all constructivists, metaphor, insofar as it functions as imagination, can create new cognitive categories and so has substantive cognitive content. But if its cognitive content is to be discussed in terms of "truth," the term will have to be reconceptualized to accommodate a constructivist ontology. Constructivists can be criticized on a number of fronts. A potent criticism is, in effect, that they have changed the subject. Instead of presenting a theory of metaphor, "they've presented a theory of cognition in which 'metaphor' is a metaphor for understanding" (Davis, 32).

This is the briefest summary of some classic theories of metaphor. Critical for this book is the large background dispute of whether we discover the world outside of language or create it. Comparison and pragmatic theories, with their commitment to literal language and truth, take the former position. Moderate interactionist theories, like Black's, try to

defrauding of certain customers; there is no such thing as a corporation apart from its members. The third fails to be literally true as well in that plants do not have wants, but they do turn toward sunlight because of complicated processes of phototropism that botanists can tell us about.

Now one possibly attractive move at this point is to say that even though none of these statements is literally true, it is a harmless sin to believe them. Surely my parents did not deceive me when they taught me about solid objects and their colors. And surely I am not living under self-deception when I act as if the table has mass and color. If this is right, one important step in the argument from patient rejection fails: it is perfectly permissible to hold beliefs that do not purport to be possibly true in the strict sense. Thus the idea that patients will and should reject interpretations conceived under this model is a nonstarter.

This move is attractive in some ways, yet I believe that it is not quite accurate. First, note that the three examples are not equivalent in all regards. It may be permissible to believe that the desk is solid and brown because, in an important realm of discourse, it *is* solid and brown. For the desk to be solid, for example, is for its atoms to resist displacement except by a certain amount of force. No physicist would gainsay this. Thus, one is

---

walk a line between the two. Constructivists usually take some form of the latter position: that we do not discover but create the world. In what follows, I do not propose a rich and textured theory of metaphor. I assume the simplest kind of understanding of metaphor. Insofar as I commit to metaphor as having some cognitive content that can be expressed in a paraphrase in literal language, I am clearly in the nonconstructivist camp. Given the suggestion of this work that patients will want some residue of literal truth, this should come as no surprise. But I do not offer a full theory of metaphor or in any way justify my choices here.

not deceived in believing that the desk is solid and brown because the belief is literally true.[9]

The second and third cases are somewhat different. To say that the corporation defrauded its customers is shorthand for saying that the actions and inactions of certain officers and employees of the business had this effect. To believe that certain officers and employees acted and failed to act in such a way as to defraud certain customers is perfectly acceptable because perfectly true. To believe, on the other hand, that a literal thing—some building on Fifth Avenue or some incorporeal entity that constituted the corporation—performed certain acts with certain intentions would be a shame. It would be normatively undesirable to hold this belief because it is simply not true.

In the same way, to say that the plant wanted to bask in the sun is just a colorful way of describing its movement in that direction. To believe that the plant turned toward the sun because of its need for sun would be acceptable because true. But a belief that the plant turned toward the sun because it literally had wants for sunlight would be a shame. Plants do not want, and to believe they do is to suffer under some deception.

But of course no one does believe that a building defrauds or that a plant has desires. The point is that in the second two cases it is not a shame to believe the two false beliefs—something to be avoided—because one does not really believe them. One automatically translates them into the true beliefs for which they are colorful shorthand; and of course it is perfectly acceptable to believe true beliefs.

Thus, the argument from patient rejection misfires in the

9. If one held a belief about the desk that a physicist could tell one was false—e.g., the atoms of the desk are contiguous to each other—one *would* be deceived, and it would be something of a shame to hold the false belief. I do not suggest that it would be a profound shame; but all things being equal, it would be normatively better not to hold the belief.

metaphor model, but for a somewhat different reason than that suggested above. It is not that it is a harmless sin to believe false beliefs in this scenario. Rather, in one case (the desk), the belief is not false, while in the other cases (the corporation and the plant), one does not believe the false beliefs, but rather the true beliefs for which they are proxies. Thus the metaphor model withstands the argument from patient rejection—at least in its classic form. Perhaps the best way to put this is to say that the analyst believes her interpretations are metaphorically true under this model and wants her patient to believe they are true in no different sense.

If the analyst does want her patient to believe the interpretations are literally true—for example, she does not inform her patient that they are only metaphorically true—she is guilty of the same failing as the story analyst. Take an interpretation of probable early sexual abuse; if that is a metaphor for the child's feelings of helplessness and domination by her parent, then right-thinking patients will want to believe it only as a metaphor. The metaphor theorist must want her patients to believe her interpretations strictly in a metaphoric sense.[10]

10. Consider the analogy to a religious belief in a good and benevolent God. Believing this may be helpful, and, because of that, a religious leader may ask one to believe it. But imagine several situations:

 1. The cleric believes that his benevolent God is a bearded figure in the sky and asks one to believe the same;
 2. The cleric believes that God is a metaphor for good and order in the world; and
    a. asks one to believe that; or
    b. asks one to believe that God is a bearded figure in the sky;
 3. The cleric is a lapsed believer, but
    a. asks one to believe that God is a metaphor for good and order in the world;
    b. asks one to believe that God is a bearded figure in the sky;
 4. The cleric is a lapsed believer; and does not ask one to believe.

Table 5.2

	Analyst Believes Interpretations True in Correspondence Sense	Analyst Believes Interpretations True in Coherence Sense	Analyst Believes Interpretations True in Metaphoric Sense	Analyst Wants Patient to Believe Interpretations True In Sense of Which Theory of Truth?
Story Model	No	No	No	Coherence or Correspondence
Clinical Psychoanalysis Model	Yes	No	No	Correspondence or Coherence
Alternative Metaphysics Model	No	Yes	No	Coherence or Correspondence
Metaphor Model	No	No	Yes	Metaphoric

Clinical psychoanalysis and alternative metaphysics theorists, by contrast, are probably indifferent to the sense of truth in which their patients believe their interpretations; a metaphoric truth taken literally is a falsehood, while the divergence between truth on a coherence and on a correspondence theory

Now, in our situation, *(1)* represents the traditional analyst (along with the clinical psychoanalysis and alternative metaphysics analysts). *(3a)* and *(3b)* are story theorists, subject to the argument from patient rejection. *(2b)* is a metaphor theorist who is subject to the same argument. *(2a)* is the metaphor theorist who seems not to be subject to this argument; the tenability of his position is the subject of this section. *(4)* is the nonanalyst.

has no such practical effect. This situation may be represented schematically (table 5.2).

The metaphor model, then, escapes the strong form of the argument from patient rejection. I say strong form because there may be a weak form of the argument under which the metaphor model is problematic. Though it is not the case on the metaphor model that the analyst asks the patient, in essence, to credit a belief that does not purport to be possibly true, she may not give him enough of the truth on this model. If the patient is dissatisfied with what he gets from psychoanalysis on this model, he may yet reject hermeneutic psychoanalysis so conceived. Thus, the argument from patient rejection may apply in a weak form.

To appreciate this argument, we may contrast the metaphoric statement, "The plant wants to be in the sunlight" with candidates for metaphoric statements in the psychoanalytic realm. I pose three such candidates: (1) You are feeling conscious envy; (2) You are feeling unconscious envy; and (3) You are an envious person. In each case, the patient believes the statement is only metaphorically true and thus does not violate the norm of avoiding belief in untrue beliefs.[11] Yet there may be problems with asking him to believe only that—that is, with limiting psychoanalytic insight to only metaphorical truths of these kinds.

When told "The plant wants to be in the sunlight," the average person believes the statement is only metaphorically true, which is to believe a series of literally true things about the plant: that, as a result of its physical need for sunlight in order

11. Below I give the most natural interpretation of these cases. Yet each could also be metaphoric in standing for something wholly other than they seem to—e.g., one calls someone envious as a metaphoric way of saying he has green hair.

to live and grow, certain physical goings on in the plant cause it to turn toward the sun. The botanist, of course, can tell a more detailed and robust story to explain the movement of the plant. The point is that nobody believes that plants have wants, inasmuch as they do not have minds that want. On the other hand, the metaphoric statement is a colorful way of saying true things about the plant.

What is one to believe when told that it is metaphorically true that one is feeling conscious envy? The claim is that it is as if one were feeling conscious envy, just as it is as if the plant wanted to be in the sunlight. But what does this mean? Perhaps it means "You are acting as one would expect a person to act if she were feeling conscious envy—for example, staying away from successful people, subtly insulting those successful people you are around, and so forth." And so for a person to be told that she is the kind of person who often feels envy in this metaphorical sense would mean that she is the kind of person who often acts in these ways.

Thus far the plant case and the conscious envy case are parallel. In neither case are we to understand the statement as being literally true: the plant does not have wants, and one is simply not feeling conscious envy. It is because the plant and the patient do not have the actual feelings that the statements are only metaphorically true. Similarly, in both cases one learns true things when told the statement: the plant moves in ways that would be explained if it did want to be in sunlight, and the person acts in ways that would be explained if she were feeling envious.

Of course, because there are no real wants or envious feelings here, citing the wants and envy is not actually explanatory in either case; each is simply a shorthand description of the bearer's behavior. This in itself may be problematic. Moreover, whereas scientists understand why plants turn toward sunlight, in my hypothetical there is no further explanation that the conscious envy story flags. Thus, the "plant's wants" story is a kind of shorthand, while the conscious envy story is at best a promissory note: we may one day discover why you are acting as if you were feeling conscious envy while you actually are not—we may one day learn, that is, what *does* explain your behavior.[12]

Now this feature of the envy story may also be problematic, and I shall return to it shortly. For now I want to note that one explanation for someone acting enviously while not consciously feeling envy is that she is feeling unconscious envy, or she has a disposition to act enviously—she is an envious sort of person. Thus, to say that it is as if one were feeling conscious envy may mean one is actually feeling unconscious envy or is an envious sort of person. The conscious envy story as metaphor, then, may bring us to the other two cases. If the metaphor model of analytic statements is true, however, these statements must also be understood metaphorically. And this means that psychoanalytic statements on this view fail to ever be explanatory.

To establish this, let us weigh the second case: "You are feeling unconscious envy." Again, one does not believe the statement to be literally true, but only metaphorically true. But what would this mean? There are at least two possibilities. First, the most appropriate reading of unconsciousness statements is already metaphoric. The contrast would be with taking the unconscious envy language on its face, in which case one might

12. Another way to put the point is that in the earlier cases of metaphors we do not in fact need the metaphors. For example, because we independently understand phototropism, we do not need the metaphor "My petunia wants the sunlight." But in the psychoanalytic cases—and often in literature—we tend to use metaphors when the thing we are getting at is not so independently discernible. As my colleague Ron Garet put it, "The metaphor is a symbol, a bridge between the known and the unknown." The question we are broaching now is whether this feature of psychoanalytic metaphors should trouble patients.

hold that unconscious envy is the same as conscious envy, except that it occurs in some inaccessible place in one's mind; perhaps a little person in one's head experiences it himself. The point is that it is hard to imagine what an actual state of envy would be like if no one were experiencing it.

Now this literal interpretation, of course, has to be wrong. A more metaphoric reading says that unconscious envy is some mental state, we know not what, that is like conscious envy in having the same kinds of antecedents and consequences, but unlike it in that one is unaware of it. On this interpretation, to say a person is feeling unconscious envy is to say this mental state is going on while avoiding the literalness of the little-person-in-the-head view. The true view of the unconscious, then, already partakes of metaphor.

The second interpretation of the way in which unconscious envy language is metaphoric takes the metaphoric reading on the last interpretation as the literal sense of statements about unconscious envy; and it denies that statements about unconscious envy are literally true in this sense. The metaphoric sense of such statements then becomes something like the following: there is some state going on in one, we know not what, that has the same kinds of antecedents and consequences as conscious envy but is not conscious and is not even mental. The metaphoric quality of unconscious envy statements then would pertain to the mentalistic connotations of the statements. I schematically represent these differences in table 5.3.

I suggest that we accept the second interpretation as the correct reading of unconsciousness statements on the metaphor model, primarily because, on the first interpretation, the view as to these statements becomes indistinguishable from *non-hermeneutic* psychoanalysis. As I noted in discussing the first interpretation, the way we should understand the meaning of unconsciousness statements is already somewhat metaphoric,

Table 5.3

	Literal Interpretation	Metaphoric Interpretation: the True View
First Reading	There is a little person in one's head experiencing the envious state which is unconscious to you	There is some mental state, we know not what, that is like conscious envy in having the same kinds of antecedents and consequences, but one is unaware of it
Second Reading	There is some mental state, we know not what, that is like conscious envy in having the same kinds of antecedents and consequences, but one is unaware of it	There is some state, we know not what, that has the same kinds of antecedents and consequences as conscious envy, but is not conscious, and is not even mental

so all psychoanalysts, when they make claims about the unconscious, wish their claims to be understood in this somewhat metaphoric sense. If we wish to preserve a distinction between hermeneutic and nonhermeneutic psychoanalysis, at least in terms of unconsciousness statements—the bread and butter of psychoanalytic interpretation—we must accept the second reading; otherwise, the metaphor model loses its claim to being distinctively hermeneutic.

Now statements about unconscious envy on the metaphor model are similar to statements about conscious envy on this model in at least two respects. First, to refer to unconscious envy is to refer to a state that has certain antecedents and consequences; in particular, these statements are helpful, if at all, only insofar as they call attention to behavioral regularities in the patient, for example, staying away from successful people and putting them down when one is around them. Second, the explanation they offer—in terms of the envious state—is really but a promissory note: we hope for an explanation in the future.

An additional feature of the unconscious envy case is that statements about unconscious envy are taken to be metaphoric in the sense of referring to a mental state. Thus the patient, in thinking he is learning about his mind, is really given a promise of some future physiological explanation. Whether these features of the unconscious envy case on the metaphor model should be acceptable to patients I shall consider below, after I have dealt with the third case.

In the third case, the analyst tells the patient, "You are an envious sort of person." Another way of saying the same thing, perhaps, is, "You have a disposition to feel (conscious and unconscious) envy and to act enviously." But what would it mean for it to be as if one had such a disposition? In what sense is the statement metaphorical here? Or put differently, what is a metaphorical disposition?

Perhaps the idea is that one does and feels these things, although one is not the sort of person to do and feel them. But recall now that the envious feelings, conscious and unconscious, are themselves only metaphorical (psychoanalysis tells only metaphoric truths about precisely such states). Thus, we should have to rewrite the statement as follows: one does things that seem envious (would be explained if one were feeling envy), although one is not feeling conscious or unconscious envy; and one does these things frequently enough that it is as if one were the sort of person to do them, although one is not actually that sort of person.

Again, the statement is at best only apparently explanatory.

Or, perhaps more accurately, it is not explanatory at all; it is a redescription of certain characteristic kinds of behavior. Moreover, it is hard to imagine what could possibly supply the missing explanation. By hypothesis, the person is not feeling envy at a conscious or unconscious level, and he is not the sort of person who acts and feels envious.

Thus, to say that someone's being an envious sort of person is a metaphor seems to be to say that the person acts in what appear to be envious ways as a result of some bizarre accident: he was given a character-altering drug (he does not have an envious character himself), is under the sway of a magic spell, or is the innocent tool of some malign other. Perhaps, most plausibly, his neurophysiology has gone haywire, and he is driven to act in ways that do not reflect his character and are not manifestations of conscious or unconscious envy—they just look that way.

The unavoidable conclusion is that characterologic statements in psychoanalysis, if only metaphorical, at most summarize certain behaviors of the person. They do not explain the behavior, although perhaps they hold out hope for some kind of explanation in the future. Perhaps more important, the explanation promised must refer to a kind of freak or bizarre accident, not to some regular feature of the person's character. The question, as before (I shall address it presently), is whether patients ought to be satisfied with these kinds of pseudoexplanations.

In order to answer this question, let me summarize the kind of self-knowledge that patients gain when analysts make interpretations on the metaphor model. When analysts name patients' conscious mental states ("You are feeling conscious envy now"), patients are not thereby learning to identify a particular state of mind they are experiencing. They must not understand their analysts literally. Rather, they are to understand them to be pointing to behavior that happens as if it were motivated by conscious envy: the patients are avoiding successful people, subtly insulting them when in their presence, and so forth.

Similarly, when told that he is feeling unconscious envy, the patient is to understand, again, that he is behaving as if he were feeling envy without knowing it, and that one day there may be some physiological explanation for the behavior. And when the patient is told that he is an envious kind of person, he is to understand that he typically behaves in ways that would be explained if he had a disposition to be envious—to feel and act enviously—but that he does not; there is some aberrational process that is going on that makes him seem that way.[13]

The point is that patients given interpretations on the metaphor model achieve a kind of pseudoinsight into their behavior; or they come to learn how they behave without learning why—without learning, that is, an explanation of their behavior. They are merely promised that an explanation adverting to physiological processes will be forthcoming. Note that the metaphor analyst cannot avoid this reduction to the physiological and remain within the realm of the mental by translating any of these statements into any of the others; as typical psychoanalytic statements, each makes ultimate reference to the physiological.

Now as an initial matter one may wonder what kind of image of people lies at the bottom of this conception of psychoanalysis. Are conscious and unconscious envious feelings no more real than plants' wants? At least on this view psychoanalysis does not purport to have discovered that they are. I will leave

13. This is the most peculiar kind of knowledge he learns because, though framed as characterologic information, that is precisely what it is *not*. The analyst's statement not only does not refer to the patient's character, but also does not refer to something that is in some sense characteristic or expectable. It points to a simple aberration.

this point for now, however, as beyond my present concerns; I will expand upon it in the Conclusion.

Another important question to pose to the metaphor theorists is, If psychoanalytic explanations are merely metaphoric in these ways, what purpose do they serve besides describing the patient's behavior? Of what benefit to the patient is an explanation of his actions couched in terms of conscious and unconscious processes and character? Are psychoanalysts mere dressed-up behaviorists on this view?

The dress, so to speak, may indeed make a difference. For example, there may be contexts in which speaking about plants' wants is apt—as when one wants to entertain as well as inform or to stress the continuity among forms of life. Similarly, there are contexts in which speaking about corporations is appropriate; the language permits shortcuts in speech.

Yet it is difficult to see how psychological talk is helpful on the metaphor model if it reduces to descriptions of behavior (together with an implicit promise of some physiological explanation). Occasional talk about plants' wants may be fine; but we would no doubt find a botany instructor who remained within a realm of wants-language inappropriate. The entertainment value of psychological talk is an insufficient justification. Finally, psychological talk might be a useful shorthand if we knew the complicated physiological story but found the task of conveying it to patients too onerous. We do not know the story, however—or even whether the various psychological terms are reasonable proxies for physiological goings-on. Given such lack of knowledge, why not drop them?

Note also that the metaphor model of hermeneutic psychoanalysis is somewhat paradoxical in placing its faith in some future physiological explanation. Hermeneutic psychoanalysis is traditionally associated with a flight from the metapsychology. Yet on this version, the only real knowledge that patients will get of themselves (beyond mere descriptions of behavior) will come from the physiological realm. The metaphor model, then, pushes psychoanalysts toward the very thing hermeneutic psychoanalysis pulls them away from.

We are now in a position to consider whether patients will reject hermeneutic psychoanalysis on the metaphor model. The argument for saying they will is twofold: first, they will be unsatisfied with the kind and amount of self-knowledge they get on this model of psychoanalysis; and second, they may fear that the metaphorical language will lead them unwittingly to believe false beliefs.

I have established that, on the metaphor model, psychoanalytic interpretations about conscious and unconscious mental states, as well as about one's character-type, reduce to statements about behavior trends with a promise of some physiological explanation in the future. But patients will arguably feel they are not getting enough in the way of knowledge to be satisfied by psychoanalytic interpretations so understood. Part of the satisfaction of psychoanalysis is coming to know one's mind better. Intimate knowledge of how one's mind works makes one feel more comfortable with oneself—less strange—and perhaps more in control. But coming to a fuller understanding of one's mind is exactly what one does not get on the metaphor model: the mind in effect drops out of the picture, and one may remain alienated from one's very self.

Not all therapies involve getting to know oneself better— behavior therapy, for example, may among other things desensitize one to stimuli one finds aversive. But a therapy that promises to set one free, as it were, through knowledge must, so the argument goes, offer more knowledge than this.

The second claim is that the metaphor model may unwittingly lead one to hold false beliefs. No one is tempted to believe that plants literally have wants for sunlight. But told that he is feeling envy, the patient may come to believe this in the ordinary, literal sense—however often the analyst stresses the metaphorical nature of the statement.[14] One problem is that we know what the language of plants' wants is proxy for, whereas in the case of psychological language metaphorically understood we do not. In any case, if patients will reject a psychoanalysis that asks them to believe untrue beliefs, perhaps they will also reject a psychoanalysis that unduly tempts them to believe untrue beliefs.

Are these arguments persuasive? The force of the first is unclear: patients do not, on the metaphor model, come to know their minds better, but they do come to know their behavior better. Presumably they will be more adept at predicting their behavior—and that is not nothing. By the same token, they achieve metaphorical insight into their minds—insight that is a kind of stand-in for some as-yet-unknown further knowledge. Perhaps patients will be satisfied with this, perhaps not.

The second argument, I think, is not persuasive: patients can simply take care not to be deceived. Asking one to be deceived is one thing; tempting one to be deceived—while taking every opportunity to prevent that—is quite another. I have faith that patients can avoid deception on this view.

The upshot is that the weak version of the argument from patient rejection is of unclear force here. The claim that patients will reject psychoanalysis on the metaphor model is obviously empirical, and I do not have strong intuitions whether they will or not. One might propose a normative argument that patients ought to reject hermeneutic psychoanalysis on this model, just as in the case of the story model. But the normative force of the arguments is markedly unequal in the two cases. Patients ought

14. Even more problematically, the patient may come to believe he was actually abused sexually, as in the earlier example.

to reject the story model because it implicitly asks them to believe interpretations that do not purport to be possibly true, and it is normatively undesirable to do so. By contrast, patients ought to reject the metaphor model, if they ought, because it gives them too little in the way of knowledge. In essence, they ought to reject the metaphor model because it is an unacceptable vision of psychoanalysis. This is a much harder argument to make, and I have at most offered some suggestions that it might be true.

The Plausibility of the Interpretations-as-Literary-Criticism Model

On the interpretations-as-literary-criticism model, psychoanalysis is hermeneutic in seeking after meaning, not causes. This version of hermeneutic psychoanalysis offers a particular interpretation of interpretation: interpretation reveals unconscious mental states but does not suppose that they are causes of the behavior interpreted. Nevertheless, these states are unproblematically real, and statements about them may be true in the most traditional sense of "truth." Thus, the interpretations-as-literary-criticism model allows that interpretations may be true in an unproblematic way; it simply denies that they reveal *causal* truths.

This model of hermeneutic psychoanalysis obviously escapes the classic form of the argument from patient rejection. On this model, the analyst does not ask the patient to believe interpretations that she herself does not believe because they do not purport to be possibly true. Thus it is not the case that patients will not and ought not to believe these interpretations; there is no normative proscription against believing the truth. The interpretations-as-literary-criticism model is subject to the argument from patient rejection, if at all, only in its weak form: if it proposes a conception of psychoanalysis with which patients will be dissatisfied.

In fact, I will point out two problems with this model. First, I will suggest that its vision of psychoanalytic interpretation as not revealing causes is seriously flawed—that it is simply in the nature of psychoanalytic interpretation to reveal causes.[15] Thus, while the interpretations-as-literary-criticism theorists reject the view that interpretations reveal meanings, not facts, they do support the view that they reveal meanings, not causes; and the latter view is as problematic as the former. Second, returning to the argument from patient rejection, I will suggest that patients may be somewhat dissatisfied with a conception of psychoanalysis under which it reveals noncausal truths by noninterpretive means.

On the interpretations-as-literary-criticism model, psychoanalysis yields patients noncausal information about themselves that they arguably ought to find valuable—and about which analysts therefore need not dissemble. An analyst tells her patient stories that are meant to reveal things about the patient's unconscious wishes and desires, but not to explain behavior in terms of these wishes and desires. Thus, the woman going to the kitchen might learn from an attempt to seek the meaning of her behavior that, without realizing it, she was hungry, was not seeing the television screen well enough, was missing her mother; although she may not learn why she went to the kitchen, she does learn a lot about herself.

Now, in invoking the example of literary criticism, analysts may be claiming to engage in the paradigmatic analytic activity

15. In saying this, I do not mean to contrast causes with reasons or motives. In fact, I am speaking of causes which *are* reasons or motives, generally unconscious. Some hermeneutic thinkers have drawn this contrast, but it has been definitively established—e.g., by Donald Davidson—as problematic. See Strenger (1991).

of interpreting behavior; it is just that our behavior, as they claim, may signify very many things about us, but at the same time those things need not causally explain the behavior. Yet this view, as I shall argue, is wrong: on this view, analysts do not in fact engage in the paradigmatic analytic activity of interpreting behavior. They cannot coherently repudiate the task of seeking causes and seek meaning instead.

That interpretation is essentially an effort to seek causes can be seen in the situations of the novelist writing scenes and the ordinary person performing actions (these situations, as we shall see below, are significantly different). Words do mean much more than their writer intended them to mean, as do actions and other psychological phenomena. Yet, unlike scenes in a novel—whose meaning may well not refer to the author's psychology—actions reveal things about the actor's internal life only to the extent that those things participated in bringing about the action.[16] In the same way, dizziness reveals that its sufferer has an inner ear problem only to the extent that that problem caused the dizziness.

It is true that thinking about the action may reveal things about the person that happen to be true even though those things did not cause the action. In the same way, thinking about the dizziness might reveal the inner ear problem even though it happens not to have caused the dizziness. But it is only by

16. Of course, actions and dreams and other psychological phenomena, like words in a novel, may have meanings that do not reveal things about their author. And we may read these phenomena for such meanings without seeking to learn more about their author—just as in reading a novel. On the theory we are considering now, however, the meanings are taken to reveal noncausal truths about the patient and to be therapeutic for that reason. I have already rejected the view that patients should accept psychoanalysis if it reveals meanings that do not purport to truth—i.e., the story view.

trying to explain these meaningful phenomena in causal terms that we arrive at these truths.

A dream, too, is like a novel in having much more meaning than its creator intended. Yet it, too, reveals things about its creator only to the extent that those things participated in the creation of the dream. The dream shows that its creator is scared only if his fear contributed to the dream-formation. If it did not, then it is only accidental that we learn from considering the dream that the person is scared.

Indeed, even that accident reveals interpretation as a cause-seeking enterprise: the interpreter theorizes that the dreamer is afraid because fear often does cause such dream-images. To interpret the meaning of behavior, that is, is at least to imagine psychological processes that might cause such behavior in a hypothetical case. When an analyst, for example, says that a girl's behavior in raising her hand in class means that she wishes to prevail over sibling-substitutes in winning the teacher/parent's approval—or alternatively, to achieve solidarity with these sibling-substitutes in showing up the teacher/parent —she is at least asserting the hypothesis that such psychological states sometimes cause such behavior, even if she is unsure that they have done so in the particular case. To find meanings simply is to find causes.

The case of a novel is different. We may seek the meaning of an action in a scene in a novel without speculating about psychological states in the author that caused the portrayal of the action. But there, we are not reading the action as evidence for certain psychological states in the author. We are reading it, rather, as evidence for certain psychological states in the character whose action it is; the action signifies things about him. But then to interpret the meaning of the action *is* to seek causes: the character's action means he is angry, for example, only to the extent that the anger contributed to the action;

and, more generally, his actions tell us about his psychological makeup only to the extent that that makeup participated in causing the actions.

Of course, the anger that causes a fictitious character's action is no more real than his action. Perhaps that explains in part why many interpretations of a novel may be equally valid; there is no reality against which some interpretations must fail.[17] The point, however, is that to interpret the imaginary behavior is to find its imaginary causes; if the behavior were real, its real meaning would be found nowhere else but in its real causes.

The case of the novel is complicated in that some people, namely, literary biographers, do interpret novels to find out about their creators[18] — about the mental states in those creators that caused their portrayal of the characters. And so art therapists interpret patients' creations to find out about their psychological states. But when interpreting a work of art aims at finding out about its creator, we reach the same conclusion as in the case of the dream and the characters in the novel: we learn about the artist from the art only to the extent that the psychological phenomena that the art reveals in fact causally contributed to the art's creation.

If a dream were interpreted not to find its causes but rather to determine the meanings of its elements in the hope that those meanings accidentally revealed things about the patient, then it would be as useful to interpret other people's dreams as the patient's to find out about him. For the meanings of the elements of any dream might accidentally reveal things about

17. Perhaps I overstate this point. There *is* the reality of the text, so some interpretations must fail. That is why I said "so many different" interpretations may be valid, and not an infinite number.

18. Some literary critics subscribe to theories that require them to do so as well — the meaning of the scene in the novel is given by the author's intent — although these theories are somewhat out of favor today.

the patient. Yet no one would regard that as an analytic interpretation. The reason we interpret the patient's own dream is that we seek to find its underlying causes.

In short, we cannot save the meaning theory by driving a wedge between causal explanations and explanations in terms of meaning. My claim is on the order of a conceptual claim about the meaning of interpreting psychological phenomena to find out about the people who experience them. To say, "x means y," where x is a psychological phenomenon and y is an underlying state of the person experiencing the phenomenon, implies that y causally contributed to the occurrence of x. And to interpret x psychoanalytically is to find these underlying y's. In this sense, "x means y" is analogous to the case in which x is a symptom of a physical disorder—"The fever means you have an infection"—or in which x is an effect of some physical process—"The earthquake means that the San Andreas Fault acted up." And it is not analogous to the case in which x is a scene in a novel: to interpret the meaning of Casaubon's endless project in *Middlemarch* need not be to say anything about George Eliot's perfectionism.

If the core case of "x means y" in the psychoanalytic context is "y caused x," even to seek meaning without causes in this context is a self-defeating enterprise; for in at least two senses to seek meaning is to seek causes. First, when one interprets a product of human activity to find out about the person who produced it, one must be trying to seek causes (although one may fail and nevertheless say true things). Second, the psychological states that one interprets some act as signifying must at least be of a sort as to be reasonably presumed causes of such behavior in a hypothetical case. Thus, to the extent that analysts are engaged in the paradigmatic analytic activity of interpretation, they cannot coherently repudiate the enterprise of seeking causes.

I can think of at least two objections to my argument that interpretation is an essentially cause-seeking venture.[19] First, a dream, say, may reveal one to be the kind of person who can do/feel/experience x, and one can learn this about oneself by interpreting the dream while being indifferent to its underlying causal mechanism. Take the case of someone who dreams of being in a state of religious ecstasy. Suppose that the person has never before had a conscious feeling of that kind. Thinking about the dream reveals to him that he is the kind of person who can experience states like that. Yet in making the interpretation, he is not making inferences about underlying causes. Perhaps the anchovies he ate before retiring played a causal role in producing his dream. But does he even care about that?

In the same way, imagine a musical illiterate who under hypnosis begins playing the piano in an inspired, creative way. Upon waking and thinking about the episode, the person would learn that, somewhere, somehow, he had the capacity to play the piano. But he is indifferent to the causal mechanism that permitted the result; he does not care that the hypnosis, say, removed his ordinary inhibitions and enabled him to tap into

19. A third objection is also possible. Imagine an author who writes a biographical novel about an analyst's patient. The analyst could then interpret the scenes of that novel and learn a good deal about the patient; but in uncovering the meaning of the text, the analyst is not revealing its causes. But this is just a mixed case of the cases described above. I have noted that one may interpret stories without uncovering the causes of their parts. Yet I have insisted that interpreting the behavior within the story is to find the causes of that behavior—of course the fictitious causes. Thus the act of interpretation implicates uncovering causes: if the behavior were real, those would be its causes. Indeed, because the fictionalized biography is a fictionalized *biography*, interpretation may disclose the true causes of the real behavior, if not of the account of it. There is just no getting round the disclosure of causes when one interprets psychological phenomena.

some deep knowledge and talent he had hidden away some-where.

But this objection, I think, misconstrues my claim that seeking meaning is seeking causes. I do not mean to imply that interpretation is after, essentially, the physiological mechanisms that were responsible for the psychological phenomena. The cause of the dream or the behavior, in my sense, is not the anchovies' gastric effects or the hypnosis's disinhibiting effects; it is the underlying psychological state that is manifested in the dream or behavior.

In this sense (to confine myself now to the dream), some underlying ecstatic state must be presumed to play a causal role in the dream-image, just as some underlying fear generally plays a role in producing nightmares. In the ordinary case, the interpreting of dreams encompasses the discovery of less obvious underlying psychological states—the religious ecstasy may be a sanitized version of the bliss of early union with mother or a defense against the terror of dying. But we can presume that some underlying ecstasy played a causal role in producing the dream-image as well. So in this case to learn from dream-interpretation that one is the kind of person who can feel ecstasy is to have uncovered meaning in the sense of cause.

A second objection to my interpretation of interpretation as a cause-seeking enterprise is that there may be kinds of interpretation that have nothing to do with discovering the underlying psychological states that cause behavior. I conceded that the interpreting of scenes in a novel may have nothing to do with pondering their causes in the author; yet I insisted that it involves pondering the causes of the behavior of the characters in the scene. But is this really true? A perfectly appropriate interpretation of *Animal Farm*, for instance, will discuss the novel as a vivid portrayal of the harms of communist dictatorship. Likewise, a Graham Greene novel may be essentially about the excesses of Catholicism. Surely it cannot be right that to interpret novels is always to reveal the psychological dynamics of the characters portrayed in the novel.

My response to this objection is severalfold. First, I agree that literary interpretation is not always about psychological dynamics. Yet it is often about them; even establishing that communist dictatorships are harmful includes portraying the psychological damage they can do—seeing the causal links between the policies and the human suffering. We also care about the effects of political regimes like the communist because, in part, of the real psychological harms they cause the people living under them.

Still, psychological harms are not the only things we care about, and psychological consequences are not the only subject of so-called political novels. For example, we may care about the excesses of the Catholic church because we do not want to commit an offense in God's eyes. Similarly, we may care about the immorality of animal experimentation portrayed in a novel because of the harm to the animals; human happiness may be utterly beside the point.

Yet while I concede that interpretation of a novel may not refer to underlying psychological causes, surely the interpreting of psychological phenomena does. Imagine interpreting a dream about animal experimentation in terms of its implicit moral message. The point of the interpretation now is not that the patient rejects animal experimentation, but that such experimentation is immoral. How does that help the patient therapeutically? Will she cease to give donations to scientific groups that experiment on animals and feel happier as a result? Surely this is not psychoanalysis—or psychology of any kind— but a form of proselytizing.

The argument is not made more plausible if we limit psychoanalytic interpretation to the discovery of psychological truths, just not causal truths about the patient. Imagine treating a patient's dream as a short story whose message is the ingratitude of children toward their parents. Hearing the analyst's interpretation of this story may help the patient deal better with his parents. In interpreting her patient's dream, then, the analyst is not trying to discover what caused the dream, but to draw moral and psychological lessons that the patient can apply to his life.

A number of responses to this argument are possible. First, interpretation here is conceded to be about discovering psychological truths. But then all the arguments I made above apply. In particular, learning about children's ingratitude toward their parents will involve the positing of underlying psychological states that constitute the ingratitude and are responsible for its ill effects. What the analyst learns, then, when she interprets as if the dream were a short story is precisely what she wants not to learn—the psychological causes underlying if not the dream, then the behavior.[20]

Perhaps more important, in applying the lesson to herself, the patient will ponder her own experience: has she felt ungrateful toward her parents in the past, and what have been the effects of her feeling this way, not least in terms of how she feels about so feeling? Even a general discussion of children's ingratitude toward their parents will produce free associations that the analyst will want to interpret. Unless the free associations themselves are treated as just another text that calls

20. It is possible here, as above, to respond that interpretation may reveal only as-if states: suppose there is no such thing as jealousy, but interpreting some text in terms of jealousy permits one to draw conclusions that will help one live better. Here, the interpretation in terms of the text's moral positively does not disclose causes; there is no real jealousy, so it can play no real causal role. But this move simply combines the metaphor model with the interpretations-as-literary-criticism model, and analysis of this case will then track analysis of those two models.

for a literary-type interpretation that yields some general moral lesson, eventually the analyst will engage in traditional interpretation that does reveal underlying psychological causes.

The alternative is to convert analysis into some form of moral training. One treats all of the patient's productions as texts that tell one how to live: don't be ungrateful to your parents. One does not explore how they apply to the patient, how he feels about them, whether they hide even deeper themes. In short, if one's aim is to discover the moral message in his productions, one is not interpreting to find out about the patient. As above, one might as well be interpreting someone else's productions—say the scenes in a George Eliot novel—and one might as well confess that this is not therapy, but moral education.

If this argument holds, then the second objection to my view falters. Although some forms of interpretation may not involve the disclosure of causes, psychoanalytic interpretation of psychological phenomena does. Indeed, I have given one case of interpretation, namely, interpretation of political texts, that does not follow the classic pattern in the case of fiction. But I want to concede now that "meaning" itself (and so interpretation) is multi-meaninged. For example, the meaning of, say, a physical symptom may refer not only to its cause, but also to its effects ("The meaning of your injury is that you will never walk again"); its psychological significance to its bearer ("Your injury means to you that you are a damaged person"); its psychological significance to others ("Your injury means to them that, while life is unfair, one can overcome even bad luck through great effort")—and many others.[21] I nevertheless want to insist

21. Take, for example, the distinction between *the Meaning of life* (meaning with a capital *M*) and the meaning of an episode, event, parapraxis, etc. (meaning with a small *m*). The hermeneuts often clearly mean to refer to "meaning," but they may sometimes seem to mean to refer to "Meaning." What about the hermeneutic claim that psychoanalytic

that, in the psychoanalytic case, the meaning of a symptom is, in its primary sense, its cause.

If this argument is correct, the interpretations-as-literary-criticism model does violence to the notion of interpretation. Thus, psychoanalysis on this model no longer proceeds via interpretation of patients' productions, and the analyst must simply give up on the paradigmatic analytic activity of interpreting. If she does so, we must turn to the second part of the analysis: whether patients will and should be satisfied with a psychoanalysis so construed—a psychoanalysis that yields only noncausal knowledge by noninterpretive means.

The first thing to be said is that, once again, this conception of analysis is descriptively inaccurate. Psychoanalysts now lead patients to believe that their interpretations reveal the underlying psychological causes of behavior. If analysts wish to adopt this version of analysis, they must change their behavior (and what they say about their behavior) on pain, again, of misleading patients.

Even if analysts change their behavior, will patients be satisfied with a psychoanalysis reconstructed on the interpretations-as-literary-criticism model? Patients, I think, may in fact be dissatisfied with purely noncausal knowledge. The patient may have a strong desire to understand a particular behavior: the woman wants to know why she went into the kitchen and is not satisfied with the incidental knowledge that, as it turns out, she is also hungry.

Indeed, as a general matter, patients seek treatment because they do and feel things that they do not like. They want to

---

interpretations are meaningful stories? Do the hermeneuts mean by this that the interpretations have a meaning, or do they mean that they give patients' lives Meaning? Greater clarity about the distinction might prove helpful.

understand themselves so they will be able to do and feel things that they will like better. They want self-understanding, in other words, because of its instrumental value: because it enables them to predict how they will feel and act and to make changes that will improve their lot.

Understanding, of course, also has intrinsic value. And knowing oneself better may make one feel happier even if one cannot further improve one's life in light of that knowledge. Still, such nonexplanatory information about oneself is less valuable than information that can figure in one's life-plans — and patients may not be satisfied with knowledge that never explains.

To repeat, the claim that patients will reject psychoanalysis so understood is clearly empirical, and I do not have strong intuitions they will. And the claim that they ought to reject psychoanalysis so understood depends on a showing that this is an unsatisfying conception of psychoanalysis — a showing that I have only begun to make. At least the claim here is much weaker than in the case of the story model, in which we can rely on the norm that one ought not to believe things that do not purport to be possibly true. Thus, this weak form of the argument from patient rejection yet again leads to equivocal results.

In short, the view that analytic interpretations give insight in the way that interpretations of art do is probably misconceived. To the extent that analysts are interpreting behavior, they cannot coherently repudiate the enterprise of seeking causal explanations under the banner of seeking meaning: meaning reduces to cause in this context. Analysts may give up the paradigmatic analytic activity of interpretation, but they will then have to alter their behavior radically; and it is unclear that what remains will be satisfying to patients — at least as satisfying as analysis currently conceived is.

6

The Weak Form of the Argument
from Patient Rejection Revisited

The strong form of the argument from patient rejection seems to me robust vis-à-vis the story model of hermeneutic psychoanalysis. That argument says that patients not only will, but also ought to, reject psychoanalytic interpretations because analysts are asking them to believe things that do not purport to be possibly true. The strong form of the argument applies to the story model alone because on all of the other models psychoanalytic interpretations purport to be true in at least some sense of "true." A more sophisticated version of the strong form of the argument, which questions whether patients will accept alternative conceptions of truth, is plausible but not without its problems.

I postulated also a weak form of the argument from patient rejection under which patients will—and arguably ought to—reject psychoanalysis on some of the other models because their interpretations fail in some other way. For example, on the metaphor model interpretations do not acquaint patients in any real sense with their minds, and on the interpretations-as-literary-criticism model they do not offer them any causal knowledge. I acknowledged my lack of any real confidence that patients will, as an empirical matter, reject these conceptions of psychoanalysis for these reasons; and that they ought, as a normative matter, to reject them. The latter claim depends on a negative evaluation of these visions of psychoanalysis, not on any simple rule against believing what does not purport to be possibly true.

I now want to examine the weak version of the argument from patient rejection more carefully. As an initial matter, consider my claim that, given the way analysis is practiced today, these visions of hermeneutic psychoanalysis seem descriptively inaccurate. But this observation is not strong grounds for dismissing these visions of analysis: for if analysts come to think about what they are doing differently, then, if they are not to mislead patients, they must explain what they are doing differently—and perhaps come to vary the way they practice.

The observation raises another point: Psychoanalysis appears to be offering patients straightforward explanations that purport to be true so that all hermeneutic views are fighting an uphill battle when they say otherwise. Why should we think psychoanalysis is doing something other than what it appears to be doing? A number of the hermeneutic commentators labored to provide us with reasons, but one was left somewhat dissatisfied by their efforts.

Indeed, one begins to suspect that the hermeneutic view is a kind of backpedaling: the failure of psychoanalysis to live up to its scientific promise, its struggles over adequate criteria of validation, its inability to adjudicate among the multiple theories that persist—these and other problems may have led the hermeneuts to propose a view of analysis that at least does not match appearances and may be simply a response to failures rather than an independently attractive view.

In any case, my criticism of the kinds of hermeneutic psychoanalysis on this basis is not unexpected, and hermeneutic analysts can easily obviate it: they can alter what they say to patients and how they practice. Truth-in-advertising requires that they do so. Analysts may be unwilling to make these changes, crucial though they are. And even if they do, one must at this point wonder whether the reconstructed versions of analysis will be acceptable to patients.

After summarizing why the new versions of hermeneutic psychoanalysis may dissatisfy patients and prompt patients to reject them, I undertake two tasks. First, I explore whether the resulting visions of psychoanalysis not only radically alter it, but in fact convert it into a therapy that is not psychoanalysis. If they do so, this adds a third prong to my empirical and normative critique of some versions of hermeneutic psychoanalysis—namely, a definitional critique. To the extent that patients want to be in analysis, they will have further reason to reject these visions of analysis.

Second, I ask whether patients will and should reject these versions of hermeneutic psychoanalysis after all, even if some of them render the therapies nonanalytical and all of them seem in principle unsatisfying in some ways. My suggestion here is that the most crucial factor may be whether the resulting therapies work. If they do, patients arguably will not and should not reject them. I nevertheless explore what their reaction should be given that there is no evidence that—or even theory why—these alternative therapies should work.

The Conceptual Gambit

I have given reasons for rejecting the story model of hermeneutic psychoanalysis and have declared the clinical psychoanalysis and alternative metaphysics models immune from this criticism. Several new versions of story analysis as well as the remaining models of hermeneutic psychoanalysis at least seemed to be subject to the weak version of the argument from patient rejection. The problems with these versions of hermeneutic psychoanalysis—why they might be unsatisfying—are summarized in table 6.1. These statements, it seems to me, would

Table 6.1

Imagine and React View	Goals-for-the-Future View	Metaphor Model	Interpretations-As-Literary-Criticism Model
Analysis does not offer insight; it is beneficial only in being cathartic (as in watching sad movies) or pleasurable (as in enjoying music in a religious service)	Analysis does not offer insight, but only goals for the future. Telling stories about the patient is an anomalous way to do so; and analysts and patients might reject casting analysts in prescriptive role	Analysis offers patients only metaphorical insight: descriptions of their behavior together with a promise for a physiological explanation in the future	Analysis offers patients only noncausal insights by noninterpretive means

constitute patients' central complaints. Behind them is a vision of what psychoanalysis is; and these versions of it do not live up to that vision. The question now is whether any of the missing aspects of psychoanalysis as traditionally understood is conceptually necessary for a therapy to be regarded as analysis.

Psychoanalysts have long debated the essential, distinguishing features of their therapy. For example, do patients need to lie on the couch for a therapy to be considered analysis? do they need four sessions a week? Some of these debates seem silly at times; and I shall explore presently what lies behind the impulse to pinpoint the defining features of psychoanalysis. For example, is it simply a guild issue?

For now, however, I want to look at more fundamental features of therapies that call themselves analysis than how the patient reclines. Perhaps I should be understood to be defining psychodynamic psychotherapies as against all other kinds of therapies, rather than psychoanalysis as against all other therapies including the psychodynamic.[1] And my concern is not to establish all of the necessary conditions of psychoanalysis, but only some of the most central ones—those of interest in our context. Indeed, the criteria I propose do not even remotely capture the richness and complexity of the analytic process. For example, patients do not merely hear interpretations of their conflicts in analysis but enact them in the transference. The characterizing of the nature of the analytic process is a difficult business, one that has generated much literature; fortunately, we do not need to take on this task in its entirety here.

It is well understood that Freud took the defining feature of psychoanalysis to be its capacity to produce relief by giving patients insight into the "exciting causes" of their behavior. In other words, Freud subscribed to what Adolf Grünbaum has dubbed the "tally thesis" and Michael Moore the "Socratic therapy thesis." The evidence is still out on the tally thesis: do patients benefit from psychoanalysis, if they do, *because* they learn the truth about themselves?

The question of how psychoanalysis produces benefit differs from the question of what psychoanalysis essentially is as a therapy, at least given our limited understanding of therapeutic efficacy. If we knew how psychoanalysis works, we could conclude that analysts should just do the things that work—that *that* was what was essential to psychoanalysis. But of course we do not know. In these circumstances, we should deem essential to psychoanalysis what we regard as crucial to its efficacy—

1. For convenience I will nevertheless continue to refer to the project as defining *psychoanalysis;* at least what we come up with will include psychoanalysis.

our best guess about how it works—taking into account the features that all activities that call themselves psychoanalysis share. In other words, the defining of psychoanalysis, as I mean the phrase, combines empirical hypothesizing with ordinary language analysis.

Under this conception of my task, it may not be necessary for a therapy to produce relief via true insight to be psychoanalysis. Many different styles of psychoanalysis seem to produce relief through widely disparate interpretations, not all of which can be right. My best guess, then, is that correct insight is not necessary to therapeutic efficacy (although of course further research is needed). Moreover, all those therapies that call themselves psychoanalytic cannot share the feature of providing patients with the true explanation of their behavior because, again, they cannot all be giving the true explanation.

It may turn out that the tally thesis is correct, and that only those therapies that furnish correct explanations are therapeutic. If so, there would be reason to limit the concept of psychoanalysis to those therapies. But because we do not have reason to think this is so today, I suggest that we weaken the requirement for a therapy to be psychoanalysis: it must purport to offer patients true interpretations of their behavior, and patients must believe the interpretations.[2] On this view, one of the defining features of psychoanalysis is that it proceeds via the acquisition of beliefs about oneself.

Two factors recommend this position. First, it is a good guess that psychoanalytic psychotherapies work via inducing patients to hold certain beliefs about themselves. It is certainly possible that the therapeutic action occurs in some wholly other way—for example, through the therapist's empathy with the patient;

2. Note that if my argument above about the story model is correct, it is only because these explanations purport to be possibly true that patients will and should believe them.

and, of course, there could be a synergy of factors that lead therapy to work. But it is a good guess that at least one of the factors is the beliefs the patient acquires; interpretation is a prominent part of all analytic activity (although naturally some analysts are more passive than others). Research may establish how psychoanalysis works, but absent conclusive data, my hypothesis is sound.

The second factor recommending this position is contained in the first: interpretation is a prominent part of all analytic activity. It would be difficult to find an analyst who would mean by "analysis" something other than helping patients come to know themselves better. Although many therapies involve, say, empathy, unless they also include interpretation, most analysts would reject them as analysis. Thus an ordinary language analysis of what we mean by the concept of psychoanalysis is likely to refer to the inducement of beliefs about himself in the patient.

If my analysis is correct thus far, we can conclude as a conceptual, definitional matter that therapy as imagining-and-reacting is simply not psychoanalysis. On that view, the therapist does not offer insight, and the therapy is beneficial only in being cathartic (as when one watches sad movies) or pleasurable (as when one enjoys music in a religious service). Beliefs about oneself do not purport to play a therapeutic role. Although this therapy could be very helpful (a point to which I will return below), it is not helpful via coming to believe things about oneself, and so it is not, as a definitional matter, psychoanalysis.

This criterion of psychoanalysis, on the other hand, does not rule out the other hermeneutic versions of psychoanalysis considered here. The goals-for-the-future view claims to work partly via beliefs: but beliefs about how one ought to be, rather than about how one is or was. Similarly, the metaphor model warrants itself to work through beliefs; it is just that here the residually true content of the beliefs refers to one's behavior, not to one's inner mental states. Finally, the interpretations-as-literary-criticism model also purports to work via beliefs, but here the beliefs are about how one is: no attention is paid to how one got to be that way.

Conceivably the criterion under which therapy qualifies as psychoanalysis should be tightened. If the therapy must work via beliefs, for instance, perhaps it must also work via beliefs about how one is—what one is like as a person. This, if true, would rule out the goals-for-the-future view, which maintains that one acquires beliefs about the kind of person one should become, not the kind of person one is. Similarly, if we added the condition that the beliefs must include some that bear on one's conscious and unconscious mental states, then therapy on the metaphor model would not be psychoanalysis because the beliefs there reduce to beliefs about one's behavior (together with a promise for some physiological knowledge in the future). Finally, if we added the condition that the beliefs must include some that relate to psychological states, conscious and unconscious, that play a causal role, then therapy on the interpretations-as-literary-criticism model would not be psychoanalysis because beliefs about causation are absent in therapy on that model.

Our final criteria would look something like this. A therapy is psychoanalysis only if

1. it purports to work via beliefs;
2. the beliefs include propositions about what kind of person one is;
3. the beliefs include propositions about one's conscious and unconscious mental states; and
4. the beliefs include propositions about mental states that play a causal role in one's behavior.

A case could be made that all four criteria are necessary, definitionally, for a therapy to be psychoanalysis, although the case is not as strong for (2)–(4) as for (1). As we saw, there are two avenues to pursue in answering the question of whether (2)–(4) are necessary, namely, the efficacy and the ordinary language avenues. In terms of the first, one can formulate a reason for thinking that all of these factors, in (2)–(4) no less than (1), are important for the therapy to be efficacious. For instance, part of the reason interpretations are beneficial is that one comes to know oneself better and therefore to feel more comfortable with oneself and more in control. Establishing the kind of person one would like to become omits these benefits. Similarly, one does not really come to know oneself if one doesn't come to know one's own mind. And knowledge about oneself that does not explain one's behavior permits one to make only incomplete predictions and postdictions about oneself.

Second, one can argue that all activities that call themselves analysis share a commitment to doing the things in (1)–(4)— that practitioners of analysis believe these things are all part of analysis. Once again, however, the case for this claim is stronger for condition (1) than for conditions (2)–(4).

At this point, however, the second criterion comes to seem problematic. If in order for an activity to qualify as analysis we require that it do all the things its practitioners think it ought to do, then significantly changed activities will no longer seem to be analysis. Ordinary language analysis is conservative, while my task here is to find out what is essential to analysis in the context of proposed modifications. Nevertheless, although some might think that the essence of an activity like psychoanalysis must await scientific findings, I believe that the issue can reasonably turn on educated guesses about efficacy in conjunction with ordinary usage.

Using these criteria, I suggest that condition *(1)* above—that analysis purports to work via beliefs—is essential, but that the case for conditions *(2)-(4)* is somewhat weaker. Although we may have reason for thinking conditions *(2)-(4)* are essential for efficacy, we do not have as strong a reason for thinking so as in the case of condition *(1)*. On the other hand, even if activities that failed conditions *(2)-(4)* looked somewhat like analysis, they would be lacking in significant ways; any activity that failed to meet *(1)-(4)*—especially *(1)*—would arguably do violence to the concept of analysis as we know it. These thoughts are tentative, and not much turns on their being right. If they are right, however, then we can say that the imagine-and-react view is clearly subject to a conceptual, definitional criticism, while the other three views are probably subject to it.

At this point, one must ask what the force of this definitional critique is. Why should anyone care whether a therapy warrants the appellation psychoanalysis? On one level, perhaps, no one should. Debates about what is essential to psychoanalysis, on this view, are much ado about nothing. Perhaps practitioners and patients of psychoanalysis get some prestige value out of the name: psychoanalysis is the highest class therapy on this view. But *we* should hardly care about that. On this view, the conceptual gambit has very little force—it is little more than a move in a guild struggle.

A more charitable view holds that we should formulate definitions of psychoanalysis carefully, as a research strategy and as a heuristic for selecting therapies under conditions of ignorance. Careful definitions of psychoanalysis expressed in terms of its therapeutically promising features and of what its practitioners take as being central are promising places to start studying the activity. Where better to study therapeutic efficacy than where we think the activity is therapeutic? Perhaps more important, lacking careful definitions of the therapy, we shall not know what we are studying. Including any therapy that simply calls itself analytic in outcome studies is likely to confound results tremendously.

It is also clear why a careful definition of analysis would be a useful heuristic for selecting a therapy. Again, we have defined as analysis what we think to be therapeutic about the activity—and one should go where one is likeliest to get the biggest therapeutic bang for one's buck. It is for this reason that the conceptual gambit figures in the argument from patient rejection. Patients should care about being in a therapy that promises to be helpful and should reject therapies that fail to meet this condition.

In short, it seems we can add a definitional component to the argument from patient rejection: To be analysis, a therapy must purport to work via inducing beliefs about oneself, including beliefs about the kind of person one is, about one's conscious and unconscious states, and about the causes of one's behavior. And one should care about being in analysis, for we have defined analysis in terms of the procedures of analysts that are likely to be therapeutic.

One final comment. In addition to asking what patients would do when faced with a therapy that is not analysis, one must wonder what hermeneutic analysts would do: would they remain committed to their theory if told it was not a theory of *analysis?*

The Empirical Gambit

Whether or not the four versions of analysis examined here are or are not analysis, a perhaps more important problem with the weak version of the argument from patient rejection remains: Should patients in fact reject any of these therapies on conceptual grounds? Clearly, only patients who are committed to being in *analysis* will do so. But even then, is not the vital question whether the therapies work? I have suggested that we should care about the conceptual gambit only because it signals that the therapy is likely to be therapeutic. But why not just cut to the chase and ask whether the various therapies are therapeutic?

Recall the summary of patients' complaints given in table 6.1. Patients might not like the idea of a therapy that works by being cathartic or pleasurable, or of one that works by helping them set goals for the future. The first may make therapy seem trivial, the second, infantilizing. Or perhaps the patients have read theoretical accounts of why analysis as we know it is likely to be therapeutic—and these new therapies fail by those standards.

But surely these considerations pale in comparison to the most important one: Does the therapy work? The weak form of the argument from patient rejection, then, contains not one, but two implicit empirical premises: patients will in fact want to reject these versions of psychoanalysis; and these versions are in fact ineffective therapeutically. If the new versions instead prove beneficial, should we not celebrate them? What does it mean to say that a therapy is trivial, so long as it works?

The argument that patients will and should reject these four versions of hermeneutic psychoanalysis may thus seem untenable. In particular, the charge of triviality is somewhat meaningless in this context, and the other charges are based, as it were, on appearances as well. Patients may not abstractly like the sound of these new therapies, so to speak, but we cannot say they will and should reject them until we know whether they work. We should celebrate any form of therapy that is effective.

This argument, however, is not so strong as I have made out. For the fact is, if we do not have reasons for thinking that these new versions of therapy are ineffective, we do not have reasons for thinking they are effective either. Absent proof of efficacy, we should at least want a theory explaining these therapies' potential for efficacy. Among those we have discussed, the therapy whose efficacy has been most studied and speculated about is psychoanalysis proper. The further these new therapies depart from traditional psychoanalysis, the less their efficacy has been studied and the less reason there is to think that their efficacy will be proved.

The upshot of this discussion of the weak form of the argument from patient rejection is that we need more research into the efficacy of both traditional psychoanalysis and new hermeneutic versions. Until the inefficacy of the former and the efficacy of the latter are proved, patients may well be right to insist on traditional psychoanalysis over these new hermeneutic versions. The weak form of the argument from patient rejection is not without merit.

7

Implications for Theoretical Psychoanalysis and Other Concluding Thoughts

In this concluding chapter I make a foray beyond the realms hitherto occupied. Thus far I have confined myself to the viability of psychoanalysis as a *practice* on the hermeneutic views. But these views also have consequences for how we are to think of psychoanalysis as a *theory* of psychology. I want now to consider these implications, raise other issues that deserve further research, and summarize my findings in this work.

Psychoanalysis purports to be not only a therapy, but also a source of knowledge about the psychology of human beings. And the versions of hermeneutic psychoanalysis have important implications for how we understand this body of what claims to be psychoanalytic knowledge.

The clinical psychoanalysis and alternative metaphysics models leave the body of clinical psychoanalytic knowledge unscathed.[1] When analysts interpret patients' behavior on these models, they are purporting to reveal true things about them. An analyst, for example, may reveal to her patient that he is feeling unconscious hostility toward his boss and that through various maneuvers of his mind the hostility is causing him to fear harm at his boss's hands. Eventually, generalizations may

---

1. Of course, at least the clinical psychoanalysis theorists, if not all hermeneuts, reject Freud's metapsychology and all the propositions contained therein.

emerge: unconscious love usually underlies such unconscious hostility, projection is ultimately the mechanism that explains paranoid feelings. The point is that because interpretations on these models purport to be true, experience over time with many patients may enable psychoanalysts to build up a body of knowledge about human psychology.[2]

The interpretations-as-literary-criticism model is in an intermediate position between the models that contemplate the possibility of psychoanalytic knowledge and those that do not. On this model, interpretations do contend that they reveal true things about patients, but they are silent on causation. Thus we may learn, for example, that Joe feels unconscious love, hostility, and fear toward his boss, but not how these feelings are linked with each other causally. And typically, we may learn true things about patients but cannot arrive at causal generalizations about them.

Such a shortcoming would seem to lead to a rather cramped body of psychoanalytic knowledge. It is true that the psychoanalyst on this model is not limited to discovering things that happen to be true of any given patient. Psychoanalysts may discover correlations among different kinds of traits of personality; for example, they may find that orderly people tend to be stingy. They can never discover why, however. Thus, although psychoanalysis on this model permits generalizations, it permits no *causal* generalizations. But this is problematic precisely because it is the task of science to reveal causal regularities — laws — so that we can better understand and predict behavior.

2. Indeed, although Grünbaum assumes that hermeneuts like Klein reject the idea that psychoanalysis can become a science, I believe that this is untrue. Klein rejects, again, the metapsychology, but he seems to contemplate that clinical generalizations can be scientifically tested. See above.

The interpretations-as-literary-criticism model does thus offer the world some scientific knowledge, but not much—its yield is somewhat disappointing.

Most problematic in terms of the quality of knowledge that psychoanalysis offers the world is the story model and all of its variants.[3] Because, on this view, interpretations do not profess to arrive at the truth about patients, analysis will lose its distinctive character of revealing unconscious sources of behavior; analysts will no longer learn about human psychology in the course of doing therapy. Psychoanalysis ceases to be a science of human behavior.

If the story theorists are right, then, their view spells a sad loss to the human sciences. Indeed, consider an ambiguity that I have glossed over: between the idea that psychoanalytic interpretations about unconscious motivations are stories and the idea that the psychoanalytic view of the unconscious is a story. If the story model commits us to the position that any given interpretation about the unconscious is a story—that is, not true—then the story model may commit us to the position that there is no unconscious at all; at least it does not give us any reason for thinking there is. Put this way, the story model is as radical a view of psychoanalysis as there can be.

The implications of the metaphor model in some respects are more equivocal than those of the story model, in some respects just as troubling. The metaphor model does not deny that psychoanalytic interpretations are true but insists that they are true only metaphorically. We have understood statements about, say, unconscious motivation on this model to refer to behavioral regularities along with a promise for a future physio-

3. Although most of the variants are not subject to the strong version of the argument from patients' rejection of hermeneutic psychoanalysis, all agree that interpretations are stories that do not purport to tell the truth about at least the patient's past, including the immediate past.

logical explanation. As such, these statements do not yield much knowledge about human nature—but they do yield some.

On this model, moreover, although psychoanalysis may remain committed to the concept of an unconscious, that concept loses some of its distinctively psychoanalytic flavor. In essence, the unconscious is no longer a mental process, but rather a physiological one that we colorfully or expeditiously refer to in mentalistic terms. Much of the appeal and interest of psychoanalysis comes from its faith in the existence of an inaccessible part of the mind whose goings-on explain a great deal of our manifest behavior. Hermeneutic psychoanalysis on the metaphor model may negate this interest and appeal.

Beyond that, one wonders how properly to understand individual motivational statements about the unconscious on this model. For example, should an unconscious delusion bearing on a decision vitiate competency to make that decision as it would if the delusion were conscious? Given that the motivational explanation is only metaphorically true, the answer is unclear.

The problem is that we do not know if the things about unconsciousness talk that seem pertinent to competency are part of the rhetorical flourish of the talk, so to speak, or go to things that are literally true. An analogy may help. Talking about plants wishing to turn toward sunlight may be part of a theory about the likely direction plants will turn if placed in the center of a room; such a theory would be perfectly fine. But if this talk became part of a theory about whether plants can have other emotions, it would not be fine. The point is that we do not know whether the parts of unconsciousness talk that seem relevant to competency are more like the first case or the second. Whether unconscious delusions should vitiate competency is a vexed question in any case. The question becomes that much more difficult if we believe unconsciousness talk is all metaphorical.

On the metaphor model, then, the unconscious loses its distinctively psychoanalytic flavor, and talk of unconscious motivation has uncertain implications for other bodies of knowledge. I have confined myself thus far, however, to the implications of this model for psychoanalytic knowledge of the unconscious.

If we go beyond this arena, the implications of the metaphor model are more disturbing. For all psychoanalytic statements on this model are metaphorical: not only statements about unconscious feelings, but also those about conscious feelings and character traits—all psychological phenomena whatever. A statement about envious feelings, for example, has the same status as a statement about my petunia's wish for sunlight. The image of humankind that results is one of people with not only no unconscious, but also no feelings or character traits. Of course, the metaphor model does not deny that these things exist. It just is not positively committed to their existence—and it tells us nothing about them.

In short, the metaphor model, unlike the story model, does yield some knowledge about psychological phenomena. At least it yields truths about behavioral regularities. On the other hand, it fails to give us the knowledge that is perhaps most important to us: knowledge of our own minds. I sum up the consequences of the hermeneutic visions of psychoanalysis for psychoanalytic knowledge in table 7.1.

Hermeneutic psychoanalysis, in short—at least in certain versions—has some limitations. Here I point to some of their problematic implications for theory, clinical no less than metapsychologic.

Of course, hermeneutic psychoanalysis has many more facets than I have explored in this work, and a more complete account would scrutinize these as well. For example, the emphasis on narrative has led to interesting and variegated work

Table 7.1

	Clinical Psycho-analysis Model	Alterna-tive Meta-physics Model	Interpre-tations As-Literary-Criticism Model	Story Models	Metaphor Model
Implica-tions for psycho-analytic knowl-edge	Same as today	Same as today	No causal knowledge	No knowl-edge at all; psycho-analys is not even committed to existence of uncon-scious	Metaphoric knowledge only; no literal truths about not only uncon-scious, but also feel-ings and character traits

on the narrative impulse in human psychology—the ways our minds work. Similarly, some hermeneutic psychoanalysts have imported a more sophisticated, contemporary theory of the metaphysical underpinnings of psychoanalysis, and we should consider not only the intellectual payoff of their work, but also its practical import. In fact, asking how the several versions of hermeneutic psychoanalysis affect practice would itself be an interesting undertaking. It appears, for example, that herme-neutic analysts tend to be relational or intersubjective or both. Is that an accidental convergence of allegiances? or does her-meneutic psychoanalysis commit one to certain practical pre-cepts? How so?

In addition to these virtues of hermeneutic psychoanalysis, one would want also to study its potential deficiencies. For ex-ample, some analysts wonder whom hermeneutic analysts treat

—whether there is a class of patients who benefit from their methods. Others wonder about the implications of conceding that psychoanalysis is not a natural science.

The work done here recommends other avenues of research. For example, it would be an interesting project to take a typical analytic session and see if practitioners adhering to each of the five models of hermeneutic psychoanalysis employed different technical interventions. Do the models have an effect on practice? I noted above that hermeneutic psychoanalysis in general seems to be correlated with certain technical precepts; it might also be rewarding to see if the various models are correlated with different positions in theoretical and technical psychoanalysis and to try to tease out whether any correlation is an accident or a concomitant of features of the models' positions.

Finally, many of the claims in this book rest on empirical speculation, and it would be useful to conduct empirical research to see whether they are borne out. *Would* patients reject mere stories? Would they want to be told that that was all they were getting? Would they think their analysts under a duty to inform them? What would they feel if told their analyst subscribed to a new theory of truth or had views that threatened to become vulgarly relativistic? It should be possible to design a study to test these things.

Although this book does not address these questions, it does, I think, accomplish a number of significant things: it distinguishes among several versions of hermeneutic psychoanalysis, permitting a more careful evaluation of each; and it explores an important criticism of hermeneutic psychoanalysis, showing that it is applicable in different ways, if at all, to the versions of hermeneutic psychoanalysis.

The criticism, in its strongest form, is central. It says that at least the story model of hermeneutic psychoanalysis asks of patients something that is normatively objectionable—to believe nontruths—and that patients therefore will and should reject that model. For psychoanalysts to withhold this information from patients would be wrong, even if therapeutically efficacious. And to offer patients nontruths but not ask them to *believe* them would be to convert the therapy into nonanalysis. The lesson of this book, then, is that psychoanalytic interpretations must make claims to truth, and if they do not, they must be rejected.

The starkest example that helps make this case is that of implanted memories of sexual abuse. If the story version were correct, therapists would be justified in offering patients interpretations of early abuse that were not thought to be true—and not informing them of the fact. Any theory that justifies this is patently wrong. As we will see in the Appendix, even now some therapists speak of recovered memories of abuse as achieving narrative truth—and of that being good enough.

In addition to the strong kind of the argument from patient rejection, we saw that there were a number of other versions—and even various strands of the strong one itself. A sophisticated strand of the strong form of the argument from patient rejection said, not that patients would reject interpretations that did not purport to truth, but that they would reject interpretations that did not purport to truth of an adequate kind. This strand of the argument might apply against the alternative metaphysics model. There were problems with the strand, however, most notably that patients would probably not care about metaphysical theories; they might not have a choice anyway about what kind of truth they were offered; and we have seen no good reasons to think that the standard alternative metaphysicians' conception of truth is indeed problematic. I myself would need to have much more powerful arguments that the alternative metaphysics view is, say, vulgarly relativistic or dependent on an inadequate conception of truth in order to credit this strand of the argument—if we could even then get around the problem that patients just might not care one way or the other.

A weak version of the argument from patient rejection predicted that patients would reject forms of psychoanalysis that offered metaphoric or noncausal truths. This version is weak because it does not turn on a proscription—with moral force— not to believe nontruths. I do not completely endorse this form of the argument because it also turns on a weaker empirical supposition that patients will not like the form of analysis offered. I have my doubts about that. Moreover, possibly they should not care that the therapy may not then be analysis, so long as it works. Of course, absent evidence that it does work, they may well insist on a treatment whose success has a longer pedigree and is theoretically explainable.

Proponents of some versions of hermeneutic psychoanalysis may argue, however, that, whatever the consequences, their views are right—and I have not argued against any of these views on its own terms. But the point is that the consequences of these views are desperately unhappy; if they are right, psychoanalysis will self-destruct. This claim does not prove that these views of psychoanalysis are not right, but it at least gives us reason to hope they are not right; the alternative is dismal indeed.

Thus, an examination of hermeneutic psychoanalysis from the perspective of the patient has borne important fruit. While one might initially have wondered why we should care what patients think, the answer is clear: if I am right that analysts are under a duty of candor, then patients have the power to doom certain versions of psychoanalysis to nonexistence.

One may have lingering doubts that patients will exercise this power. Perhaps the analysts who hold the objectionable views will find nothing objectionable themselves about asking patients to believe mere stories. Perhaps they will not accept being under any kind of duty to disclose their beliefs. Still, analysts of other persuasions might inform the public, or the law might impose an obligation of disclosure. Even then, one might think that patients are so under the sway of transference that they will accept anything their analysts offer them.[4] If this is so—and one wonders whether transference is really that powerful at the beginning of a treatment—then we have bigger problems than objectionable forms of hermeneutic psychoanalysis to deal with. I intend in another work to address these kinds of ethical dimensions of the analyst/patient relationship. In any case, I can simply modify my argument to say that well-analyzed patients will (and all patients should) reject the story model of hermeneutic psychoanalysis.

Although this book, then, does not offer a comprehensive treatment of hermeneutic psychoanalysis, it does adduce some important distinctions and an important critique. Most crucial, it has tendered some reasons for believing that patients would not approve of the story model of hermeneutic psychoanalysis. In looking at hermeneutic psychoanalysis through the lens of what patients will think, we have come to some other insights as well, insights concerning the nature of metaphorical truth in this arena, the nature of psychoanalytic interpretation, the

4. Geha (1993b), in response to Sass's critique of his paper (1993), makes the opposite kind of argument: patients would reject many things if their analysts told them these things at the beginning of the analysis— e.g., that they would be led to believe an Oedipal story of themselves. It strikes me, however, that this is, first, probably untrue and, second, of a different order from being told their analysts are offering them non*truths*. There are moral proscriptions against believing false things, and patients would be right to reject mere stories in this sense. The same is decidedly not true of the Oedipal theory.

nature of psychoanalysis itself, and the implications of hermeneutic psychoanalysis for theory. The focus on patients, then, allows one to make important contributions to discussions not only of hermeneutic psychoanalysis, but also of issues that have long interested psychoanalysts of all stripes.

APPENDIX

THE REALITY OF THE STORY MODEL
AND THE APPLICABILITY OF THE
ARGUMENT TO ITS VARIANTS

The story model of hermeneutic psychoanalysis, as we have seen, seems most vulnerable to the strong form of the argument from patient rejection. But does anyone really hold the story model, or have I constructed a straw man for purposes of knocking it down in this book? A number of the hermeneuts I have submitted as story theorists hold equivocal positions; Steele and Viderman, for example, could also be alternative metaphysicians or interpretations-as-literary-criticism theorists. Spence and Loch, two prime story theorists, seem to hold that interpretations are true in some sense, even if not in another, so perhaps they, too, should be regarded as alternative metaphysicians. And although Sharpe does seem to be a story theorist, the need to answer his article alone seems scant justification for an entire book.

I shall respond to these objections in a number of ways. First, I will look at two main story theorists, Spence and Loch, to show either that they definitively are story theorists or that their version of psychoanalysis is vulnerable to the strong form of the argument from patient rejection even if they hold an alternative metaphysical conception of one form of the truth of interpretations: the argument applies even to this weaker, mixed story/alternative metaphysics model. Second, I will show from some of Spence's other writings that he unqualifiedly envisions analysts offering their patients falsehoods. In addition, I will show that many clinicians have appropriated Spence's notion of narrative truth to refer, essentially, to fantasies. Indeed, as noted above, the notion has come to be applied even in the false memory controversy (by Spence himself, among others), in which it refers to what are plainly false memories of abuse in the ordinary sense. Further, I point to indications that the best reading of Steele and Viderman is as story theorists and reiterate why we should think Sharpe without doubt a story theorist. Thus, the best interpretation discloses a number of analysts to be story theorists.

It is simply wrong that the target of the principal argument of this book is one lone writer—as noted, a number of hermeneuts seem to hold the problematic view. Indeed, as the reference to the false memory controversy implies, the general problem is more widespread. Although most therapists do not have postmodern philosophical reasons for the positions they take on truth, many seem to hold that the truth of their patients' memories and of their own reconstructions is unimportant. It *is* important, the immense difficulties of establishing it notwithstanding.

APPLICATION OF THE STRONG FORM OF THE ARGUMENT TO SPENCE AND LOCH

The argument that Spence and Loch are not really story theorists runs as follows. Let's look at Spence. Spence denies that interpretations are historically true, but he insists that they may be "narratively true." Perhaps, for Spence, historical truth refers to truth understood on a correspondence theory, whereas narrative truth refers to truth understood on a coherence theory. Is he not, then, most appropriately classified as an alternative metaphysics theorist, and not a story theorist at all? Spence does, after all, speak of narrative truth as the truth of being coherent and as involving the "fitting [of an] expression into the patient's life story" (1982a, 165). To be narratively true is to be true in the way that narratives are true—that is, all the parts of the story cohere.

This is an interesting interpretation of Spence. Yet it is, I think, finally implausible because Spence speaks as if there were such a thing as historical truth; it is just that interpretations rarely (if ever) achieve it. Thus Spence says that an interpretation's narrative truth may have priority over its historical truth—as if it may have historical truth. He also says that an interpretation's historical truth may, at times, be "relatively unimportant" (1982a, 276). Further, he speaks of interpretations' not having "clear correspondence with an event in the patient's life" (1982a, 275), again as if there were, at times, such correspondence. Even his analogy to art seems to contrast art forms with other statements on the ground that the latter may correspond with the external world.

The point is that, although a coherence theory of truth may be a plausible metaphysical position on the nature of truth, it is not plausible to think that some items in our ontology—at least some items in our ontology of the empirical world—are true on this theory, while others are true on a correspondence theory.[1] If it is the nature of truth that it consists of, say, correspondence with reality, then if, for instance, statements about elephants are true in this way, statements about giraffes can hardly be true in any other way. Maybe this is an overstatement; maybe mental events, for example, are relevantly different from physical events, so that it does make sense to think an alternative theory of truth applies to them. Even if so, however, Spence seems

1. We may, by contrast, have a different theory of truth for items not in the empirical world. Thus, in certain forms of mathematics, truth may be a function of an entity's role within a system.

to allow at times that there is such a thing as the truth of an interpretation of a patient's mental states on a correspondence theory, and it is wholly implausible that some of these interpretations should be true on this theory and others on another theory. My point is that if narrative truth, for Spence, is "truth according to a coherence theory," then there should be no such thing as historical truth. In other words, for a coherence theorist even historical truths are truths by virtue of their coherence with other items in the theory.

If this is right, theorists like Spence and Loch do hold that interpretations are mere stories that do not purport to be possibly true, and not that they are accounts true on a coherence theory of truth. The story model really does have adherents.

This reasoning seems compelling, yet it may nevertheless be wrong in its reading of these thinkers. Loch, in fact, explicitly says that his second kind of truth is truth on a theory other than the traditional—on a coherence or a pragmatic theory, for example. Either, then, the reasoning above is unconvincing or Loch is holding an incoherent position—as is Spence, on this interpretation. It remains true, however, that Spence and Loch could be alternative metaphysicians as regards interpretations and not vulnerable to the strong argument from patient rejection, even if open to the other criticism about the incoherence of their position.

But I now want to suggest that Spence and Loch, so long as they believe (as they do) that interpretations *can* be true—or, therefore, false—on a correspondence theory, remain subject to exactly the strong form of the argument from patient rejection even if they are alternative metaphysicians as to the truth of interpretations. That is, even if the pure form of the story model is not true as to them, they hold a mixed theory that is subject to exactly the same argument as is the story model.

There are several variations on this argument. Here is how

the first runs: If as a therapist you believe that your interpretations can be true or false on both a correspondence and, say, a coherence theory, then if a particular interpretation is true on a coherence theory but false on a correspondence theory, and you know or should know that your patient will believe it on a correspondence theory, you have an obligation to tell your patient. You have the same obligation, indeed, that you would have if the interpretation were false and there were no sense in which it was true. The argument against the story theory was designed for the latter case, but it applies equally when the patient will believe something is true in a particular way, and it is false in that way.

Although somewhat orthogonal to my central concern, an interesting question arises here. Suppose you believe your interpretations are true on a coherence theory (you are an alternative metaphysician), but you know or should know that your patient believes them on a correspondence theory. Do you have an obligation to disabuse your patient of her false belief? I believe not: it is only when you believe that the correspondence theory is a valid theory, and your interpretation is in fact false on that theory, that you are obliged to so inform your patient. When you believe, on the other hand, that the correspondence theory is false, incoherent, or otherwise wanting—that there is no such thing as correspondence truth—then you have no obligation to inform your patient of her misconceived view because she is not believing a false interpretation you have offered her as truth; the interpretation is not false.

But why should the analyst not have to disabuse the patient of her false or delusory view of truth as much as of her false or delusory interpretive belief? On the face of it, these situations seem to differ. It seems inappropriate for analysts to engage their patients in discussions about philosophical theories of truth. To do so would be outside the scope of one's implicit contract with the patient to do therapy, so to speak. It would no doubt be of little interest to most patients. The therapist is not an authority on theories of truth and does not know the patient's theory to be false, and it would not necessarily be generally conceded to be so; the therapist simply thinks it is. Perhaps most important, in offering an interpretation she knows to be false, the therapist is implicitly holding it out as true and inviting the patient to believe it. A conversational implicature, so to speak, of offering an interpretation to a patient is that one thinks it is or might be true. If one does not think this and fails to so inform the patient, one is being deceptive. By contrast, to present an interpretation to a patient is to make no implicit or explicit representations about the correct theory of truth. The analyst has no hand in bringing about the patient's (putatively) delusory belief and hence is under less of an obligation to set the record straight, that is, to disabuse the patient of her false belief.

If this argument is convincing, Spence and Loch — and those who might be called mixed story/alternative metaphysics theorists generally — are as subject to the strong form of the argument from patient rejection as pure story theorists generally.

Indeed, there is an argument that, even if these theorists do inform their patients of their theory, their patients still both will and should reject their interpretations. This second variation on the strong version of the argument from patient rejection as applied to this mixed view runs as follows: If interpretations can be true (or false) on both a correspondence theory and a coherence theory, patients both will and should want them to be true on the correspondence theory. The idea would be that they would not want to believe interpretations that are false on the correspondence theory.

But this contention seems to come to immediate grief as soon as we recall the metaphor theory. I suggested that patients might be perfectly happy to accept interpretations that were true metaphorically but false on a correspondence theory, on condition that they were informed of this fact.

There may be an important difference between these cases, however. We know what it is to believe a metaphoric truth without lapsing into believing a falsehood; one believes the (un-problematically) true things for which the metaphor is proxy and believes the residue as metaphor. Thus, it is easy to see how one can believe the relevant belief in the correct way, without lapsing into believing a falsehood. But do we even know what it means to believe some proposition p as a truth when it is true on a coherence theory but false on a correspondence theory? More important, is it possible to believe the proposition in the correct way, without lapsing into believing the relevant false belief? In short, it is hard to know what this even means, and, more important, whether people can do it.

The central difference between the metaphor theory and this mixed story/alternative metaphysics theory, then, is that patients are likely to hold false beliefs on the latter theory but not on the former. Yet I must point out a number of qualifications to this argument. First, I may be wrong in supposing that people will not be able to understand, in the correct way, a proposition that is true by coherence and false by correspondence—perhaps I simply cannot. Second, I may be supposing that patients will be tempted to believe the interpretation in the correspondence way because that is the way people's minds work—I have already considered the difficulties with this supposition in the discussion of the alternative metaphysics theory. Third, I may be implicitly supposing that a difference between this theory and the metaphor theory is that one gets some correspondence truth on that theory, and patients will want that. This at least needs argument. Fourth, this third argument may suppose that patients will care on what esoteric theory of truth an interpretation is true; so long as it is true on some respectable theory, they may not be in the least bit concerned.

I now want to suggest a third variation on the original argument, however, that will take up these last two concerns. Even if patients informed of the truth of interpretations on a coherence theory and of their falsity on a correspondence theory can make sense of this idea and avoid believing the interpretations in a false way, they still will and should want interpretations that are true on a correspondence theory, as they think that is a better theory of truth. The idea here is that the correspondence theory is more robust—and more psychologically satisfying to boot. Perhaps it is unavailable,[2] in which case patients must be content with what is available. But on the mixed theory, recall, it *is* available: it is a coherent notion that is true to the concept of truth, so to speak. Thus, patients will insist on *it*. Moreover, to the claim that patients likely will not care a whit about theories of truth, one may respond that the correspondence view is the commonsense view, and people will indeed care to have their expectations satisfied. (They may not want to have the conversation, but once they have it, as I argue they must, they will care about the outcome.) This variation of the argument, then, has some plausibility.

A fourth and final variation of the argument is the following: Patients will and should reject the mixed story/alternative metaphysics view because the kind of truth it offers is inadequate. This argument is easiest to make when the theory of truth offered is wanting by anyone's standards. Thus Loch sometimes speaks as if truth in his second sense is what sustains one—what makes one feel better. But that sounds not at all like truth, but rather like a cheering fiction. When this

2. This is the case on the alternative metaphysics view, so this argument is not available there.

argument is applied to more philosophically respectable theories of truth, it is problematic. In all, however, even if Spence and Loch hold this mixed story/alternative metaphysics theory, it remains true that their theory is subject to the strong form of the argument from patient rejection just as much as if it were a pure story view.

Spence and Others as Pure Story Theorists

I want now to offer further evidence from some of Spence's later writings (Loch's writings are far less voluminous) that he holds that interpretations may be unambiguously false on what he sees as truth in its paradigmatic sense.[3] He does so, of course, without indicating any awareness that it may therefore be problematic to offer these interpretations to patients for them to believe—at least without disclosure of their status.

Consider Spence's article "Narrative Truth and Theoretical Truth" (1982). Even the abstract of this article shows his position in no uncertain terms:

> Although Freud was inclined to believe that every effective reconstruction contained a "kernel of truth," it is by no means clear how this kernel can be identified and separated from the set of equally likely *fabrications* which make up a good part of the patient's life story. If we have no sure way of identifying historical truth, we may be seriously handicapped in our attempt to frame theoretical laws. What may be effective in a particular clinical in-

---

3. The reader will recall, however, that by the time of *The Freudian Metaphor*, Spence seems to have changed his position. Even there, he still uses the concept of narrative truth in the objectionable way.

stance (narrative truth) may not automatically generalize to the larger domain of clinical theory. (43)[4]

Plainly historical truth (the kernel of truth) here is identified with the truth. The contrast is with fabrications. At best, narrative truth is something that is therapeutically effective. As such, it does not lead to theory development because narrative truths are not, in essence, truths.

Spence makes the further claim in this article that "while narrative fit can be highly persuasive in the immediate clinical situation, its compelling quality does not necessarily indicate the presence of more general truths" (48). Thus, narrative truth (or fit) is here contrasted with truth. And so "true and false happenings (in the sense of historical truth) can both be smoothly fitted into a patient's developing story, and the goodness of fit cannot be used to distinguish the first from the second" (48–49). Again, historical truth refers to the truth, and something false can narratively fit. A few sentences later, narrative truth is contrasted with "historical *validity*" (48–49) (emphasis added), and Spence seems to suggest that aesthetic appeal might be more important than a "strict representation of reality" (48–49).

That historical truth, for Spence, is the truth and narrative truth something quite different, is clear from other statements as well. Consider his claim that "among the elements of the narrative account, some may be true in the sense of having actually happened (historical truth), and others may be true

4. Emphasis added. Spence makes this claim thus in the article: "It is by no means clear how the 'kernel of truth' can be identified and separated from the set of equally likely fabrications which make up the patient's life story, and if we have no sure way of identifying historical truth, we are seriously handicapped in our attempt to frame theoretical laws" (1982b, 51).

in a narrative sense, but false from the standpoint of history" (50). Historical truth is what actually happened, and narrative truths can be historically false. And again: "Implicit in the notion that narrative truth can be distinguished from historical truth is the conclusion that narrative truth can be based on nonhistorical premises" (60). Thus, interpretations may "work for nonfactual reasons" (60).

In short, "Narrative Truth and Theoretical Truth," written in the same year as *Narrative Truth and Historical Truth* and said to be an outgrowth of the earlier work, shows Spence believing that it is acceptable to offer patients interpretations that are false yet satisfying. Historical truth, for Spence, just *is* truth, and narrative truth is something effective, pleasing, useful to believe—but not quite truth.[5]

Spence continues the theme that narrative truth is not truth in his article "Narrative Appeal vs. Historical Validity" (1989). Once again, many interpretations offered to patients may be persuasive but false: "Some—indeed many—of our interpretations might easily be false; they nevertheless maintain their power to persuade because they contain the elements of narrative persuasion plus (sometimes) a soupçon of historical truth" (518). An interpretation, if supplied "with the right amount of conviction, . . . will be taken as true—whether or not it is" (519). Indeed, analysts may ask, "How many *delusions*, masquerading as interpretations, are we peddling every day?" (519) (emphasis added).

Later Spence continues to align narrative truth with persuasive appeal, the power to heal—and to contrast it with truth: "Much of the time, I would suggest, what passes for recon-

5. Indeed, Spence's 1983 article is called "Narrative Persuasion" rather than "Narrative Truth." Perhaps the change in terminology is significant. See Spence (1983).

struction is largely narrative truth; it has its own persuasive appeal and therapeutic clout, but does not necessarily represent a true recovery or faithful reworking of the past" (520). And so the therapist's own narrative truth "has the power to heal. But this should be kept separate from the true recovery of the past" (520). And again, an interpretation may have a good chance to "succeed"—"but it may be entirely *delusional*" (521) (emphasis added).

Spence's article "Narrative Truth and Putative Child Abuse" (1994) leaves no doubt that narrative truths are not true: a false memory of early child abuse may be deemed narratively true. Thus "memories of early child abuse can be read in at least two distinct ways—as true accounts of an unspeakable event or as metaphors for a wide range of boundary violations which belong to both past and present" (289) (from abstract). "In the hands of a master craftsman, narrative truth can paper over any number of logical and scientific lapses" (293).

Spence discusses many of the ways these memories can go wrong; for example, original memories can be "tampered with" (294). And "even though the adult witness or patient knows the difference between fact and fantasy, he or she is in no position to partition the retrieved memory into initial observations—historical truth—and the subsequent leveling and sharpening of the remembering process which produces narrative truth" (295). False memories of abuse may be narratively true. Narrative truth is something that persuades, that seems true—but is not.

This brief review of some of Spence's work subsequent to *Narrative Truth and Historical Truth* illustrates beyond a doubt that he is not referring to two different literal versions of truth, like a correspondence and a coherence version (if we can even make sense of the notion of two coexisting versions of truth), but rather is holding that historical truth just is truth, full stop, and narrative truth is something that does not fully deserve that name. Spence, in his writing, seems to identify historical truth with truth—and to contrast truth with narrative truth. If this is so, the fourth variation of the argument above may be available as against Spence: patients will and should reject interpretations that are only narratively true because narrative truth does not fully deserve to be thought of as truth. At the very least, Spence seems aware that analysts may offer patients interpretations that are not true, at least by a correspondence theory—indeed, that are fantasies or delusions under this theory; yet he evinces no awareness that this is problematic—and that analysts might be under an obligation to inform their patients of this fact.

My interpretation of Spence is bolstered by the fact that many therapists have read his concept of narrative truth to mean fantasy in the context of false memories of child abuse. For example, in "Historical Versus Narrative Truth: Clarifying the Role of Exogenous Trauma in the Etiology of MPD [multiple personality disorder] and its Variants" (1989), George Ganaway speaks of the concept of narrative truth in the false memory context: "As in psychodynamic psychotherapy with other disorders [than MPD], the reconstruction of memory is subject to so much defensive distortion as to require the label of narrative truth, or psychical reality, as opposed to historical truth, or fact-based reality (Spence, 1982)" (1989, 210).[6]

Michael I. Good makes the same identification in "The Reconstruction of Early Childhood Trauma: Fantasy, Reality, and

6. Spence himself correctly warns against a too-fast identification of narrative truth with psychical reality and historical truth with material reality, in part on the ground that there can be fact-based no less than fantasy-based descriptions of psychic reality no less than of material reality. See "Narrative Truth and Theoretical Truth" (1982b, 50). It remains true that insofar as one is discussing material reality—as one is in the abuse context—to identify narrative truth with psychic reality is to identify it as fantasy.

Verification" (1994). He speaks of the "contrasting perspectives of historical (actual, material) truth as opposed to narrative (intrapsychic) truth in psychoanalytic reconstruction" (1994, 79) (in abstract). Similarly, in "The Reconstruction of a Repressed Sexual Molestation Fifty Years Later" (1995), Milton Viederman discusses the "current public concern about childhood molestation and abuse," which "has fueled the debate in psychoanalysis about historical versus narrative truth" (1995, 1169) (in abstract). The narrative theory in its purest form, according to Viederman, insists "that truthfulness regarding early experience is not the domain of psychoanalysis properly speaking and only meaning and coherence are pertinent" (1995, 1170).

In "A Narrative Approach to 'Repressed Memories'" (1995), Theodore Sarbin transparently uses Spence's concepts of narrative and historical truth to refer to the difference between fantasy and reality; therapy may be concerned with fantasies that resonate with the patient, but courts of law must be concerned with the facts—historical truth: "In the forensic setting, the narrative truth that flows from the recovery of repressed memories is not enough; historical truth is required. I discuss the role of imagining in the construction of rememberings and the difficulties in establishing the historical truth of any remembering" (51) (in abstract). Thus, "until recently, therapists could be satisfied when they helped their clients achieve a formulation of self that met the criteria for narrative truth; now, therapists must keep in mind that the legal system may require them to assist in establishing historical truth because their clients or the alleged victimizers may appeal to the courts to legitimize their respective narratives" (52). Sarbin identifies the distinction between narrative truth and historical truth with that between "therapeutic coherence and forensic coherence" (61). If called on to be a witness, "the therapist must recognize that narrative truth, or therapeutic coherence, although an acceptable goal in reconstructing a failing self-narrative, may not be acceptable in the forensic context. For the triers of fact, historical truth is paramount" (61). That narrative truth is not, for Sarbin, truth becomes apparent when he states that recovered memories of sexual abuse might better be labeled *"believed-in imaginings"* (64).

Finally, Theodore Shapiro, in "On Reminiscences" (1993), once again suggests that a focus on narrative truth means a diminution in the importance of remembering—which implies that one recovers truth: "Recently, psychoanalysts have focused on narrative truth and hermeneutics with diminished attention to the role of remembering in symptom formation and treatment" (395)(in abstract). Shapiro decries the idea of analysts becoming "poets of the couch" (408).

From this brief review of the use made of Spence's notion of narrative truth by a number of contemporary writers, it should be obvious that narrative truth is essentially a fantasy that resonates with the patient. A number of the commentators I have quoted from are troubled by the idea that narrative truth is sufficient unto itself, although some, at least for purposes of the therapeutic context, are quite happy with it. In any case, the argument against the story model of hermeneutic psychoanalysis is an argument against any version of therapy that does not aim at the truth, whether this posture is motivated by a postmodern turn in theory or not. This, of course, is not to imply that achieving truth or knowing what to do therapeutically when it is unclear is an easy matter.

The argument of this book against the story model, then, is not directed at a lone article, namely, Sharpe's "Mirrors, Lamps, Organisms and Texts." I do think it is clear that Sharpe is a story theorist. Recall his thesis about the indeterminacy of psychoanalytic interpretations. And if nothing else, his conclusions on why interpretations are efficacious leave no doubt as to his view: interpretations are effective not because they are true—indeed, no "sense" can be attached to this notion—but as placebos. In the same way, an ideological or religious conversion may be enormously satisfying and helpful without being "a conversion to a set of true doctrines" (1988, 196).

A case can likewise be made that both Steele and Viderman are story theorists, even though they could also conceivably be alternative metaphysicians or interpretations-as-literary-criticism theorists. For instance, among other things, Steele says that "truth is not the correct statement of a historical fact" (1979, 398)—a rather storylike thing to say. Viderman states, among other things, that interpretations are not either true or false—they "cannot be contained in an alternative binary proposition of truth or untruth" (1979, 266). Another very storylike thing to say. Thus, there is evidence that at least Sharpe, Steele, Viderman, Loch, and Spence—not to mention those clinicians who have latched onto the concept of narrative truth in thinking about their practices—are story theorists. The story theory is fully deserving of an extended critique. It is not a straw man. Indeed, so much is the theory not a straw man that some think it obviously and unproblematically true.

I entered a caution in the Introduction to this book that the story theorists may have distorted the hermeneutic position. Nevertheless, they are usefully thought of as hermeneuts for my purposes, inasmuch as that is how they are classified in psychoanalytic circles. Furthermore, they sound a lot like the other hermeneuts. This may suggest that the truly hermeneutic position threatens to become an implausible story position if care is not exercised. It may also be important when exploring whether other, more classically hermeneutic theorists are vulnerable to the more sophisticated form of the argument from patient rejection.

References

Aldrich, Virgil. 1958. Pictorial meaning, picture-thinking, and Wittgenstein's theory of aspects. *Mind* 62:70–79.

Aristotle. 1984. *Rhetoric*. Translated by W. Rhys Roberts. *Poetics*. Translated by Ingram Bywater. 1st ed. New York: Modern Library.

Aronson, Gerald. 1992. Review of *Freud Reappraised: A Fresh Look at Psychoanalytic Theory*, by Robert Holt. *International Review of Psychoanalysis* 19:242–45.

Atwood, George E., and Robert D. Stolorow. 1984. *Structures of subjectivity: Explorations in psychoanalytic phenomenology*. Hillsdale, N.J.: Analytic Press.

Balkin Jack, personal communication.

Beardsley, Monroe C. 1958. *Aesthetics*. New York: Harcourt, Brace.

Black, Max. 1954. Metaphor. *Proceedings of the Aristotelian Society* 55:273–94.

———. 1962. *Models and metaphors*. Ithaca, N.Y.: Cornell University Press.

———. 1979. How metaphors work: A reply to Donald Davidson. In *Metaphor and thought*, edited by Andrew Ortony. New York: Cambridge University Press.

———. 1993. More about metaphor. In *Metaphor and thought*, 2d ed., edited by Andrew Ortony. New York: Cambridge University Press.

Blight, James. 1981. Must psychoanalysis retreat to hermeneutics? Psychoanalytic theory in the light of Popper's evolutionary epistemology. *Psychoanalysis and Contemporary Thought* 4:147–205.

Bruner, Jerome. 1990. *Acts of Meaning*. Cambridge: Harvard University Press.

Cioffi, Frank. 1988. Exegetical myth-making in Grunbaum's indictment of Popper and exoneration of Freud. In *Mind, psychoanalysis and science*, edited by Peter Clark and Crispin Wright. New York: Blackwell.

Cohen, Ted. 1979. Metaphor and the cultivation of intimacy. In *On metaphor*, edited by Sheldon Sacks. Chicago: University of Chicago Press.

Davidson, Donald. 1978. What metaphors mean. In *On metaphor*, edited by Sheldon Sacks. Chicago: University of Chicago Press.

Davis, Paul. N.d. Metaphor and truth: A brief survey (paper on file with author).

Draeger, John H. 1983. The problem of truth in psychotherapy: A phenomenological approach to treatment. *Social Science and Medicine* 17:371-78.

Eagle, Morris. 1980. Psychoanalytic interpretations: Veridicality and therapeutic effectiveness. *Nous* 14:405-25.

———. 1984. *Recent developments in psychoanalysis: A critical evaluation.* New York: McGraw-Hill.

Edelson, Marshall. 1985. The hermeneutic turn and the single case study in psychoanalysis. *Psychoanalysis and Contemporary Thought* 8:567-614.

Fast, Irene. 1993. Are narrative structures basic to mental organization? A tentative yes. Paper presented at APA, Division 39, Spring meeting.

Fingarette, Herbert. 1963. Meaning and being. In *The self in transformation: Psychoanalysis, philosophy, and the life of the spirit.* New York: Basic Books.

Fisher, David J. 1990. Philosophical and psychoanalytic hermeneutics: Towards a play of interpretations (paper on file with author).

Freeman, Mark. 1985. Psychoanalytic narration and the problem of historical knowledge. *Psychoanalysis and Contemporary Thought* 8:133-82.

Friedlander, Saul. 1992. *Probing the limits of representation.* Cambridge: Harvard University Press.

Gadamer, Hans Georg. 1975. *Truth and method.* New York: Crossroad.

Ganaway, George K. 1989. Historical versus narrative truth: Clarifying the role of exogenous trauma in the etiology of MPD and its variants. *Dissociation* 2:205-20.

Geha, Richard E. 1993a. Transferred fictions. *Psychoanalytic Dialogues* 3:209-43.

———. 1993b. On the "mere" fictions of psychoanalysis: Reply to Sass. *Psychoanalytic Dialogues* 3:255-66.

Good, Michael I. 1994. The reconstruction of early childhood trauma: Fantasy, reality, and verification. *Journal of the American Psychoanalytic Association* 42:79-101.

Goodman, Nelson. 1968. *Languages of art.* Indianapolis: Bobbs-Merrill.

———. 1978. *Ways of worldmaking.* Indianapolis: Hackett Publishing.

———. 1979. Metaphor as moonlighting. In *Metaphor and thought*, edited by Andrew Ortony. New York: Cambridge University Press.

Grünbaum, Adolf. 1984. *The foundations of psychoanalysis: A philosophical critique.* Berkeley: University of California Press.

———. 1988. Précis of the foundations of psychoanalysis: A philosophical critique. In *Mind, psychoanalysis and science,* edited by Peter Clark and Crispin Wright. New York: Blackwell.

Habermas, Jürgen. 1971. *Knowledge and human interests,* translated by Jeremy J. Shapiro. Boston: Beacon Press.

———. 1975. *Legitimation crisis.* Boston: Beacon Press.

Hanly, Margaret F. 1996. Narrative, now and then: A critical realist approach. *International Journal of Psychoanalysis* 77:445-57.

Henle, Paul. 1958. Metaphor. In *Language, thought, and culture,* edited by Paul Henle. Ann Arbor: University of Michigan Press.

Hester, Marcus B. 1966. Metaphor and aspect seeing. *Journal of Aesthetics and Art Criticism* 25:205-12.

Hinman, Lawrence M. 1990. *Quid facti* or *quid juris?* The fundamental ambiguity of Gadamer's understanding of hermeneutics. *Philosophy and Phenomenological Research* 40:512-35.

Hobbes, Thomas. 1968. *Leviathan.* Harmondsworth: Penguin.

Holt, Robert R. 1976. Drive or wish? A reconsideration of the psychoanalytic theory of motivation. In *Psychology versus metapsychology,* edited by Merton Gill. New York: International Universities Press.

Holzman, Philip S. 1976. Theoretical models and the treatment of the schizophrenias. *Psychological Issues* 9:134-57.

———. 1985. Psychoanalysis: Is the therapy destroying the science? *Journal of the American Psychoanalytic Association* 33:725-70.

Holzman, Philip S., and Gerald Aronson. 1992. Psychoanalysis and its neighboring sciences: Paradigms and opportunities. *Journal of the American Psychoanalytic Association* 40:63-88.

Horner, Elinor A. 1995. The meeting of two narratives. *Clinical Social Work Journal* 23:9-19.

How, Alan R. 1985. A case of creative misreading: Habermas's evaluation of Gadamer's hermeneutics. *Journal of the British Society for Phenomenology* 16:132-44.

Ingram, David. 1984. Hermeneutics and truth. *Journal of the British Society for Phenomenology* 15:62-78.

Inwood, Michael J. 1995. Hermeneutics. In *Oxford companion to philosophy.* New York: Oxford University Press.

Jay, Martin. 1982. Should intellectual history take a linguistic turn? Reflections on the Habermas-Gadamer debate. In *Modern European intel-*

lectual history: Reappraisals and new perspectives, edited by Dominick LaCapra and Steven L. Kaplan. Ithaca: Cornell University Press.

———. 1992. Of plots, witnesses, and judgments. In *Probing the Limits of Representation,* edited by Saul Friedlander. Cambridge: Harvard University Press.

Johnson, Mark. 1981. Introduction: Metaphor in the philosophical tradition. In *Philosophical perspectives on metaphor,* edited by Mark Johnson. Minneapolis: University of Minnesota Press.

Khatchadourian, Haig. 1968. Metaphor. *British Journal of Aesthetics* 8:227–41.

Klein, George S. 1976a. *Psychoanalytic theory: An exploration of essentials.* New York: International Universities Press.

———. 1976b. Freud's two theories of sexuality. In *Psychology versus metapsychology,* edited by Merton M. Gill and Philip S. Holzman. New York: International Universities Press.

Lakoff, George. 1987. *Women, fire, and dangerous things: What categories reveal about the mind.* Chicago: University of Chicago Press.

Lakoff, George, and Mark Johnson. 1980a. *Metaphors we live by.* Chicago: University of Chicago Press.

———. 1980b. Conceptual metaphor in everyday language. *Journal of Philosophy* 77:453–86.

Levin, Samuel R. 1993. Language, concepts, and worlds: Three domains of metaphor. In *Metaphor and thought,* 2d ed., edited by Andrew Ortony. New York: Cambridge University Press.

Loch, Wolfgang. 1977. Some comments on the subject of psychoanalysis and truth. In *Thought, consciousness and reality,* edited by Joseph Smith. New Haven: Yale University Press.

Locke, John. 1721. *An essay concerning human understanding.* London: Printed for A. Churchill and A. Manship.

Loewenstein, Era A. 1991. Psychoanalytic life history: Is coherence, continuity, and aesthetic appeal necessary? *Psychoanalysis and Contemporary Thought* 14:3–28.

McCarthy, Thomas. 1978. *The critical theory of Jürgen Habermas.* Cambridge: MIT Press.

Mendelson, Jack. 1979. The Habermas-Gadamer debate. *New German Critique* 18:44–73.

Moore, Michael. 1989. The interpretive turn in modern theory: A turn for the worse? *Stanford Law Review* 41:871–957.

Morgan, Jerry L. 1993. Observations on the pragmatics of metaphor. In

Metaphor and thought, 2d ed., edited by Andrew Ortony. New York: Cambridge University Press.

Morse, Stephen. 1982. Failed explanations and criminal responsibility: Experts and the unconscious. *Virginia Law Review* 68:971–1084.

Novick, Peter. 1988. *That noble dream: The "objectivity question" and the American historical profession.* Cambridge: Cambridge University Press.

Nuyen, A. T. 1992. Rorty's hermeneutics and the problem of relativism. *Man and World* 25:69–78.

Ortony, Andrew. 1993. Metaphor, language, and thought. In *Metaphor and thought,* 2d ed., edited by Andrew Ortony. New York: Cambridge University Press.

Phillips, James. 1987. Grunbaum on hermeneutics. *Psychoanalysis and Contemporary Thought* 10:585–626.

————. 1991. Hermeneutics in psychoanalysis: Review and reconsideration. *Psychoanalysis and Contemporary Thought* 14:371–424.

Radnitzky, Gerard. 1973. *Contemporary schools of metascience,* 3d ed. Chicago: Henry Regnery.

Ricoeur, Paul. 1970. *Freud and philosophy: An essay on interpretation,* translated by Denis Savage. New Haven: Yale University Press.

————. 1978. The metaphorical process as cognition, imagination, and feeling. In *On Metaphor,* edited by Sheldon Sacks. Chicago: University of Chicago Press.

————. 1981. *Hermeneutics and the human sciences: Essays on language, action and interpretation,* edited and translated by John B. Thompson. Cambridge: Cambridge University Press.

Rorty, Richard. 1979. *Philosophy and the mirror of nature.* Princeton: Princeton University Press.

Rothberg, Donald J. 1986. Gadamer, Rorty, hermeneutics, and truth: A response to Warnke. *Inquiry* 29:355–61.

Rubovits-Seitz, Philip. 1986. Clinical interpretation, hermeneutics, and the problem of validation. *Psychoanalysis and Contemporary Thought* 9:3–42.

Sarbin, Theodore R. 1995. A narrative approach to "repressed memories." *Journal of Narrative & Life History* 5:51–66.

Sass, Louis A. 1993. Psychoanalysis as "conversation" and as "fiction": Commentary on Charles Spezzano's "A relational model of inquiry and truth" and Richard Geha's "Transferred fictions." *Psychoanalytic Dialogues* 3:245–53.

Sass, Louis A., and Robert L. Woolfolk. 1988. Psychoanalysis and the hermeneutic turn: A critique of narrative truth and historical truth. *Journal of the American Psychoanalytic Association* 36:429–54.

Schafer, Roy. 1976. *A new language for psychoanalysis.* New Haven: Yale University Press.

———. 1980. Action and narration in psychoanalysis. *New Literary History* 12:61–85.

———. 1983. *The analytic attitude.* New York: Basic Books.

———. 1984. Misconceiving historiography and psychoanalysis as art. *International Forum for Psychoanalysis* 1:363–72.

———. 1992. *Retelling a life.* New York: Basic Books.

Searle, John R. 1979. *Expression and meaning.* New York: Cambridge University Press.

Shapiro, Theodore. 1993. On reminiscences. *Journal of the American Psychoanalytic Association* 41:395–421.

Sharpe, Robert. 1988. Mirrors, lamps, organisms and texts. In *Mind, psychoanalysis and science,* edited by Peter Clark and Crispin Wright. New York: Blackwell.

Spence, Donald P. 1976. Clinical interpretation: Some comments on the nature of the evidence. *Psychoanalysis and Contemporary Science* 5:367–88.

———. 1982a. *Narrative truth and historical truth.* New York: W. W. Norton.

———. 1982b. Narrative truth and theoretical truth. *Psychoanalytic Quarterly* 51:43–69.

———. 1983. Narrative persuasion. *Psychoanalysis and Contemporary Thought* 6:457–81.

———. 1987. *The Freudian metaphor: Toward paradigm change in psychoanalysis.* New York: W. W. Norton.

———. 1989. Narrative appeal vs. historical validity. *Contemporary Psychoanalysis* 25:517–24.

———. 1994. Narrative truth and putative child abuse. *International Journal of Clinical and Experimental Hypnosis* 42:289–303.

Spezzano, Charles. 1993. A relational model of inquiry and truth: The place of psychoanalysis in human conversation. *Psychoanalytic Dialogues* 3:177–208.

Steele, Robert S. 1979. Psychoanalysis and hermeneutics. *International Review of Psycho-Analysis* 6:389–411.

Strenger, Carlo. 1991. *Between hermeneutics and science: An essay on the epistemology of psychoanalysis.* Madison, Conn.: International Universities Press.

Terwee, Sybe. 1987. Grünbaum's foundations of psychoanalysis. *Psychoanalysis and Contemporary Thought* 10:347–72.

Thompson, John B. 1996. Hermeneutics. In *The social science encyclopedia,* 2d ed., edited by Adam Kuper and Jessica Kuper. New York: Routledge.

Viderman, Serge. 1979. The analytic space: Meaning and problems. *Psychoanalytic Quarterly* 48:257–291.

Viederman, Milton. 1995. The reconstruction of a repressed sexual molestation fifty years later. *Journal of the American Psychoanalytic Association* 43:1169–95.

Warner, Martin. 1973. Black's metaphors. *British Journal of Aesthetics* 13:367–72.

Warnke, Georgia. 1987. *Gadamer: Hermeneutics, tradition, and reason.* Stanford: Stanford University Press.

Wellmer, Albrecht. 1993. Truth, contingency, and modernity. *Modern Philology* 90:109–24.

Index

Alternative metaphysics model: definition of, 11, 81; and argument from patient rejection, 14, 163–75; and argument from patient rejection (sophisticated form), 14, 167, 168–69, 168n, 171–74, 227–28; and truth, 14, 81, 100, 114, 115–16, 135n, 163, 164, 164n, 166–68, 168–70n, 172, 182, 220–21; and Steele, 97, 97n, 231, 246; and Viderman, 98, 231, 246; and hermeneutic psychoanalysis, 99–107, 119; and Schafer, 100–3, 164n, 175; and Fingarette, 103–7, 164n; and Geha, 107n; and hermeneutics, 168, 168–70n; metaphor model compared to, 175; and psychoanalytic theory, 220–21, 225; and story model, 231, 236, 237; and Spence, 232–33, 234

Analysands. *See* Patients

Argument from patient rejection: and psychoanalysts, viii–ix, 121; and story model, viii, 11–13, 14, 99, 115n, 120–21, 123–39, 145–48, 147, 164–66, 226, 229; and hermeneutic psychoanalysis, 1, 11–12n; and truth, 2, 13, 14, 80, 121, 127–30, 134, 135–39, 164–65, 167–68; structure of, 11–13, 120–21; and alternative

metaphysics model, 14, 163–75; and clinical psychoanalysis model, 14, 83n, 163–65, 174; and mixed hermeneutics, 18, 18n; and interpretations-as-literary-criticism model, 120n, 194–206; examples supporting, 129–34; and unconscious, 130n; and metaphor model, 133, 175–94

Argument from patient rejection (sophisticated form): cogency of, 12n; and alternative metaphysics model, 14, 167, 168–69, 168n, 171–74, 227–28; and story model, 120, 207; and Habermas, 173n

Argument from patient rejection (strong form): cogency of, 12n; and metaphor model, 14–15, 183; and interpretations-as-literary-criticism model, 15; normative component of, 15n; and story model, 120, 207, 222n, 231, 232–39; and Habermas, 173n; and Loch, 232, 234, 236, 239; and Spence, 232–39

Argument from patient rejection (weak form): cogency of, 12n, 228; and metaphor model, 14, 183, 193, 207, 210, 213–14, 215; and interpretations-as-literary-criticism model, 15, 194–95, 206,

Argument (weak form) (*cont.*)
207, 210, 214; merit of, 15–16;
normative component of, 15n;
and story model, 120, 162n, 206,
209, 212n; and hermeneutic
psychoanalysis, 208–9, 219; and
conceptual gambit, 209–17; and
empirical gambit, 217–19
Aronson, Gerald, 12n
As-if views: and psychoanalysts,
149–52; belief version of, 150–
53, 156n, 158; and placebo effect,
150–51, 154; imagine-and-react
version of, 153–58, 210, 213, 216;
and interpretations-as-literary-
criticism model, 203n

Beardsley, Monroe C., 175n
Behaviorism, 5, 137n, 172, 191, 192
Black, Max, 176–77n, 178n
Bruner, Jerome, 9n

Causes: and hermeneutic psychoanalysis, 12n, 19; and interpretation, 15, 196, 197, 198–203, 200n,
205, 206; and Steele, 59, 60,
61; and metaphor model, 175;
and interpretations-as-literary-
criticism model, 194, 195–96,
195n, 221–22; and meaning,
196–99, 196n, 201, 205
Cioffi, Frank, 73n
Clinical psychoanalysis model:
definition of, 11, 81; and argument from patient rejection, 14,
83n, 163–65, 174; and hermeneutic psychoanalysis, 82–85,
83n; and interpretation, 86, 114,
163, 164, 182, 220–21; and Steele,
97n; metaphor model compared

to, 175; and psychoanalytic
theory, 220–21, 220n, 225
Clinical theory, 20, 22–25, 26, 26n
Cohen, Ted, 176n
Collingwood, R. G., 48
Consciousness, 6, 7
Constructivism, 42–43, 101

Davidson, Donald, 195n
Davis, Paul, 176n
Dilthey, Wilhelm, 3

Eagle, Morris, 12n, 94, 95, 119
Edelson, Marshall, 12n

False memories, 242, 243–44. *See
also* Sexual abuse memories
Fast, Irene, 9, 9n
Fingarette, Herbert: and hermeneutic psychoanalysis, 49–59,
54n; and interpretation, 49, 53,
54, 55, 56–57, 104, 105n, 106–7,
116; and alternative metaphysics
model, 103–7, 164n; and goals-
for-future view, 159, 159n
Fisher, David James, 6–7, 7n
Freeman, Mark, 80n, 119
Freidlander, Saul, 169n
Freud, Sigmund: and psychoanalysis as natural science, 5–6n;
Klein on, 22, 25n; Schafer on,
26, 27, 34–35, 39, 47; Fingarette
on, 50, 51, 55, 58; Steele on,
59, 61, 113; Viderman on, 62–
63; Loch on, 65; Spence on,
69, 73, 74, 90, 92, 109n, 239;
Grünbaum on, 73n; Sharpe on,
75–76, 78; and metapsychology,
82; and hermeneutic psychoanalysis, 116; and definition of

psychoanalysis, 211; and clinical psychoanalysis model, 220n

Gadamer, Hans Georg, 4, 16, 169-70n
Ganaway, George, 243
Garet, Ronald, 153-54n, 185n
Geha, Richard, 47-48, 102n, 107n, 229n
Glover, Edward, 68
Goals-for-future view, 158-62, 159n, 161n, 210, 213, 214
Good, Michael I., 243-44
Grünbaum, Adolf, 12n, 13n, 73n, 211, 221n

Habermas, Jürgen, 4, 6-7, 18, 169n, 170n, 172-73n
Heidegger, Martin, 3-4
Hermeneutic psychoanalysis: models of, vii-viii, 10-11, 13, 16, 19, 114-19; and patients, viii-ix, 124n, 229-30; and argument from patient rejection, 1, 11-12n; characterizations of, 5, 6-8, 7n; and differences among hermeneuts, 8-9, 18, 80, 80n, 115n, 118-19; criticisms of, 12-13n, 226-27; and metaphysics, 88; and interpretation, 116-18; and argument from patient rejection (weak form), 208-9, 219; effectiveness of, 218-19; limitations of, 224, 225-26; and narratives, 224-25. *See also specific models and psychoanalysts*
Hermeneutics: and language, 1, 19, 118-19; categories of, 2, 81, 117-18; history of, 2-6, 2n; and interpretation, 2-3, 4, 6n, 8;

hermeneutic circle, 4, 7, 47; and natural sciences, 5, 7n, 8; hermeneutic spiral, 8; and truth, 16-17, 168-70n; mixed hermeneutics, 18, 18n; and meaning, 19, 204-5n; and Schafer, 36-37; and Steele, 61; and alternative metaphysics model, 168, 168-70n
Hinman, Lawrence M., 170n
Historical truth: and sexual abuse memories, viii, 145; and narrative truth, 9; and Loch, 64, 64n, 65, 95; and Spence, 66-69, 69n, 70n, 71, 72, 75, 90-93, 90n, 108-9, 109n, 232-33, 234, 239-43, 240n; and Sharpe, 69n; and story model, 86; and Viderman, 98
Holt, Robert R., 83n
Holzman, Philip S., 12-13n, 83n
Homer, 3
How, Alan R., 169n
Human sciences, 3, 5, 6, 8, 12n, 16, 27

Idealism, 135, 136, 137, 172
Imagine-and-react view, 153-58, 157n, 210, 213, 216
Ingram, David, 170n
Insight: and Fingarette, 50, 55-56, 58; and psychoanalysts, 122-23; and imagine-and-react view, 155, 156, 157, 157n, 158, 210, 213; and metaphor model, 183, 190; Freud on, 211; and psychoanalysis, 212
Interpretation: and hermeneutics, 2-3, 4, 6n, 8; and psychoanalysis, 5-6, 10, 122, 212-13; and

Interpretation (*cont.*)
meaning, 10–11, 204–5n; and
truth, 10, 13, 14, 80, 93, 122,
123–27, 127n, 135–49, 151–52,
227, 234–35, 238; and causes, 15,
196, 197, 198–203, 200n, 205,
206; and Schafer, 30, 32–33, 36,
46, 47, 76, 84–85, 102–3, 110;
and Fingarette, 49, 53, 54, 55,
56–57, 104, 105n, 106–7, 116;
and Steele, 59, 59n, 60, 61–
62, 96, 96–97n, 110, 113, 116;
and Viderman, 62–64, 70, 72,
90, 97–98, 112, 112–13n; and
Loch, 64n, 65, 95–96, 234; and
Spence, 66–75, 90–95, 90n,
109n, 110, 233–34, 239, 241, 243;
and psychoanalysts, 68, 121, 122,
140, 161; and Sharpe, 75–79, 110,
116, 245–46; and Klein, 83–84;
and story model, 85–87, 87–88n,
95n, 115–16, 121n, 123–24, 134,
134n, 135–41, 164–65, 170, 182,
222; and clinical psychoanalysis
model, 86, 114, 163, 164, 182,
220–21; and alternative metaphysics model, 100, 114, 115, 163,
164, 166–68, 182, 220–21, 237;
and metaphor model, 108, 114–
15, 175, 181, 182, 189–90, 222,
236–37; and interpretations-as-
literary-criticism model, 111,
114, 120n, 194, 195–96, 205, 221;
and hermeneutic psychoanalysis, 116–18; and placebo effect,
141–42, 142n, 145; and as-if
views, 149, 151, 152–53, 154; and
imagine-and-react view, 157;
and goals-for-future view, 159n,

161; comparison of dreams and
novels, 196–201
Interpretations-as-literary-criticism model: definition of, 11,
82; and argument from patient
rejection (strong form), 15; and
argument from patient rejection
(weak form), 15, 194–95, 206,
207, 210, 214; and Steele, 97,
113–14, 231, 246; and Viderman,
98, 111–14, 112–13n, 231, 246;
and hermeneutic psychoanalysis, 110–14; and argument from
patient rejection, 120n, 194–
206; and causes, 194, 195–96,
195n, 221–22; and as-if views,
203n; and psychoanalytic theory,
221–22, 225
Inwood, Michael, 3

James, William, 9n
Jay, Martin, 169n
Johnson, Mark, 178n

King, Rodney, 132, 133
Klein, George: and hermeneutic
psychoanalysis, 20–26, 20n, 22n,
25n; and clinical psychoanalysis
model, 83–84, 83n, 175; Viderman on, 112n; Grünbaum on,
221n
Klein, Melanie, 62
Knowledge: and hermeneutic
psychoanalysis, 12n; and metaphor model, 15, 191–92; human
sciences versus natural sciences,
16; and truth, 127; and story
model, 138; and alternative

metaphysics model, 163; and psychoanalytic theory, 220–25

Lakoff, George, 178n
Language: and hermeneutics, 1, 19, 118–19; and Steele, 8, 59, 96; and story model, 16, 86; and Schafer, 27, 36, 39–40, 44, 102; and Fingarette, 54n, 56; and Viderman, 62, 97–98; and interpretations-as-literary-criticism model, 110, 111–12
Loch, Wolfgang: and truth, 60, 64–66, 64n, 95, 108n, 167, 234; and hermeneutic psychoanalysis, 64–66; and story model, 95–96, 231–32, 234, 236, 246; and metaphor model, 108n; and argument from patient rejection (strong form), 232, 234, 236, 239
Loewenstein, Era, 118–19

McCarthy, Thomas, 169n, 173n
Meaning: and hermeneutic psychoanalysis, 1, 5, 6, 10, 12n; Strenger on, 8; Bruner on, 9n; and interpretation, 10–11, 204–5n; and hermeneutics, 19, 204–5n; and Klein, 20, 21–26, 22n, 83–84; and Schafer, 27–28, 40, 84; and Fingarette, 49–59, 103–5; and Steele, 59, 61; and Loch, 66; and Spence, 74, 92, 94; and alternative metaphysics model, 81, 100, 114; and clinical psychoanalysis model, 81, 82, 114; and story model, 81, 85, 114, 123, 126; and interpretations-as-literary-criticism model,

82, 110–11, 114, 194, 195–96; and metaphor model, 82, 108, 114; and Morse, 98–99n; and psychoanalysts, 122–23; and goals-for-future views, 158–62; and causes, 196–99, 196n, 201, 205
Mendelson, Jack, 169n
Metaphor, 41, 49–50, 53, 175–79n
Metaphor model: definition of, 11, 81–82; and argument from patient rejection (strong form), 14–15, 183; and argument from patient rejection (weak form), 14, 183, 193, 207, 210, 213–14, 215; and hermeneutic psychoanalysis, 107–10; and interpretation, 108, 114–15, 175, 181, 182, 189–90, 222, 236–37; and Loch, 108n; and Spence, 108–9, 109n; and argument from patient rejection, 133, 175–94; and conscious envy, 184–85; and unconscious, 185–88, 222–24; and envious disposition, 188–89; and psychoanalytic theory, 222–24, 225
Metaphysics, 88–89, 135n, 174–75
Metapsychological theory: Strenger on, 8; and Klein, 20, 22, 23–25, 175, 221n; and Schafer, 26–27, 84; and clinical psychoanalysis model, 82, 83, 83n, 220n; and metaphor model, 191
Moore, Michael, 80n, 88, 137n, 169n, 211
Morse, Stephen, 98–99n

Narratives: and psychoanalysis, 7,

Narratives (*cont.*)
9–10, 9n; and Schafer, 26, 31–
47, 100, 110; and Steele, 59–60;
and metaphor model, 107–8;
and hermeneutic psychoanalysis,
224–25
Narrative truth: and sexual abuse
memories, viii, 145–48, 227; and
historical truth, 9; and Schafer,
44; and Spence, 66–69, 67n,
90, 91–92, 108–9, 109n, 110,
148, 232–33, 234, 240–43, 245;
and Sharpe, 77–78; and Sarbin,
244–45; and story model, 246
Natural sciences: and hermeneutics, 5, 7n, 8; psychoanalysis
as natural science, 5–6n, 6, 8,
12–13n, 226; and knowledge,
16; and Schafer, 27, 36, 84; and
clinical psychoanalysis model,
82; and alternative metaphysics
model, 99; and metaphor model,
175
Novick, Peter, 169n
Nuyen, A. T., 169n

Ortony, Andrew, 177–78n

Patients: and hermeneutic psychoanalysis, viii–ix, 124n, 229–30;
and viability of therapy, 15, 228–
29; and Fingarette, 57, 58; and
Steele, 60, 61, 62; and Viderman, 63; and interpretation,
122; and meaning, 123; complaints of, 209–10, 218. *See
also* Argument from patient
rejection
Perspectivism, 42–43, 99, 101
Phillips, James, 80n

Placebo effect: and Sharpe, 78, 89,
246; and argument from patient
rejection, 121; and interpretation, 141–145; and as-if view,
150–51, 154, 162
Positivism, 5, 30, 34–36, 42, 48,
100, 163
Psychoanalysis: as hermeneutic
discipline, 1, 5–6, 10; and interpretation, 5–6, 10, 122, 212–13;
as natural science, 5–6n, 6, 8,
12–13n, 226; as mixed hermeneutic discipline, 6, 18; narrative
function of, 7, 9–10, 9n; and
hermeneutic psychoanalysis
models, 16; and Schafer, 30,
31–34, 42–43; effectiveness of,
46–47, 218–19; and Fingarette,
49, 54, 56, 58; and Loch, 64, 65;
and story model, 87, 139–40, 222,
225; and sexual abuse memories, 148; and imagine-and-react
views, 153; and metaphysics,
174–75; and understanding,
205–6; definition of, 210–13,
215, 216–17; criteria for, 213–
16; theoretical implications of,
220–25
Psychoanalysts: and argument
from patient rejection, viii–ix,
121; and Steele, 61; and interpretation, 68, 121, 122, 140, 161;
and insight, 122–23; and story
model, 139–40; and as-if views,
149–52; and imagine-and-react
view, 155; and goals-for-future
view, 159–61, 161n; and truth,
235–36

Reality: and Schafer, 28–29, 33, 36,

37–39, 42–44, 43n, 47, 49, 100–1, 101n; second reality, 33, 100–1n; and Fingarette, 49–52, 54n, 56, 57, 59; hidden reality, 49–52, 56, 57, 103–4, 105, 106; and Steele, 60–61; and alternative metaphysics model, 99; and Geha, 107n; and story model, 136
Relativism, 168, 169n, 170n, 171
Ricoeur, Paul, 4, 6–7, 18
Rorty, Richard, 5, 9n, 169n, 170n
Rothberg, Donald, 169n
Rubovits-Seitz, Philip, 80n

Sarbin, Theodore, 244–45
Sass, Louis A., 229n
Schafer, Roy: early Schafer, 26–30, 83, 84; and truth, 28, 29–30, 43–47, 46n, 84–85, 101–2, 166; later Schafer, 30–49, 43n, 100; Sharpe on, 76; and alternative metaphysics model, 100–3, 101n, 164n, 175; and interpretations-as-literary-criticism model, 110; and story model, 119
Schleiermacher, Friedrich, 3
Searle, John, 70, 177n
Sexual abuse memories: and story model, viii, 145–48, 227, 232; and metaphor model, 181, 193n
Shapiro, Theodore, 245
Sharpe, Robert: and historical truth, 69n; and hermeneutic psychoanalysis, 75–79; and interpretations, 75–79, 110, 116, 245–46; and story model, 89, 231, 232, 245–46; and goals-for-future view, 159, 159n
Sherwood, Michael, 68, 69, 91
Spence, Donald: Schafer compared to, 32; and hermeneutic psychoanalysis, 66–75; and historical truth, 66–69, 69n, 70n, 71, 72, 75, 90–93, 90n, 108–9, 109n, 232–33, 234, 239–43, 240n; and narrative truth, 66–69, 67n, 90, 91–92, 108–9, 109n, 110, 148, 232–33, 234, 240–43, 245; and story model, 86, 89–95, 134n, 231–32, 236, 239–46; and truth, 90–91, 94, 108, 167, 231–34, 239–43, 240n; and metaphor model, 108–9, 109n; and examples, 131; and goals-for-future view, 159, 159n; and argument from patient rejection (strong form), 232–39
Steele, Robert: and hermeneutic psychoanalysis, 8, 59–62; and interpretation, 59, 59n, 60, 61–62, 96, 96–97n, 110, 113, 116; and story model, 96–97, 114, 231, 232, 246; and clinical psychoanalysis model, 97n; and interpretations-as-literary-criticism model, 97, 113–14, 231, 246
Story model: and argument from patient rejection, viii, 11–13, 14, 99, 115n, 120–21, 123–39, 145–48, 164–66, 174, 226, 229; and sexual abuse memories, viii, 145–48, 227, 232; definition of, 11, 81, 114; empirical and normative components of, 13, 121, 123–29, 136; and language, 16, 86; and hermeneutic psychoanalysis, 85–99, 119, 170–71n, 246; and interpretation, 85–87, 87–88n, 95n, 115–16, 121n, 123–24, 134, 134n, 135–41, 164–65, 170,

Story model (*cont.*)
182, 222; and Spence, 86, 89–95,
134n, 231–32, 236, 239–46; and
psychoanalysis, 87, 139–40, 222,
225; and Sharpe, 89, 231, 232,
245–46; and Loch, 95–96, 231–
32, 234, 236, 246; and Steele,
96–97, 114, 231, 232, 246; and
Viderman, 97–98, 112, 113n, 114,
231, 232, 249; and Fingarette,
105, 106; and argument from
patient rejection (sophisticated
form), 120, 207; and argument
from patient rejection (strong
form), 120, 207, 222n, 231, 232–
39; alternate versions of, 149–62,
222; and as-if views, 149–58; and
imagine-and-react view, 153–58;
and goals-for-future view, 158–
61; and argument from patient
rejection (weak form), 162n,
209; metaphor model compared
to, 175, 181, 182, 193–94; and
alternative metaphysics model,
231, 236, 237
Strenger, Carlo, 8
Subjectivity: and psychoanalysis,
7, 12n; and alternative metaphysics model, 14, 168, 169n,
170n, 171; and Schafer, 27, 29;
and Fingarette, 57

Texts: and hermeneutics, 3; Ricoeur on, 4; and psychoanalysis,
5, 6, 8, 12n; and Schafer, 31, 33,
48; and Steele, 61
Thompson, John, 2–3
Truth: and argument from patient
rejection, 2, 13, 14, 80, 121,
127–30, 134, 135–39, 164–65,

167–68; and understanding, 5;
Bruner on, 9n; and interpretation, 10, 13, 14, 80, 93, 122,
123–27, 127n, 135–49, 151–52, 227,
234–35, 238; and hermeneutic
psychoanalysis, 12n; and normative undesirability of belief
in nontruths, 13, 14, 14–15n, 121,
136–37, 140, 141n, 160, 162, 180,
180n, 193–94, 206, 226–27; and
story model, 13, 16, 81, 86–87,
115–16, 123, 134, 135–39, 164–
65, 170, 170–71n, 182, 206, 222,
226–27, 235, 237; and alternative metaphysics model, 14, 81,
100, 114, 115–16, 135n, 163, 164,
164n, 166–68, 168–70n, 172, 182,
220–21; and interpretations-as-
literary-criticism model, 15, 82,
111, 114, 203; and hermeneutics,
16–17, 168–70n; and Schafer, 28,
29–30, 43–47, 46n, 47–49, 84–
85, 101–2, 166; and Fingarette,
54, 55, 56–57, 106–7; and Loch,
60, 64–66, 64n, 95, 108n, 167,
234; and Steele, 60–61, 96; and
Viderman, 62, 64, 98, 112; and
Sharpe, 76, 78; and clinical
psychoanalysis model, 81, 83,
83n, 86, 163, 164, 182, 220–21;
and metaphysics, 88–89, 135n;
and Spence, 90–91, 94, 108, 167,
231–34, 239–43, 240n; and Geha,
107n; and metaphor model,
108–9, 175, 176–81, 182, 222, 236–
37; and as-if views, 149; and
imagine-and-react view, 157;
and psychoanalysis, 211; and
psychoanalysts, 235–36. *See also*
Historical truth; Narrative truth

Unconscious: and Fingarette, 51–54; and Viderman, 62, 98; and clinical psychoanalysis model, 82–83, 83n; and Steele, 96n; and Schafer, 102–3; and Spence, 109n; and interpretations-as-literary-criticism model, 111; and argument from patient rejection, 130n; and metaphor model, 185–88, 222–24; and story model, 222

Understanding, 3–4, 5, 8, 74, 126, 205–6

Viderman, Serge: and hermeneutic psychoanalysis, 62–64, 70, 72; and Spence, 90, 98; and story model, 97–98, 112, 113n, 114, 231, 232, 249; and interpretations-as-literary-criticism model, 98, 111–14, 112–13n, 231, 246

Viederman, Milton, 244

Warnke, Georgia, 169n
Wellmer, Albrecht, 170n
White, Hayden, 169n